I LOVE

I LOVE

THE STORY OF VLADIMIR MAYAKOVSKY AND LILI BRIK

ANN & SAMUEL CHARTERS

FARRAR STRAUS GIROUX   NEW YORK

TO RITA RAIT,
a true friend of Mayakovsky and the Briks

Copyright © 1979 by Ann and Samuel Charters
All rights reserved
Printed in the United States of America
Published simultaneously in Canada
by McGraw-Hill Ryerson Ltd., Toronto
Book design by Kathleen Westray
First printing, 1979
Library of Congress Cataloging in Publication Data
Charters, Ann.
I Love : the story of Vladimir Mayakovsky
and Lili Brik.
Bibliography: p.
1. Maîàkovskiĭ, Vladimir Vladimirovich, 1894–1930
—Relationship with women—Lili Brik.
2. Brik, Lili ÎUr'evna.
3. Poets, Russian—20th century—Biography.
4. Mistresses—Russia—Biography.
I. Charters, Samuel Barclay, Joint author.   II. Title.
PG3476.M312C45   1979   891.7'1'42 [B]   79–92

CONTENTS

ACKNOWLEDGMENTS

THIS BOOK COULDN'T HAVE BEEN WRITTEN WITHOUT THE assistance of Lili Brik (1891–1978), who helped with interviews, photographs, manuscripts of memoirs, and printed material, and also arranged for us to interview Nora Polonskaya, the actress who was with Mayakovsky at the time of his suicide in 1930.

Rita Rait, a fine translator who is widely known in the Soviet Union for her translations of William Faulkner, J. D. Salinger, and Kurt Vonnegut, Jr., was of considerable help in the interviews with Lili, her friend for nearly sixty years, and she has added much information of her own to this book. She read the manuscript in its final stages and was able to correct a number of errors as well as to clarify some of the contradictory aspects of Mayakovsky's life, though there were points of interpretation with which she disagreed. She also checked the translations of the poetry.

Also important to any understanding of Mayakovsky's life is Tatiana Yakovleva Lieberman, who discussed her relationship with the poet in the last years of his life. Her assistance is gratefully acknowledged.

It was a Swedish student of Russian literature, Bengt Jangfeldt, who supplied Lili Brik's address in Moscow in 1972. At that time Bengt was writing a doctoral thesis on Mayakovsky and the Futurist movement. He is now a lecturer at Stockholm University and has generously furnished information throughout the writing of this book. His own published work on Mayakovsky and the Futurists has been of use to us, and he also helped in some of the interviews with Lili, as well as translated and corrected factual errors in an early draft of the manuscript.

We would like to acknowledge the help of our other translators, Rimma Vinnehova, Lars Kleberg, Alexandra Eiche, and Stig Fredrikson. Tomas Tranströmer and Gunnar Harding in Stockholm, and Irene Kirk, Gennady Smakov, and Joseph Brodsky in Connecticut, gave their opinions and encouragement during the writing and research of this book; Hugh Clark, Associate Dean of the University of Connecticut Research Foundation, helped with funds for the translations. The staff of the University of Connecticut Library and Anders Ryberg at the Nobel Library in Stockholm kindly assisted in locating printed material. All the photographs in the book are from the archives of Lili Brik.

It was originally my idea to write a book about the love affair between Lili Brik and Vladimir Mayakovsky because I was impressed by Lili's personality when I first met her. But when I began sorting out the pieces of her story from the various sources I'd accumulated, I found that Mayakovsky's relationship with Lili and Osip Brik was so complicated, and a clear perspective on their lives in the Soviet Union during the early years of the Revolution was so difficult to attempt in the dense undergrowth of fallible human memory and strongly held political opinion, that the book I began as a short, lyrical description of a love affair turned into a long project that took more than six years to complete. After the first draft, Sam took over organizing the material and writing the new drafts, which I revised. For years he had been so deeply interested in Mayakovsky's poetry that on our first trip to Moscow he was more involved with the poet and his life there than he was with the city itself. Later he worked with Rita Rait, who lived with us for six weeks during the summer of 1978, refining the translations of the poems to bring the tone closer to Mayakovsky's own work.

As during the writing of our other books, our children Mallay and Nora Lili have had to be endlessly patient with our distraction. They remember Lili simply as the generous woman who filled a corner of her living room with every stuffed animal she could find in Moscow as gifts for them when they came to visit her.

ANN CHARTERS

INTRODUCTION

ON A SUNNY, WARM AFTERNOON IN APRIL 1972, ON A TRIP
to Moscow with our four-year-old daughter Mallay, we stopped at the
Metro Station at Red Square to buy flowers from a peasant woman,
then took a taxi to the apartment of Lili Brik, to meet her for the
first time. When we had talked for several hours, Lili said, "But you
didn't bring your books. You must be writers yourselves or you
wouldn't have come. Where are your books?" We returned the next
day with books for her, and immediately Lili sat down on a sofa to
ask questions about the American writers from the 1950's whose
photographs were in the book *Scenes Along the Road*. In the
spontaneity of her responses we sensed how she must have encouraged
Mayakovsky's work during his lifetime.

During the next two years we returned to Moscow and Peredelkino
to tape interviews with Lili about Mayakovsky and their life together. It was soon apparent on repeated trips to the Soviet Union
that Lili's role in the poet's life was not often publicly acknowledged.
The most dramatic incident occurred in the newly opened Mayakovsky Museum in Moscow, where the authorities' use of a heavy,
ornate desk could symbolize the official treatment of Mayakovsky's
involvement with Lili and her husband, Osip Brik. It is a carved
black walnut desk that belonged originally to Brik's father. When
his parents moved to a smaller apartment they didn't have room for
it and they offered it to Osip, who gave it to Mayakovsky. It sat
in the poet's workroom for a few years, until he bought two identical
brown wooden desks in the spring of 1926, one to go in a new apartment he shared with the Briks and the other to go in his own small
room, since the big desk took up too much space. He passed the desk
on to a friend who was publishing some of his books, Vasily

Katanyan. In the museum the guides take parties of visitors to the imposing desk and identify it proudly as the desk at which Maya-kovsky sat as he wrote his "immortal" poem "Vladimir Ilyich Lenin." However, Mayakovsky wrote the Lenin poem on Osip Brik's battered desk in their communal apartment. The only poem he wrote at the carved walnut desk in his workroom was a long love lyric for Lili called "About This," composed during an anguished separation in the winter of 1922–23. The museum guides never mentioned Lili, the owners of the desk, or the actual poem that was written on it.

The museum itself is still another symbol of the effort to separate Lili from Mayakovsky's life. Until the mid-1970's the museum was in the last apartment where the Briks and Mayakovsky had lived together, and their shared life was obvious in the arrangement of the rooms with their simple furnishings. The new museum is purposely free of Lili's presence. The small workroom where Mayakovsky died is part of the new museum—the guides don't mention suicide—and if they are questioned about the people who shared the large apartment where the Soviet Union's most famous poet of the Revolution actually lived, these people are dismissed as his "neighbors." Lili's photograph was on the cover of the original edition of the poem he wrote on the walnut desk for her, and when the book is exhibited sometimes her photo is also described by the guides as that of the "neighbor" or as one of his "many loves."

Why has there been this effort to eliminate Lili's presence in Mayakovsky's life? Today he is almost a mythic figure in the Soviet Pantheon, and his life and work are part of the official canon of the Revolution. But it is impossible for the Soviet cultural authorities to reconcile the figure of the Mayakovsky they've created with the reality of his life with Lili. Perhaps it is because Lili was Jewish, and despite the official denials, anti-Semitism is still a virulent force in Soviet life today. She was also married, and Mayakovsky lived with both Lili and her husband while he and Lili were lovers. This is difficult to reconcile with the official Soviet morality. Finally, the most important political influence on Mayakovsky was Lili's husband, Osip, who was the poet's closest intellectual companion in the years they were together. In a society that is dominated by the legend of Lenin, it is officially impossible to accept the fact that the leading poet of the Revolution was so closely influenced by a Jewish intellectual.

The relationship between Mayakovsky and the Briks also presented difficulties for many Soviet critics, who saw Lili as an "evil genius" in Mayakovsky's life. To them she and Osip Brik were a corrupting influence, and it was because of their hold over him that he was never able to join the new society with the complete acceptance that the government demanded of its writers and artists. To others who were less concerned with Mayakovsky's political attitudes, like the poet Anna Akhmatova, Lili and her husband seemed selfishly to be living off him and his work. There have been foreign writers who spoke of her "strange hold" over him, and there have been others who have questioned her role in the difficulties he faced in his last months.

Despite the controversy over Lili's place in Mayakovsky's life, she was often recognized informally by many people while we were in Moscow and Peredelkino visiting her. On a bitter December afternoon in 1974, eighty-three years old and bundled up in furs against the wind, she took us to an exhibition re-creating the display "Twenty Years of Work," which Mayakovsky had first presented in the headquarters of the Writers' Union in Moscow in 1930. A group of students on an official tour of the exhibition immediately saw her, and there was a sudden scurrying to come to her, to take her hand. She was asked to sign copies of the program, to pose for photographs alone, and finally to stand with the whole group for a picture of all of them together. After a first brief greeting, the officials present at the exhibition stood carefully to one side, though they were surrounded by the drawings and photos of Lili on the walls and shelves that had been part of Mayakovsky's original exhibition.

When she was recognized on a more public level, the moments were often spontaneous and emotional. For some months a staged reading of Mayakovsky's poems had been running at a Moscow theater, and she attended with us one night in the summer of 1973. The actor who was to read one of the love poems written to her learned that she was in the audience, sitting in the second row, and when the moment for the poem came, he went forward to the edge of the stage and leaned over the footlights to recite it to her.

It has been impossible for the Soviet government to remove Lili Brik completely from Mayakovsky's biography. His poetry is dedicated to her, much of his early work is a series of passionate love poems to her, and she was involved in every aspect of his life. She died in her summer dacha in Peredelkino in August 1978, shortly before her eighty-seventh birthday. Perhaps after her death it will be possible to conceal more of the traces of her love affair with the poet, as has already been done in the official museum in Moscow, but the poetry itself lives, and her presence is an indelible part of it.

You're occupied with your balance sheets,
The tragedy of the Council of Home Industry,
You the Flying Dutchman
Soaring over the gangway of every song and verse.

The burlap storm of tents
Blew up like the unruly Dvena in motion,
When you, the winged one,
Emerged starboard to larboard with me.

And you, writing clichés about oil?
Dumbfounded and bewildered I wonder
What therapist
Could give you back your wrath.

I know your course is genuine,
But how could you be blown
Under the roofs of such poorhouses
From your sincere course?

BORIS PASTERNAK
A POEM WRITTEN TO MAYAKOVSKY
ON THE FLYLEAF OF A BOOK

PART ONE

It was one of the first warm days of April, the tentative beginning of spring. People in Moscow were out in the streets, their coats open, moving less hurriedly in the liquid air. At a few moments past ten in the morning, when the man in the small room close to the government printing offices shot himself, the first sound was the scream of the girl in the corridor outside his closed door. Then the sound began to echo across the city. Within a few minutes the corridor was filled with people, then the stairways into the building, then the street outside. By the time the ambulance had come to take his body back to his apartment, the sound had echoed over the roofs, through the telephone wires, into rooms, apartments, offices, onto the sidewalks, into the squares and avenues. As the ambulance made its way through the streets with the body, people followed in cars, in taxis, and in streetcars. It was April 14, 1930, and Vladimir Mayakovsky, the most famous poet of the Soviet Union, a public personality who had come to stand for the Revolution itself, had committed suicide at the age of thirty-six.

The shabby workroom where he'd spent the night was splattered with blood, the stains spilling across the couch that was close to the door, across the chair, the littered desk. He'd left a letter on his desk and it was passed from hand to hand; then it was given to the men from the newspapers to copy and the copies were hurried to the printers. Most of the letter was concerned with his literary and business affairs, but the third paragraph read simply, "Lili, love me." Who was Lili? The people crowding into his room knew, as did the people who came later to cry over his body at his apartment. Her name was Lili Yuryevna Brik, the wife of a literary theorist and critic named Osip Maximovich Brik. For the fifteen years she and the poet had lived together she had been the subject of some of the most fevered and tumultuous love poetry written in this century.

But who was she? Why in his letter had he asked, for the last time, "Lili, love me"? When he shot himself she was traveling outside the country, but in two days she was to return. In their apartment the people clustering around the body said in choked whispers, "If only Lili had been here . . . if only Lili had been here . . ."

I

Lili Brik, 1914

Osip Brik, 1916

If I am destined to be a tsar—
on the sunny gold of my coins
I order my people:
mint
your precious face!
And there
where the world has faded into tundra,
where the river trades with the North wind,
there I'll scratch Lili's name on my chain
and kiss it again and again in the gloom of hard labor . . .

You who have robbed my heart,
depriving it of everything,
who have demanded my soul in delirium,
dearest, accept my gift,
perhaps I'll never create anything else . . .

"THE BACKBONE FLUTE"

LONG AGO TOLSTOY WROTE THAT HAPPY FAMILIES ARE all alike, and certainly Lili Brik was born into a happy family, with parents who adored her and gave her everything she wanted. Her life was always sheltered and comfortable, completely unlike Mayakovsky's. Her father, Yury Alexandrovich Kagan, was a lawyer who specialized in arranging contracts for actors and musicians in theaters throughout Russia; her mother, Yelena Yuryevna, was a musician, an amateur pianist. Lili was their first child. She was born in Moscow on November 11, 1891 (October 30, Old Style pre-Revolutionary calendar). Two years later her mother conceived another child, but she miscarried after an incident in which Lili choked on something stuck in her throat and nearly suffocated. Lili felt that the loss of this second child made her parents especially indulgent with her; her sister Elsa (later to become the Prix Goncourt novelist Elsa Triolet) wasn't born until Lili was nearly six.

Lili was raised with a nursemaid and a language tutor. Her parents spoke German fluently—her mother was originally from Riga, her father from a small village in Lithuania—but Lili learned German as a second language, after Russian. The tutor tried to teach her French, but she was too lazy to learn much, and since she didn't like to practice the piano either, her music lessons never progressed very far. There was a good income from her father's legal practice, and the family enjoyed a large apartment, servants, and long trips during summer holidays. Her parents indulged her so much that she became spoiled. Once when a friend of her mother's came for a visit and was drinking tea, Lili stared at the guest and told her, "With a face like that you don't go visiting." High-spirited and strong-willed, Lili was allowed to say what she pleased, and she had already begun to think of herself as privileged when she was still young.

Lili was taller than her mother before she was a teenager,

though she never became a tall woman. As her face matured she became beautiful, with the strong line of her jaw balanced by her high, pale forehead, widely spaced hazel-brown eyes, and finely molded mouth. She had luxuriant red hair which was first braided in a heavy plait, but by the time she'd had her picture taken after finishing high school (the Russian "Gymnasium"), she wore it loose in soft waves to her shoulders. She went back to a single long braid a few years later, or pinned it in a coil in back of her head.

In school Lili was clearly intelligent, but she was unmotivated, interested only in her mathematics class, where she got top grades. After graduating from the Gymnasium she studied mathematics for a year, grew bored with it, and switched to the Institute of Architecture to begin a course in sculpture and drawing. When she decided she was serious, she begged her father for permission to study in a private sculpture studio in Munich. Lili later remembered that she was one of the best students in the class, but the sculpture lessons came to an end after a year. Her parents visited her in Munich and saw her hands, which had become rough and red after her work with the clay. Lili's father exclaimed, "But you had such beautiful hands!" and she was persuaded to come home.

Lili's life with a private French tutor and sculpture lessons in Munich was very different from the one her father had known as a boy in a poor Jewish household where the women were illiterate and their lives regulated by Orthodox customs. But Lili was still a Jew, and her parents couldn't protect her completely from experiencing anti-Semitism as she was growing up.

I remember some incidents. Once I took a train to visit my aunt in the Caucasus. In the compartment next to mine was an army officer whose adjutants were transporting geese, boxes of them in the corridor of the train. I left my compartment and sat down on a box among the aides. The soldiers began talking to me, and somehow during the conversation I said I was Jewish. They were very embarrassed by it, but one of them told me,

"For a woman it's not so terrible to be Jewish. You can get married to a Russian and everything will turn out all right."

Once something else happened, again with army officers. Our French governess married a Russian officer and they took me to the races with them. One of their friends, another officer, liked me very much. While we were drinking lemonade it came out again that I was Jewish. He stood up and left without even paying for the lemonade. I turned to the governess and said, "Who are you introducing me to? You put me in a very foolish position." She apologized. "I assure you it was an accident. He didn't expect to meet you."

Considering what was happening to Jews elsewhere—the terror of the pogroms swept Russia when Lili was in her early teens—Lili was fortunate to live a life of privilege in Moscow, where anti-Semitism was only an occasional social embarrassment. She thought of herself as a Jew because her parents were Jewish by birth, but the family were atheists, completely disinterested in Zionism, and they celebrated Christmas and Easter holidays in the Russian style with parties and special food. Some of their friends were formally assimilating by becoming Christians, but the Kagans' life in Moscow was so sheltered that being Jewish seemed to be more a distinction than a problem.

When Lili was twelve and thirteen, boys were already interested in her and she loved the attention. Once she went to the theater with two boys who liked her and she sat between them during the performance. She had a fur muff in her lap, but her hands were underneath it, and at the intermission she looked down to see the boys holding each other's hand inside the muff, each of them thinking he was squeezing her hand. At a pre-Lenten costume party at the home of a wealthy tea merchant she met a boy who was to be a friend when they were older, Boris Pasternak. Her relationships with the boys she met were casual and uninvolved, but at fourteen she fell in love with the man she was to marry, Osip Maximovich Brik.

Osip Brik was born on January 16 (January 4, O.S.), 1888. He was four years older than Lili, a student in the graduating class of a boys' Gymnasium. His sister Vera was a class ahead of Lili and introduced them by bringing Lili to a study circle on Political Economy directed by Osya, as he was called by his family and friends. He was short and physically slight, with a sensitive, scholarly face behind his glasses. Like many adolescents during that period he had become a Marxist, and had been readmitted to school in the fall of 1905 after being expelled for revolutionary activities during the unsuccessful uprising of the previous spring. After Osip's lecture, his sister asked Lili, "How do you like my brother?" Not sure she understood, Lili answered carefully, "As a lecturer I like him very much."

At Christmas, shortly after her fourteenth birthday, the Briks invited her to their house for a party. They were also Jewish, from the same social class as Lili's parents, although Osip's father was wealthier. He was a very successful dealer in antiques and jewelry, especially interested in dark corals, which he bought in Italy and sold throughout Russia. Osip's mother, who could speak several languages and was an admirer of the writing of Alexander Herzen, encouraged her son's interest in socialism. After the Christmas party Osip took Lili home in a cab. As soon as they were alone he put his arm around her and asked, "Don't you think, Lili, that there is something more than friendship between us?" As she recalled later, "I didn't quite feel it myself then, but I liked the question."

Lili was still so young that Osip's question didn't seem real to her, but after a few months she began to feel she must be in love with him. That summer, in 1906, Lili went with her family to the Black Forest in Germany for a vacation. Lili sent him her address, but when she didn't get an answer she decided he hadn't gotten it and wrote a second letter and then a third. At last she got an answer. He didn't say it directly, but his meaning was clear: he'd made a mistake and didn't love her as much as he'd thought, he was never going to marry, but instead would dedicate his life to the Revolution. Lili was in despair. She began losing her hair and developed a nervous facial tic that came back in later life whenever she was greatly upset.

When she returned to Moscow in the fall she didn't see Osip, and as the months passed she thought of him less often. She met other young men, among them a talented composer, a friend of her mother's, who was married. It developed into a serious affair that finally ended in considerable unhappiness. In her late teens she became engaged to a number of her suitors in an effort to resolve the emotional uncertainty in her life.

All my young admirers proposed marriage to me, and I said yes several times, but Fate always decided a different way for me. Each time, right after I'd accepted a proposal, I'd meet Osip Maximovich on the street or in the theater, and I'd always break the engagement afterward.

Osip hadn't forgotten Lili, but he had lost touch with her because of his university studies. In 1911, at the end of her year studying sculpture in Munich, he found her again in Moscow.

When I returned from Munich to Moscow, I went with a young man who was very rich and very nice. I went to the Art Theater with him. Brik found out that I was in Moscow and he phoned my house. Mama told him, "Lilichka is at the Art Theater tonight." The Briks lived very close to the theater, and Osya came there, couldn't get a ticket, but waited for me to come out during intermission. We planned to meet at a restaurant the following day. We took a private room at the restaurant —I was nearly twenty years old then, old enough to go into a private room—and Osip Maximovich said to me, "Lilichka, marry me." By that time my feelings had cooled toward him and I'd begun to forget him. I answered indefinitely, but he persisted. He said, "Lilichka, let's try." "All right," I answered, "let's try."

Osip left Moscow on a trip to Central Siberia for his father's business, while Lili and her mother prepared for the wedding. They found an apartment in a fashionable neighborhood near what is now Gorky Street and bought furniture. Her father ordered linens and the wedding dress from a German firm he represented in Moscow. All this time Lili and Osip had a stormy correspondence, with many quarrels and reconciliations, but in the end they were married, although it was never officially registered. To please their parents, they agreed that a rabbi who was a friend of Lili's father could come to the Kagan apartment and marry them under the traditional Jewish canopy.

The wedding took place on March 26, 1912, with only their immediate families present. Lili had told the rabbi to make it a brief ceremony, and when he finished he said drily, "I hope I've not delayed you young people."

Mama said the main thing she remembered about the wedding was my teeth. I was wearing a very low-cut dress, not exactly proper for a wedding dress, although I'd covered my shoulders and head and even my face with a thin silk scarf. But Mama could see how much I was laughing during the ceremony, and that's why she said she remembered only my white teeth. We ate roast beef for the wedding dinner, but our cook forgot to prepare the horseradish and she wept in the kitchen about it. In later years after Mama let her come work for me, each time she prepared roast beef she always said, "This time I haven't forgotten the horseradish."

After the wedding dinner Lili and Osip went to their new apartment, where they found that her mother had left flowers and two bottles of champagne on the table next to their bed. In the beginning the marriage was successful.

The only year of real happiness in my life was the first year I spent together with Osya. This was in 1912. We traveled to Uzbekistan and liked it so much that we planned to spend a few years living there, but nothing came of it. At that time there were harems and women went around in veils. When I visited a harem, the women pulled up my skirt to look at what I wore underneath. I spent whole days at the bazaars, shopping and eating wonderful hot pancakes and grapes. At the bazaar one of our friends, an Uzbek bookseller, was impressed by our companion, the poet Lipskarov. When I told the bookseller he was a poet, he said, "Aha, he is a 'shoar,' a man who speaks from the heart." I still remember this word meaning "poet" in the Uzbek language.

When they returned to Moscow Osip studied law and continued to travel occasionally for his father. There was enough money for them to do as they pleased, and in spite of Brik's Marxist beliefs they lived like a fashionable newly married couple. Lili's father had given her a generous dowry of thirty thousand rubles, which they spent in the first year of their marriage. They had decided not to have children since "it was too big a responsibility." Later Lili laughed at their extravagance.

We spent ten thousand on furniture and twenty thousand on living like kings. We visited the theater, went to the races, traveled wherever we liked, and even rented expensive cars. One morning Osya's father Maxim Pavlovich called on us unannounced, and the doorman told him, "They are not in, as usual on Sundays. On Sundays they go to the races."

We lived this way until 1914, when Osya was drafted. With the help of one of our friends, Sobinoff, a tenor singing at the Bolshoi Theater, a very nice man, Osya entered the Automobile Corps. We moved to Petrograd, putting most of our furniture into storage.

In Petrograd during the first year of the war, Brik found his duties with the Automobile Corps dreary and tiring. His assignment demanded all his time, and Lili felt he might have dragged on with it until the Revolution if his command hadn't suddenly decided that Jews didn't belong in the Automobile Corps. All the Jews were ordered to assemble within twenty-four hours to be sent under escort to the village of Medved to a disciplinary force, and from there to the front.

At first Lili was in tears, and then she told Osip that he must protest; he couldn't allow himself to be treated like a criminal under military escort. If he went along with the others, she threatened she'd no longer be his wife and that she'd never forgive him. There was little he could do. He put himself in the hospital, and while he was there the Jews were sent to Medved. When Osip came out, the command didn't think it was worth wasting two guards on a Jewish conscript. He stayed in the apartment, waiting for his orders, but they never came. For a time he continued to wear his uniform, but then he started to go out on the street in civilian clothes. In the confusion of the war the Russian Army simply forgot about him.

During the first months in Petrograd the Briks didn't know anyone, and Lili was often bored. She would sleep late and then wander in the art galleries at the Hermitage, returning home in the late afternoon after looking at shop windows along Nevsky Prospect. In Moscow her father was ill with cancer, and she would often go back to see her parents and younger sister, Elsa. But time passed slowly.

Osip did have a distant relative in Petrograd, a very wealthy man whose wife once asked Lili to come along on a visit to Tsarskoe. Lili agreed, since she'd never seen the little village where the Tsar and his family had their summer palace. The train to Tsarskoe was full, and they had to sit at different ends of the car. Directly across from her Lili noticed a peculiar man who glanced at her now and then. He wore a broadcloth cassock with a bright-colored silk lining, high boots, and a beautiful beaver hat, and he carried a stick with an expensive knob. Lili was fascinated by him, because with all his fine clothes he had a dirty beard and black fingernails. She stared at the man for so long that finally he turned his glance directly on her; his eyes were clear blue and cheerful. Then he hid his face in his beard and sniffled.

Lili smiled, and they began to flirt, but when she left the train she rejoined her relative, and would have forgotten the flirtation if they hadn't run into the man again on the station platform. Her relative nodded toward him and whispered to Lili, "That's Rasputin."

After looking at summer houses they went back to the station to wait for the train to Petrograd, and they met Rasputin again. He hurried up to them, followed them into the same car when the train arrived, and talked almost entirely with Lili on the trip back to Petrograd, asking her to visit him whenever she could. When she came home, Lili told Osip about the encounter. She was excited by the opportunity to visit Rasputin, but she couldn't talk her husband into it. He refused, wondering how she could be interested in another meeting. Lili sighed, and all that happened was that for the next couple of days she saw Rasputin in every man on the street "if his eyes seemed that clear shade of blue." Jokingly, Brik told her that honest people had brown eyes, like theirs.

There were many flirtations the first months in Petrograd. "Flirtations," Lili said, "but no affairs." She loved Osip, but their marriage was no longer completely satisfying to her. He came back from his military duties too tired to think of anything but sleep, and their physical relationship had gradually ended.

> For nearly a whole year Osya and I didn't live as man and wife because he was in the army and we were separated. He got up terribly early in the morning and went to his job. He came home tired and went to bed early, and he never liked sleeping in the same bed with me. He said he couldn't rest.

There doesn't seem to have been any conscious decision on Osip's part to end their sexual relationship. It hadn't been that strong a factor in their marriage for him. Also, after their first year together, he turned to a cousin, Isadore Roumer, for intellectual companionship, since Lili had no serious interest in theoretical political discussions. She was so jealous that her nervous facial tic came back to trouble her. To justify their new relationship Brik told her that they had to revolutionize the institution of marriage. This was a fashionable subject in Marxist circles of the period, when Russian intellectuals argued that all human relationships could be structured rationally and systematically. In a "new marriage" neither partner was to be the property of the other, and each was to be free to experience life as fully as possible.

As if to test this theory, Lili drank too much at a party one evening and went off to a hotel with another man. Hours later she returned to Osip and confessed unhappily that she'd done something foolish. His response was to tell her, "Don't worry about it. Just go take a hot bath." Lili was deeply upset by his indifference, especially since his passive acceptance of her infidelity made it clear that the physical side of their relationship had completely ended. She continued the affair for several weeks in an effort to arouse his jealousy, but Osip never responded. Then, since she didn't really like the other man, she abruptly broke off with him. A few months later the Briks were to meet Mayakovsky.

2

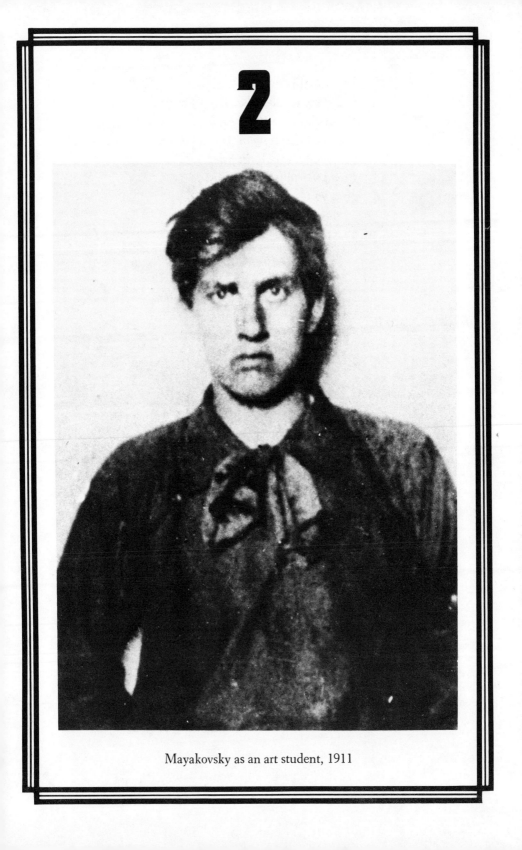

Mayakovsky as an art student, 1911

I splashed paint from a glass
and smeared over the chart of everyday.
I showed on a dish of aspic
the jutting cheekbones of the ocean.
On the scales of a tin fish
I read the calls of new lips.
And you—
          could you play a nocturne
on a drainpipe flute?

                    "BUT COULD YOU?"

MAYAKOVSKY DESCRIBED HIS CHILDHOOD, BUT IT was after he'd become a public monument and everything he said was expected to match the slogans carved around the monument's base. Although his family had been minor Russian gentry, at the time of his birth his father was a forester in Russian Georgia. The father's name was Vladimir Konstantinovich, his mother was Alexandra Alexeyevna; there were two older sisters, Ludmilla and Olga. When Mayakovsky was born on July 19 (July 7, O.S.), 1893, the family lived in a simple three-room house built of logs at the foot of a steep grassy hill. The land sloped sharply away from the house, which was surrounded by gardens, orchards, and vineyards. His mother remembered the mountains and forests, the isolation of the houses, and the howling of the packs of jackals that came out of the woods at night. There were no close neighbors. The remote village of Bagdadi, where they lived, was without schools, teachers, or doctors. The oldest daughter, Ludmilla, was sent away to school in Tiflis. In 1899, when Volodya (as Mayakovsky was called at home) was almost six, they moved to a brick house close to the ruins of an ancient Georgian fortress, and it was here that his memory of childhood began.

First house remembered distinctly. Two stories, upper was ours. Lower was small winery. Once a year carts of grapes. Grapes were pressed. I ate. They drank. All round was territory of extremely ancient Georgian fortress near Bagdadi. Around the fortress was a feudal wall in the form of a square. At the corners of the walls were stands for cannons. In the walls were turrets. Beyond the walls, pits. Beyond the pits—woods and jackals. Overhanging the woods were mountains. I grew up. Would run up the highest. Hills lowered to north. In the north a gap in the hills. There I dreamed was Russia. I was intensely drawn there.

He remembered that at first he was taught "by mother and all sorts of female relatives," but his mother said that he taught himself to read when he was six. The family agreed on his difficulties with arithmetic—"Arithmetic seemed implausible," he explained—but his reading also went very slowly.

Certainly some of his reading difficulties were due to the awkwardness of learning two languages at once. He was being instructed in Russian, and the family spoke Russian at home, but they lived in a Georgian village and he spoke Georgian with the people around him. To help him prepare for school, his mother finally took him to the town of Kutais, where they rented rooms in the home of an irritable landlord who shouted at the young Mayakovsky when he forgot to walk on the carpets and stepped on the polished wood floors: "Why do you have to walk on the floor? Can't you see the carpets? You're not in the forest now!"

In May 1902, when Mayakovsky was finally ready to try the examinations for entrance into the Gymnasium, his familiarity with the Georgian language almost caused him to fail. Later, in his autobiography, *I Myself*, he described the exam humorously, exaggerating its importance as if it affected his entire life, but at the time it was a very difficult experience for him.

Moved from Bagdadi to Kutais. Gymnasium entrance examinations. Passed. I was asked about anchor (on my sleeve). Knew well. But the school priest asked, "What does 'oko' mean?" I answered, "Three pounds" (which it means in Georgian). The polite examiners explained that "oko" is the Ancient Church Slavonic for "eye." Because of it I almost failed. That's why I began to hate everything ancient, everything churchy, and everything Slavonic. Possibly from this sprang my Futurism, my atheism, and my internationalism.

On the last day of his examination he came down with a high fever which was diagnosed as typhoid. He was ill for months, and when he'd recovered the doctor advised him never to drink unboiled water, a warning which instilled in Mayakovsky a lifelong preoccupation with sanitation and cleanliness. When he was twelve he began to read revolutionary articles, pamphlets that his sister brought from Moscow, and he took part in his school's demonstrations in the revolution of 1905. He began to do better at school, reading Gorky and Marx, following the well-worn path of the village rebel.

> Socialism. Speeches. Newspapers . . . I used to get up at six. Read like a drunkard . . . All my life have been impressed by the capability of socialists to disentangle facts and systematize world . . . Was taken to a Marxist study circle. I found myself in the middle of the Erfurt Programme. About Lumpenproletariat. Began to consider myself a Social-Democrat. I sneaked out my father's guns and brought them to the Social-Democratic committee . . . Used to go to Rion and make speeches with pebbles in my mouth.

The next year tragedy struck Mayakovsky's family. His father pricked his finger on a pin fastening some papers together and, in those years of primitive medicine, fell victim to blood poisoning and died suddenly; his death strengthened Mayakovsky's obsession with germs and sanitation. Since his father was a year from his pension at the time of his death, the family was left destitute on a dispensation of ten rubles a˙ month. They sold their furniture for food; then in desperation borrowed two hundred rubles from a friend and left for Moscow, even though they had no friends there and no prospects for work. They reached Moscow on August 1, 1906, shortly after Mayakovsky's thirteenth birthday, and moved into a bare apartment in a poor neighborhood.

Mayakovsky's commitment to the Revolution was suddenly intensified by the poverty and unhappiness of his adolescence. He had lost his father and been taken out of his own Georgian background to a shabby district in a vast, dirty city, and he reached out recklessly for something of his own. He was in the same city as Lili, but while she was going to parties and dances, his family was struggling to get enough to eat. His mother petitioned for an increase in her small pension, but she had to take tenants into their apartment to pay the rent. Mayakovsky's sisters decorated wooden boxes and eggs in the style of folk handicrafts and he helped with the glazing and delivered their work to stores early in the morning before going off to school. They made very little money, but everything helped.

Already old for his years, Mayakovsky was moving toward an activist revolutionary role. By 1908, at the age of fourteen, he had become so involved with the ideas of his mother's tenants, most of whom were Marxists, that he joined the Social-Democratic Workers Party, the Bolsheviks. Expelled from school for not paying fees, Mayakovsky began distributing propaganda materials full-time under the name "Comrade Constantine." On March 29, 1908, he was arrested for the first time, in a raid on an illegal printing press.

> *First arrest.* I was ambushed in Gruzino. Our illegal printing works. Chewed, swallowed notebook. With addresses and binding. Presnaya police station. Secret police. Sukhochevskaya police station. The examiner Boltanovsky (apparently considered himself cunning) made me take dictation: I was charged with writing proclamation. Hopelessly misspelled the dictation. Wrote "Soshaldimocratic." Probably trick fooled them. Released on bail.

According to official records, he was released less than two weeks later because of his age, but he was considered important enough to be kept under surveillance by police spies for the next several months. He returned to his studies in technical school while continuing to work for the Party. He was arrested again on January 18, 1909, and in a search of his room a pistol was found. This time he was held for a month, but again released because of his age. Six months later, on

July 2, 1909, Mayakovsky went to offer his assistance to the wife of a man who was tunneling into a Moscow prison to free political prisoners, and suddenly he fell into a police trap. Although Mayakovsky had drawing materials with him as an ostensible reason for his visit, his previous arrests weighed heavily against him.

In prison he rebelled against the authorities by mocking the police, jeering at their orders, and demanding to be allowed to see other prisoners. Then, after a trip to the toilet, he refused to return to his cell for thirty minutes, shouting at his guard until the other prisoners began to join in the disturbance. As punishment, on August 18, 1909, he was transferred to solitary confinement in Moscow's bleak Butyrki Prison and held there until the end of the year.

Mayakovsky tried to pass off the experience as a kind of study period, when he had time to read Byron, Shakespeare, and Tolstoy and to fill a notebook with his own poetry, but in a poem written many years afterward he described his deeper emotions at being locked in a solitary cell at the age of sixteen, with the threat of three years' exile looming over him when he left prison.

> Youths have a lot of cramming to do.
> We teach grammar to every big fool.
> But I
> was kicked out
> of the Fifth Class
> and was thrown around the Moscow jails.
> In the narrow
> world of your
> apartments,
> curly-haired rhymers are bred for bedrooms.
> What could you find in these puggy rhymesters?
> But where I
> was taught
> to love
> was Butyrki Prison.
> What is it to me to yearn for the Bois de Boulogne?

What is it to me to sigh over a seascape?
Me, I
fell in love
with a "Funeral Home"
through the peephole of cell 103.
Those who look at the sun every day
shrug:
"What's so special about those ordinary sunbeams?"
But I
for a yellow jumping speck
of sunshine on the wall
would give now—everything in the world.

For the rest of his life he hated the number 103, the number of the cell where he'd stood with his eye pressed to the peephole, trying to see a reflection of the sun.

Again it was his age that helped him. Without his knowledge his mother went to St. Petersburg to plead for his release on the grounds that he was a minor. She was successful and he was freed on January 9, 1910. In the photographs that were attached to his card in the secret-police files he looks young and afraid, despite a half-defiant glitter in his eyes and the hard set of his mouth, his lips tightly clenched. A long coat hangs from his skinny shoulders to his ankles. He is very thin, with large ears and the faint shadow of a mustache. Through neglect he had bad teeth; they were little more than brown stumps and he always kept his mouth tightly closed for photographs. His sister Ludmilla remembered that he came home in the evening after his release from prison and that while he was washing his hands he kept embracing his family with soapy fingers, saying how happy he was to be with them again. He didn't have a warm winter overcoat—it had been pawned—but when he'd eaten something he rushed out into the January night to say hello to his friends wearing his thin flapping school jacket.

For the next few months the Tsar's police could consider that the imprisonment had been successful. Mayakovsky dropped his membership in the Party and was never to join again, even after the Bolsheviks came to power in 1917. He had decided during his seemingly endless days in Butyrki that if he involved himself completely in the Revolution he wouldn't have time for anything else. He wanted to study, and he turned to art, since he felt that his efforts at writing poetry had been a complete failure.

He began with the same academic training that Lili had already finished. While she was in Munich, he was "doing heads" in the studio of Pyotr Kyelin, who prepared students for the examinations required for entrance into the Moscow Institute of Painting, Sculpture, and Architecture, where Mayakovsky was accepted in 1911, a year after his release from prison. During his time with Kyelin he filled out, grew a mustache, and in his dark student blouse he didn't look any different from the others in his class.

When he entered art school in the late summer of 1911, he was eighteen. Like many adolescents raised by a mother who was strongly protective, he was both self-assured and desperately insecure, the two moods alternating unpredictably. He moved out of the family apartment and took a room of his own on the outskirts of the city, but his mother arranged a credit for him at the market where he could charge up to ten rubles a month on her account. To save the streetcar fare he walked the long distance between his room and the shop, buying a cheap sausage and measuring it off into small pieces so he wouldn't eat it all at once and go hungry before the next trip. The ration was half an inch for breakfast and supper, and an inch for lunch.

Mayakovsky quickly became restless and dissatisfied with the mediocrity of his classes. The art school was located across the street from the post office, and he used to say that only this saved it from getting lost in Moscow. One night, bored at a Rachmaninoff concert, he got up to leave and recognized someone else from the school who looked as bored as he was. This was an older, dandified student named David Burliuk who'd antagonized Mayakovsky in their art classes by his patronizing manner. Meeting each other at the door, they began to talk, and when Mayakovsky found that Burliuk was as dissatisfied as he was, they struck up an immediate friendship. With this encounter Mayakovsky was drawn into the creative path he was to follow for the rest of his life.

David Burliuk was not only ten years older than Mayakovsky, he'd also come from a different background. His father was an estate manager and their life was comfortably bourgeois. He and his two brothers and sisters had been able to study whatever they liked, and by the time he drifted into the art school in Moscow he'd already studied art for two years in Germany and one year in France. David and his brothers Vladimir and Nikolai had become involved with the avant-garde art movements and David was one of the exhibitors in the famed Blaue Reiter exhibition in Munich in 1911–12. Despite this achievement he kept moving from one place to another, throwing himself into painting, organizing, writing, and promoting the talents of the people associated with him.

Perhaps part of Burliuk's restlessness grew out of an inner dissatisfaction with his own work. Although he participated in the early avant-garde exhibits and was close to most of the important artists working in new directions in Russia, like Larionov and Goncharova, his own painting was diffuse and tentative. He was influenced by nearly every school of modern painting without ever finding a style of his own. But to Mayakovsky he was a model of success and assurance. Shortly after their first meeting, as they were walking through the dark Moscow streets, Mayakovsky recited some lines from one of his own poems, saying that a friend of his had written it. Burliuk stopped, looked him up and down, and yelped: "You yourself wrote it. You're a brilliant poet!"

While Mayakovsky was sure that his poem wasn't worth such enthusiastic praise, he was also very pleased: "That evening, quite unexpectedly, I became a poet." Swept along by his own enthusiasm, Burliuk introduced him the next morning to someone else as "my brilliant friend, the famous poet Mayakovsky." Then as he was walking away he turned back to the thoroughly confused Mayakovsky and shouted, "Now write, or you'll put me in a ridiculous position."

Mayakovsky was quickly drawn into Burliuk's group of artists and writers, which already included the young poet and pioneer pilot Vassily Kamensky and Velimir Khlebnikov, a poet of startling and eccentric genius whom Kamensky had brought into the group in 1909. As editor of the magazine *Vesna* (*Spring*), Kamensky had published a poem of Khlebnikov's in 1908, the first Futurist avant-garde work to be published in Russia. With his usual immediate response to new ideas, Burliuk published a collection of his friends' drawings, poetry, and articles called *A Trap for Judges* in the spring of 1910, the year before he met Mayakovsky. The anthology, printed on the back of wallpaper as a protest against the fancy printing of the period, went generally unnoticed—partly because only about twenty of the three or four hundred copies ever got out of the printer's shop due to the artists' difficulty in paying the bill.

Burliuk had a little money from his father, and he didn't hesitate to support someone he thought could be interesting.

> *Beautiful Burliuk.* I think of David with everlasting love. Wonderful friend. My real teacher, Burliuk made a poet out of me. Read French and German poets to me. Thrust books at me. Used to walk and talk without stop. Never let me out of his sight. Gave me fifty kopeks daily, so I should not starve while writing.

The small coterie that Mayakovsky had joined was one of the many groups of Russian writers and artists trying to follow the great wave of new writing and art that had sprung up in Europe the decade before. Much of what they did was expressed as a strident bohemianism that spent its energy writing noisy manifestos and wearing ridiculous costumes, but at the same time there was a definite purpose behind it, even if many of the results were confused and undirected.

They wanted to break away from the oppressive weight of the Symbolist writers who dominated Russian literature, writers like Valery Bryusov, Andrei Bely, and Alexander Blok. They wanted to create a new poetry using the language of the streets and the sounds of words themselves. They wanted to be free of the "stagnant swamp" of the Symbolists' vague language and visionary dreaming. Later, Burliuk and his followers were to deny strenuously that they'd been influenced by other European avant-garde groups, but as early as 1909 there had been discussions in the Russian press of the Italian Futurists, another group with some of the same attitudes, whose spokesman, F. T. Marinetti, toured Russia. Burliuk's friends first called themselves "The Coming Men," but the press called them "Futurists," which after a while they accepted. Since Cubism was the counterpart in art, they came to use both words, and for a time they were also known as Cubo-Futurists.

In their obstreperous self-advertisement they often had their picture taken, and Mayakovsky's face began to appear in the group. At first he looked out of place. Except for Khlebnikov, the others were much more affluent than he was. They wore good suits and warm coats, and Burliuk usually affected a monocle. Volodya looked like what he was, a poor art student in a loose blouse with a flowing tie, a long shabby coat, and a floppy, wide-brimmed hat. He was growing a scraggling beard, and often in the pictures he looked hungry, his face thin and drawn, only his dark eyes charged with their intense vitality.

During this time Mayakovsky began to take a few lessons to help him recite poetry more effectively. He was coached by Burliuk, who'd recently married and was living with his wife, a music student, in the Romanovka Hotel in Moscow. The hotel was filled with students from the Music Conservatory because practicing was allowed until midnight. Usually Volodya visited Burliuk in time for tea; then he'd leave the table with its copper samovar and plates of cookies and candied fruit to stand in the middle of the room so he could watch himself pose in the dim mirror hung on the grimy red damask wall. As he did his vocal exercises and struck attitudes, his voice mingled with the sounds of practicing from the young singers and instrumentalists who lived in the decrepit hotel.

In December 1912, the Moscow Futurists put together a new anthology. It was titled *A Slap in the Face of Public Taste* and was conceived as another protest against the current literary fashion. The poems and articles were printed on gray and brown wrapping paper, and the cover was bound with a rough sackcloth material. At the beginning of the anthology the poets placed a manifesto of their program which had the same title as the collection, a blast at everything in Russian culture that had come before them: "The past suffocates us. The Academy and Pushkin are more incomprehensible than hieroglyphics. Throw Pushkin, Dostoevsky, Tolstoy, etc., overboard from the steamship of modernity."

A Slap in the Face of Public Taste contained the first poems of Mayakovsky to be published, "Night" and "Morning." They are obviously youthful works, exaggerated and posturing, with a tone of egotistic self-assurance that was already part of his public performance. This time Burliuk's efforts attracted attention, and an emotional debate was carried on in the press about the Futurists' aesthetic ideas. The poets themselves emphasized the outlandishness of it all with their sophomoric clowning, parading on the streets in eccentric costumes with their faces painted and wooden spoons in their buttonholes, or giving readings with a grand piano suspended upside down over their heads. Mayakovsky's costume was usually his famous yellow blouse (a loose shirt in a peasant style that his mother and sisters had sewn for him), a green overcoat, and a top hat.

> The Yellow Blouse. Never had suits. Had two blouses—hideous kind. A tried method was to ornament with a tie. No money. Took a piece of yellow ribbon from my sister. Tied it around my neck. Furor. So the most conspicuous and beautiful thing about a man was his tie. Evidently if you increased the size of the tie you increased the furor. As sizes of tie are limited I had to resort to cunning. I made a tie-shirt and a shirt-tie. Impression: irresistible.

Burliuk and his friends toured the large cities of Russia, usually having to defend themselves against persistent clamor from the audience. Once, in Kishinev, they hired fifty young boys to rush through town shouting, "The Futurists are coming!" but the boys mixed up the words "Futurists" and "Footballers," which are close in Russian, and ran through the streets calling, "The soccer team is coming." One of Mayakovsky's personal moments of success came during a reading in Georgia, when he addressed the audience in his native Georgian. They were so pleased at hearing something in their own language that they were almost ready to accept anything he had to say. As a local newspaper expressed it, "One could agree with many of his comments about the evolution of the arts."

Mayakovsky had already begun a long work, an experimental verse-play that was filled with his posturing, his vanities, and his hunger for attention, but it was also tinged with a pervading sense of loneliness, even if he did express himself with an overblown cry of self-pity. The play, called *Vladimir Mayakovsky: A Tragedy*, was presented in December 1913 as part of a small Futurist theater festival in Luna Park in St. Petersburg. All the characters were dressed as puppets who pushed canvas figure-frames in front of them, except Mayakovsky, who played the central figure. Although he later said that he was "booed to shreds," the play was actually a popular success, with the sold-out audience enjoying it as much for the Futurist novelty as for the play itself.

The play was short, only two brief acts with a prologue and epilogue, and often it was more farcical than tragic. Despite its occasional gaucheries and insistent egoism, it was one of the surest strides forward he had taken in his poetic development, and its themes were to appear in some of his greatest poetry of the next years. He, the poet Vladimir Mayakovsky, was the central character, and everyone else in the play was reduced to a dominant characteristic: the old man with scrawny black cats, the man with one eye and one leg, the man without a head, the man with two kisses. The action of the play was often obscure, but the theme was explicit: a celebration of his genius as a poet, and the apotheosis of the Poet offering himself as a sacrifice for the sufferings of all mankind. Perhaps the most affecting moment was at the end of the play, after all the

characters brought the Poet their tears, which he jammed into a
suitcase, saying,

> I
> with my load
> walk on;
> stumble,
> crawl
> to the north
> to where
> in the vise of infinite longing
> the fanatic ocean
> is eternally
> tearing its breast
> with the fingers of waves.
> I'll drag myself there—
> exhausted;
> and in my last delirium
> I'll throw your tears
> to the dark god of thunder
> at the source of bestial faiths.

There was no one in all creation with more integrity or loftier
purpose than himself, Mayakovsky told his audience. The soul was
prosaic by comparison.

> By the way
> I did find her once—
> the soul.
> She came out
> in a blue dressing gown,
> and said:
> "Sit down.
> I've been waiting for a long time for you.
> Wouldn't you like a glass of tea?"

The play was awkwardly touching, though he tried to return the audience to the usual mood of Futurist banter with an epilogue that began

> I wrote all this
> about you—
> poor drudges!
> It's too bad I had no bosom: I'd have fed
> all of you, like a sweet little old nanny.
> But right now I'm a bit dried up— . . .

and ended

> . . . at other times, what pleases me
> more than anything
> is my own name:
> Vladimir Mayakovsky.

At that moment he was a twenty-year-old poet declaiming on a small stage in a St. Petersburg park, gesturing in front of a stark backdrop painted to suggest a spider's web of city streets. Despite some hisses and booing from the spectators, he held the stage with a deep voice so powerful that it could shout down anyone else's. For a poet who'd been writing for less than two years, his presence and his authority were startling. Mayakovsky playing himself before an audience seemed to have discovered a role that suited him for life.

Notoriety had come so quickly that he was often spoiled in public, expecting attention as a normal part of his life. With people outside the Futurist group he posed and wheedled, demanding that they listen to him and then often being loudly insulting when they did.

As well as being talented, he was also good-looking and ardently physical. He threw himself hungrily at the girls who ventured close and he was often successful with them. As Burliuk noticed humorously, there were lots of girls. "In the early months of our acquaintance he tried to impress me with his achievements in debauchery. He was full of young, untapped, inexhaustible vigor, but he had to content himself with the love of townswomen, unfaithful to their husbands while on vacation—in hammocks and on seesaws—or with the young, unbridled passion of girl students . . ."

The involvements didn't last. He'd had so much attention that he was quickly bored with the girls who were swept away by him. The excitement for him was as much in the loud pursuit of the girl as it was in his enjoyment of whatever she gave him. But at the same time he seemed to be looking for something else, for a relationship that would be more than a brief affair. His poetry, despite its verbal audacities and determined posing, reflected a deep inner despair.

By the time he wrote *Vladimir Mayakovsky: A Tragedy*, there seemed to be two opposite sides to Mayakovsky's character. He exaggerated the public Mayakovsky, the flamboyant, arrogant dandy, because he was afraid of his double, wary of the softness of his private feelings, which often threatened to overwhelm him. As a child he felt lonely and unloved, and the shattering experience of five months' confinement in prison at the age of sixteen had contributed to his lack of emotional balance; he had frequent thoughts of suicide. His insecurity was expressed in his boorish postering as a Futurist and his callousness in his many love affairs, deliberate attempts to deny his emotional vulnerability.

Yet his need for a place, for close friendship, was as intense as his need for an audience for his poetry. He hated to be alone, and he spent hours with girls he wasn't having an affair with, just to have somewhere to go. At the same time that Lili was beginning the second year of her marriage, Mayakovsky was a familiar figure in the apartments of many people in Moscow. Eventually at one of these apartments he met Lili's sister, Elsa, who knew almost nothing about him except that he muttered verses under his breath all the time, and that he seemed to be searching for somewhere to feel at home.

3

Lili Brik and her sister, Elsa, 1918

I,
with a foot swollen from searching,
have walked all through
your country
and several other lands too,
in the cloak and mask of darkness.
I was searching
for her,
the soul no one had seen,
in order to put her healing flowers
into the wounds of my lips.

VLADIMIR MAYAKOVSKY: A TRAGEDY

E LSA, AT SIXTEEN, HAD NONE OF THE STYLISH BEAUTY she developed when she was older. During these years she was just Lili's little sister. She was short and plump, without Lili's distinctive beauty, though her eyes, a deep blue in contrast to Lili's dark brown, were in their way as striking. The two sisters were very close and very competitive. Where Lili was lazy and unmotivated in school, Elsa worked hard, did well, went on to teacher training while she continued to study music and art. It was as a student that she met Mayakovsky. He baffled her. "This first time I was impressed not by his verses, not by the man reciting them, but by all this together, as a phenomenon of nature, as a thunderstorm."

While Elsa didn't understand him, she liked him. Mayakovsky used to telephone her, but at first she refused to see him. Some weeks later when they met by chance on the street, he was dressed in a ridiculous top hat and embroidered frock coat, swinging a cane. He lifted his eyebrows, smiled, and asked if he could come to visit her. Elsa knew her parents wouldn't approve, and she didn't quite trust him herself, but she said he could come to the Kagans' apartment.

When Mayakovsky showed up at the front door, he startled the housekeeper with his Futurist costume, though she was used to the theatrical people who were the lawyer's clients. He was as arrogant as ever. The first thing he did was to inspect the apartment, and he insisted that Elsa had to take down the reproduction of Böcklin's Symbolist painting "The Island of the Dead," which he told her was impossibly bourgeois. He recited his lines for the play *Vladimir Mayakovsky* and his poems, and when Elsa asked him to be quiet while she concentrated on her schoolwork, he kept on scribbling poetry on bits of paper as she did her lessons. He was obsessed with his play, but when he showed her passages from it, she was unimpressed and corrected his spelling mistakes. If she practiced the piano, he followed her into the living room, pacing back and forth, still mumbling verses. Once he showed up at the apartment when Elsa wasn't at home, and he left his oversized calling card, which looked to the Kagans like an advertisement (his name was in large yellow block letters). Elsa's mother returned it to him, saying, "Vladimir Vladimirovich, you forgot your signboard at our house yesterday."

Perhaps the Kagans let him have the freedom of their house because they sensed his desperation. If they knew that he sometimes walked the streets all night after he left their house because it was too far to return to his shabby room on the outskirts of Moscow, they never said anything to him about it. They probably did have some idea that he was virtually homeless, for his deepest need seemed to be for the family itself, for the emotional life he felt there. It was enough for him simply to be allowed to sit in their rooms.

It wasn't only his family's poverty. His mother and sisters didn't understand his painting and poetry or his Futurist friends Kamensky and Burliuk; his mother wanted him to become a doctor. At the Kagan apartment Mayakovsky could keep up his pose, he could wear his outlandish costumes and mutter and pace the floor in young self-consciousness, without worry.

But finally the visits became too much. Elsa's father was sick, and when Lili came home she told her sister, " A certain Mayakovsky comes to see you . . . Mother cries because of him." The next time he telephoned, Elsa told him he couldn't come to the house. They began to meet outside the Kagan apartment in the billiard room of the Society for Free Aesthetics in Moscow, where Volodya played billiards with great concentration, losing again and again despite the fact that he made up his own rules for the game. Once when Elsa came there after he hadn't heard from her for a long time, he recited a little poem he'd written about her and the Kagan apartment.

> There stands a house,
> it's full of windows,

to the right of Pyatnitskaya.
And that meany witch
lives
there and doesn't write to me.

For people as young and self-absorbed as they were, the outbreak of World War I in the late summer of 1914 came at first as a light-hearted distraction. The streets were crowded with men in black who had tucked their trousers into high boots, conscripts being mobilized and marched in large groups with a policeman carrying a heavy ledger at their side.

> *War.* Took it excitedly. At first thought of it in its decorative and noisy aspects. Draw posters to order, of course entirely military. Then poem "War Is Declared."

> *August.* First battle. The horror of war stared us in the face. War horror. War is disgusting. The rear even more disgusting. To speak about the war one must see it. I went to enlist as a volunteer. They didn't take me—politically unreliable.

In the first weeks of spring, 1915, Elsa, her mother, and her father moved out of Moscow to the family's summer dacha in Mala-khova. Her mother agreed to let Mayakovsky visit with Elsa in the country, but on condition that she take one of her aunts as a chaperone when meeting him at the small country station. Elsa was so embarrassed at having the older woman with her that she delayed her departure, hoping Mayakovsky would get impatient and take a train back to Moscow. When they finally arrived they found him still waiting, furious that Elsa had tried to stand him up. The next time he came to Malakhova, he insisted that she find a way to see him alone. Again she was hours late, but Mayakovsky still waited, smoking cigarettes in the evening shadows of the tall pine trees beside the station. They went for a walk along the empty dacha-lined country road, Mayakovsky so angry with Elsa that he kept at a distance, refusing to walk along beside her, reciting lines to himself. She was contrite, and for the first time she began to listen to him.

> In the darkness his voice, not addressing me, slid in verse along the fences. I had become used to the fact that Volodya was constantly creating verses, both silently and aloud, when he was with me. I didn't pay any attention to his being a poet, but suddenly that evening in Malakhova I was awakened as if a bright light had been switched on. I was enlightened when suddenly I heard the words, pronounced softly,
>
> Listen!
> If they light up the stars—
> That means—somebody needs them, doesn't it?
>
> I stopped and asked excitedly, "Whose verses are these?" "Ah, you like them—now you see!" said Volodya triumphantly. We walked farther, then we sat somewhere on a low bench under the starlit sky while Mayakovsky recited his verses for me for a long time. That night the marvelous, enormous, infinite feeling of awe and the most faithful friendship were lit in me. Immediately it became clear and simple that I could meet with Mayakovsky secretly and without the slightest pang of conscience. I used to come to Moscow, to our empty apartment smelling of mothballs, with the rugs rolled up, the two grand pianos wrapped up like horses covered with sheepskins . . .

Mayakovsky was giving her what Lili later described as his "treatment," but Elsa was still too young for him, too sheltered by her mother, and too concerned with doing well in school. Lili always vehemently insisted that there was never anything between them except an adolescent flirtation, saying, "Nothing like that could have happened," but she was concerned at the time. Mayakovsky made it very clear to everyone that many girls came and went in his life.

Early in 1914, a few months after meeting Elsa, he fell desperately in love with a girl, Maria Alexandrovna Denisova, whom he'd seen for a few hours in Odessa on the Futurists' tour with Burliuk and Kamensky. In the typical impetuous style of his romances, he proposed to her immediately, and was so excited about her that he wanted to leave the tour in Odessa, abandon Burliuk and Kamensky and the theaters and posters waiting for them in Kiev, and spend the rest of his life making love to Maria in Odessa. After she was hours late to an assignation in his hotel room and refused to hear of his plans for a future together, Mayakovsky sullenly joined Burliuk and Kamensky and resumed the tour.

Back in Moscow, Mayakovsky was involved with a girl named Sonia Shamardina, and he took Elsa to the room of an art student with whom he was having an affair, a girl named Tonya Gumilina. All of these girls were to become part of a long poem he was writing, at first titled "The Thirteenth Apostle," but eventually published as "The Cloud in Trousers."

This was not only a period of intense personal confusion for Mayakovsky, but also one of turbulent artistic growth. Some of the work of the months before he met Elsa seemed to be straining for effects, his syntax and vocabulary forced out of his exhibitionism. What was to be his own distinct voice as a poet was a muting of this theatricalism. He still used it, but he learned to include himself and his own emotions in it, as if consciously allowing expression to his inner, private self. The outbursts of his first poems had tried vainly to conceal his responsiveness and vulnerability to life, but in poems like "Listen," the poem he read to Elsa in Malakhova, his emotions were clearly exposed.

> Listen!
> If they light up the stars—
> That means—somebody needs them, doesn't it?
> It means—someone wants them to be there?
> It means—someone calls those tiny spits pearls?

And straining
Through the blizzards of noontime dust
Bursts in to God
Afraid that he is late,
Weeps,
Kisses His veiny hand
Begs
That there positively must be a star!

Her perception of Mayakovsky's genius made it easier for Elsa to be close to him, but her mother and Lili were still upset at their friendship. Although Lili hadn't met him, she and Osip had seen him in 1913 at a ceremonial dinner for the well-known Symbolist poet Konstantin Balmont, when Mayakovsky had broken in with shouted interruptions and had given a mocking speech entitled "From Your Enemies." Later in the evening Lili was standing close to a group around Mayakovsky while he studied a portrait of Tolstoy by Repin that was hanging on the wall and sneered, "You'd have to be a clod to paint like that." Lili thought his behavior was scandalous. "Both of us, Brik and me, but especially me, were indignant over Mayakovsky and the others. They couldn't even appear in public without the police coming to quiet things down."

One day early in the summer of 1915 Lili took the train from Petrograd to visit her family at their summer house, and for the first time she met Mayakovsky. She was sitting on a bench near the dacha with Elsa on a warm, overcast evening when suddenly a figure stepped out of a grove of trees a short distance away. She saw a cigarette, and then a deep voice said, "Elishka, let's go for a walk." Without a word Elsa immediately stood up and went off with him. A half hour passed, an hour, it began to rain, but still Elsa didn't come back and Lili became worried. She knew that the deep voice belonged to Mayakovsky, and she shared her mother's uneasiness, especially since Elsa had confided to Lili that he often "made advances" to her. Elsa treated their meetings as a joke and cheerfully refused to agree with her sister that Mayakovsky should behave himself, but Lili didn't like leaving them unchaperoned on an evening walk in the woods together. She knew she couldn't go inside the dacha without Elsa.

Finally Elsa returned and formally introduced Mayakovsky to her sister. In the murky darkness, Lili couldn't see much of him, only that he was very tall—Elsa didn't even come up to his shoulder—but she did notice that he had "a beautiful voice." They were so late she scolded Elsa, who turned and said, "You see, Volodya, I told you she'd be angry!" He didn't answer, just disappeared as he'd come, with a burning cigarette in his hand.

There were no other meetings between them in the country, but Lili saw him once again, this time wearing his top hat, on Nevsky Prospect in Petrograd, surrounded by young people. "He looked terribly insolent to me."

Lili's father died of cancer of the pancreas early in July 1915, and after helping with the funeral in Moscow, the two sisters returned to the apartment in Petrograd. Mayakovsky was now living closer to Petrograd himself—with friends in Finland at the resort town of Kuokkala, two kilometers from the Russian border. Finland had been a Russian province for more than a hundred years, and it was a popular vacation area for many Russians, who took the short train journey from Petrograd. The months Mayakovsky spent in Kuokkala were to be an important turning point in his poetic career.

Mayakovsky's friend, the literary critic Kornei Chukovsky, had a two-story summer house facing the bay. Away from the distractions of Moscow, he threw himself into the composition of "The Cloud in Trousers." Kuokkala was a country resort in the sparse pine woods on the shores of the Gulf of Finland, with a gritty beach that had huge stones protruding irregularly from the water. At high tide the waves covered the rocks, and at other times they lay scattered on the sand in long, uneven loops, as if strung on a chain. Mayakovsky jumped on the rocks murmuring lines from his poem in progress, sometimes running for several minutes, leaping from stone to stone as if carried by a strong wind. He would interrupt the running to walk slowly on the beach, taking long steps, stopping to light a cigarette, but never breaking off his quiet, concentrated, rhythmical monologue. This work went on five hours every day for nearly two months, except for a few trips to Petrograd or Moscow.

At first Mayakovsky kept the entire long poem in his head, never bothering to write down the verses in a notebook, sometimes jotting a few key lines on empty cigarette boxes as he paced the beach. Every evening he ate dinner with Chukovsky or one of his friends— the theater director N. H. Evreinov, or the artists Repin and Punin— and after dinner Mayakovsky always recited the entire poem from the beginning, adding the half dozen new lines written that day. Some evenings he'd reject a line after he'd read it to an audience, and the next day he'd "walk" a more effective one on the beach.

On July 19 (July 7, O.S.), Mayakovsky celebrated his twenty-second birthday. He was young, already well known, and creating lyric poetry of startling originality in "The Cloud in Trousers," but he was continually unhappy. He was pouring his feelings into the poem, and yet the creative effort didn't resolve his essential insta-bility. His lack of emotional balance was felt by everyone close to him that summer, his arrogance and insecurity jostling each other and erupting to cause unexpected scenes.

Despite the publication of excerpts from "The Cloud," he was so desperate to find a publisher for the entire poem that he even dragged Chukovsky back to Moscow to help him impress a wealthy man he hoped would put up the money. At first everything went well. Mayakovsky tried to be polite, but at the end of the dinner their rich host drunkenly burst into loud praise of the poetry of the Futurist Igor Severyonin, and told Volodya that he should write something in the other poet's "refined" style. Mayakovsky banged his glass down on the table and turned to his friend. "Please forgive me, Kornei, for bringing you to this sweet-smelling place."

Later in the summer Mayakovsky was invited to have breakfast with Maxim Gorky, who was at his summer house in Mustamyaki, also in Finland, not far from where Mayakovsky was staying in Kuokkala. Gorky was back in Russia during this period of relative political relaxation, allowed to write and edit a literary journal despite his opposition to the war. In April 1915 he'd written an article on Futurism in the *Journal of Journals*, Number 1, particularly praising Mayakovsky, whom he'd heard reading at the popular Petrograd literary café, the Stray Dog, two months before. Gorky's support would be very important.

On the morning of the breakfast Mayakovsky arrived at Gorky's dacha early, excited and tense. He paced the floor waiting for Gorky to come downstairs and chatted nervously with his wife, who was impressed by Mayakovsky's extraordinary height. She thought he was very good-looking, but when he smiled at her and she saw his bad teeth, she thought sadly, "So young and no teeth." She turned to leave the room to bring in the trays of food for breakfast—coffee, fresh bread, ham—when Volodya stopped her with an abrupt question: "Aren't you afraid I'll steal your silver spoons?" This was such an odd thing to say that she hesitated and then answered carefully, "No, I'm not afraid. And frankly, our spoons are not silver, anyway."

Alone with Gorky, after breakfast and a few glasses of wine, Mayakovsky began to recite passages from "The Cloud," standing up near the table. As he read he became more and more agitated, his voice rushing over the phrases, his body swaying rhythmically from side to side. Finally he was so overcome with emotion at his own words that he broke down and was unable to finish the poem. Gorky was both impressed and alarmed.

> When I told Mayakovsky that in my opinion he had a great but probably hard future, and that his talent called for a lot of work, he answered gloomily, "I want the future today," and again, "Without joy I have no need for a future, and I feel no joy." He behaved very nervously and was clearly deeply disturbed. He seemed to speak with two voices; in one voice he was a pure lyricist, in the other sharply satirical. It was clear that he was especially sensitive, very talented, and very unhappy.

Gorky instinctively sensed the split in Mayakovsky's personality, and his insight that the poet seemed to speak with two voices was especially acute. Mayakovsky's response was characteristically uncompromising. Different from the others whom Gorky later encouraged, like the brilliant young short-story writer Isaac Babel, Mayakovsky didn't need inspiring words to give him the courage to be a writer. He might seem to Gorky to lack balance and discipline, but he had total confidence in himself; what he wanted was a publisher. It wasn't until the end of 1915 that he was invited to contribute to Gorky's magazine *The Chronicle*, but he was too impatient to wait even these few months.

Restless after finishing "The Cloud in Trousers," Mayakovsky still felt close to Elsa. One day in early July he left Kuokkala and went to the Briks' apartment, expecting to find her, but only Lili was at home. She was in black, mourning her father, and he blurted out, "You've gotten thin, catastrophically." She was angered by his rudeness, but he persisted, disturbed enough to insist on reciting a short poem to her. He bragged that his poems were great even if she didn't understand them, and that nobody beside himself and Anna Akhmatova was writing brilliant poetry in Russia.

Lili thought his manners were terrible. "I had learned as a child that it was bad manners to brag," and she told him as politely as she could that although she hadn't read any of his poems, she'd try to read them if he had any with him. Mayakovsky showed her "Mother and the Evening Killed by the Germans." She looked at it carefully and returned it without comment. Surprised, he asked, "Don't you like it?" She realized authors should be praised, but she was so angered by his insolence that she answered, "Not particularly." He finally left, each of them irritated with the other.

A week later he was back in the apartment. Elsa brought him for tea, insisting that Lili and Osip must "meet" him and listen to his poetry. As Elsa remembered:

I think that then, that very evening, the fates of those who were listening to Mayakovsky's "The Cloud in Trousers" were shaped. The Briks' attitude toward the poem was rapturous. They fell in love with the verses without reservation. And Mayakovsky fell in love with Lili without reservation.

It was July 15, 1915, the date that Mayakovsky described in his autobiography as the "Most Joyful Date" in his life.

4

Mayakovsky, 1915

Formerly I believed
books were made like this:
a poet came,
lightly opened his lips,
and the inspired fool burst into song . . .

"THE CLOUD IN TROUSERS"

THE SETTING FOR THEIR MEETING WAS IN ITSELF almost symbolic of the point the Briks had come to in their lives. Their Petrograd apartment was a mixture of fashionable bohemianism and middle-class elegance, their three very small rooms on the seventh floor of an old building on Zhukovsky Street in a shabby neighborhood not far from Nevsky Prospect. A wrought-iron street lamp illuminated the entranceway on the cobblestone street, and a battered sculpture of a horse's head stood in a niche in the stable wall in the courtyard. A long trudge up interminable flights of steep stairs led to their apartment. Although most of their furniture was in storage in Moscow, the rooms were so small they seemed cramped anyway. The living room off the tiny entrance foyer was filled with a long, low sofa with silk cushions and a piano, with an automobile Osip had made out of playing cards sitting on top of it. On the walls were Japanese fans and a large oil painting by Boris Grigoryev, a portrait of Lili lying on the grass in a dress and laced boots in front of a flaming sunset, which Mayakovsky later titled "Lili Spilled Out." Across the narrow corridor were two smaller rooms which the Briks had tried to enlarge into a combination dining-and-sitting room by removing the connecting door. Their bedroom also opened off the entrance foyer, furnished with two separate beds covered with thick expensive quilts that had come from their Moscow apartment.

The atmosphere was strained when Elsa and Mayakovsky came in. He knew that the Briks didn't like him, but his immature assertiveness forced him to try to get their attention. Unwilling to sit down to make polite small talk, he hulked in the doorway to the dining room as the others settled at the table for tea. Lili leaned over to Elsa and whispered, "Please, I beg you, tell Mayakovsky not to bore us today. Tell him not to read us any poetry." But Elsa had brought him there so that they could hear his poetry, and she insisted. Mayakovsky was so used to reluctant audiences—his friends in Kuokkala had gotten very tired of hearing "The Cloud" every evening after dinner —that he would have recited anyway. He stood leaning against the door frame, facing them as they sat uncomfortably at the table, paying no attention to what they were saying, waiting for the right moment to begin his poem. As the seconds passed, he took a small notebook out of his coat pocket with intense self-absorption, leafed through the pages, then put it back in his pocket. He looked around the narrow little room as if it were a public auditorium and said abruptly in his deep voice, almost as if he were challenging them to go on ignoring him,

> Your thought
> musing on a softened brain
> like a bloated lackey on a greasy couch,
> I'll tease with a bloody morsel of heart
> and taunt to my heart's content, arrogant and caustic.
>
> In my soul there isn't one gray hair,
> and no senile tenderness in it!
> Having thundered the world with the might of my voice
> I walk—handsome,
> twentytwoyearsold.

The opening lines of the prologue to "The Cloud in Trousers" were a strident continuation of the bombastic exaggeration that the Futurists had used again and again to attract attention, a mixture of insult and grandiose posturing that either made people immediately angry or just as immediately sympathetic—but it was impossible to listen to it without some response. For the Briks, crowded at the table in their small dining room trying to keep their eyes on their teacups while a towering, disheveled poet recited loudly into their faces, the effect would have been overpowering whether they liked it or not. The poem, however, was not the usual Futurist compound of rhetoric and assertion. A few lines later—still insisting he could tell them something no one else could—Mayakovsky said suddenly,

> if you wish—
> I'll be irreproachably tender:
> not a man, but—a cloud in trousers.

It was for them the first suggestion of the deeper strain of personal lyricism that was as strongly centered in Mayakovsky as his futurist theatrics. He swept on to the first section of the poem, exposing the emotional pressures that were gnawing at him as if there in the doorway he'd suddenly pulled off his shirt. For the Briks it was a moment like the one Elsa had experienced a few months before at the dacha in Malakhova, when "a bright light had been switched on."

> You think malaria makes me delirious?

> It happened.
> In Odessa, it happened.

> "I'll come at four," Maria said.

> Eight.
> Nine.
> Ten.

The poem's first section was a long, merciless description of his own despair as he waited for the faithless Maria to come to him and who, when she did show up hours later, said only, "D'you know, I'm getting married." Lili was never to forget the sound of his voice as he spoke the line "You think malaria makes me delirious?" By this time they were staring at him, teacups forgotten, listening to his voice flow on in rhythmical cadences as he stood without moving from the door frame, not paying the slightest attention to them. The second and third sections of the poem were less personal, but in the

fourth section he came back to the despair that had colored the
opening, and his performance came to an end with a typical mixture
of braggadocio and tenderness.

Hey, you!
Heaven!
Take off your hat!
I'm coming!

Not a sound.

The universe sleeps,
resting a huge ear on its paw
with mites of stars.

With the last words he sat down at the table, leaned close to
Lili, and asked in a suddenly personal manner—still continuing the
theatricality of the reading—if he could have a cup of tea. Lili was
unable to speak; she just sat staring at him. Silently she poured a
cup of tea from the samovar, and just as silently Mayakovsky accepted it.

Brik was the first to speak. He told Mayakovsky that it was the
finest poetry he'd ever heard and that he felt Mayakovsky was already a great poet, even if he never wrote another line. For Brik the
poem was a brilliant revolutionary statement, and he was stunned by
the intensity and originality of Mayakovsky's poetic images. Osip
took the notebook that "The Cloud" had been copied into and read
the poem over to himself, while Mayakovsky smiled, stirred jam into his
tea, and looked at Lili and Elsa with his large brown eyes. Suddenly
he took the notebook from Osip's hands, put it on the table, opened
to the first page, and asked Lili, "May I dedicate it to you?" Very
carefully he wrote her name under the title of the manuscript.

Lili was flattered, but she was also surprised, because they had
not gotten along well, and besides, she thought that Mayakovsky had
been courting Elsa. But for Elsa he was still too overpowering; he
made up funny poems to her as a schoolgirl. With Lili there had

been an immediate sexual current that they had first felt as antagonism. She tried to protest. "How can you dedicate a poem to one woman when you've written it about another?" She remembered:

He answered then that the poem least of all had anything to do with Maria. "I was interested in many women but I never promised the poem to anyone, and my conscience is clear if I dedicate the poem to you." He told me that while he was writing he was in love with several women. The image of Maria in the poem was not only connected with the Maria from Odessa; in the fourth part originally it was also about a different girl named Sonia. He changed the name Sonia to Maria because he wanted the image of the woman to be a collective image, and he chose the name Maria since it seemed to him to be the most womanly.

Brik kept the notebook for the rest of the evening, reading passages of the poem over and over. Elsa stayed with Lili at the table drinking tea and murmuring occasionally, "I told you so." Brik asked where the poem was going to be published. "Ah, nobody will print it," Mayakovsky answered. He was being a little ingenuous, since the prologue and the fourth section had already been published in February in the first issue of *The Archer*, an almanac that contained, side by side, writings by major Futurists and Symbolists. But as Mayakovsky knew too well, no one had been willing to bring out the entire poem. "How much will it cost if we print it ourselves?" Brik asked, and with that question threw his lot—and Lili's—in with the Futurists.

The next morning Mayakovsky rushed to a printer and found out that it would cost 150 rubles to print a thousand copies. The money could even be paid in installments. Osip gave him the first installment out of his pocket and said, "Bring the poem to the printer. I'll get the rest of the money later." Since Brik had become the publisher, they went over the manuscript together, working with a general rule that they would take out anything that was superfluous, even punctuation. The book was to be set simply, with a plain cover, and Osip drew up a contract promising to pay Mayakovsky fifty kopeks a line "forever."

With Lili, Mayakovsky refined the dedication. He wanted to change it, first to "Liljika," a word he coined from the diminutive of Lili, "Liletjka," and the word "Litjiko," which means "little face." She didn't like it, but he wanted to discard the formal "To Lili Yuryevna Brik," so they settled on the simple "To Thou, Lilya."

Mayakovsky never returned to Kuokkala. He left his things behind him—even his dirty clothes at the laundry—and moved into a room in a small hotel in Petrograd called the Palais Royal in order to be nearer to the Briks. His book was promised for September, but before it was ready there was a gathering at the apartment, a few friends talking and drinking on a warm evening, and Lili and Mayakovsky sat hidden from the others on a windowsill behind the heavy drapery. She thought he looked "suntanned and very handsome." Mayakovsky held her hands, whispering to her, then began stroking her legs and feet until she agreed to meet him the next day, when they could be alone in his room.

From the beginning of their love affair Mayakovsky felt more bound to Lili than she felt to him, though she found him exciting. Probably she was not thinking beyond the moment, and at first she tried to keep a distance from him. She remembered, "For a long time I couldn't say Volodya to him. I always said Vladimir Vladimirovich, and I said 'Vi' (the formal Russian 'you') to him, not 'thou.' But he said 'thou' and 'Lilya.'"

But Mayakovsky was so ardently possessive that there was no question of keeping what had happened a secret, and she went back from his hotel room to wait for her husband. She told Osip that she loved Mayakovsky and that they had become lovers and asked, "What am I to do?" Brik answered, "I quite understand you. How is it possible to refuse Mayakovsky?" And then he said, "But we must never part from one another." And with his plea he decided the course of their lives.

Mayakovsky went on living at the Palais Royal. Lili came to him in the afternoons and he went to the Briks' apartment at night to play cards and talk to Osip. Brik showed no jealousy, rather, a sense of relief that Lili had turned to Mayakovsky instead of troubling him with her unhappiness over their lack of physical intimacy. Besides, Brik admired Mayakovsky's new poem so much that, when they had worked together preparing it for the printer, he had told Mayakovsky that they would be "friends for life." Both Lili and Osip could recite "The Cloud" by heart themselves before it came out. For Lili, waiting for the finished book was like waiting "for a rendezvous," and she and Brik were elated when they saw the first copies, simply printed with a bright orange cover, as they'd planned. Later Lili had her own copy bound in an expensive blue leather cover stamped in gold, with an elegant white moiré lining.

By this time Brik felt so close to Mayakovsky that he began trying to imitate him. He would walk with wide, swinging steps, he talked with a bass voice, and he wrote verses such as:

and as I'm waiting for my simple coffin
when life's last strength slips,
"The Cloud in Trousers" will be the last word
that passes my lips.

In the late fall Mayakovsky left his hotel and moved to a small room on Nadezhdinsky Street. But when he wrote his mother on November 9, 1915, to tell her he'd moved, he asked her to send his mail to the Briks.

I am well as usual. Working as usual too. I moved from the Palais Royale. So now please write to me at 7 Zhukovsky Street, Apartment 42, c/o Brik, for Mayakovsky. Dearest Mama, I have a great favor to ask of you. Redeem and send me my winter coat and send me, if possible, some warm underwear and a couple of handkerchiefs . . .

Mayakovsky began to bring his friends to meet the Briks. A member of the Moscow Futurist group, Viktor Shklovsky, had volunteered for the Army, but despite his requests to be sent to the front, he remained in Petrograd as an instructor in an armored unit. Shklovsky had been close to Mayakovsky before his meeting with the Briks, and he could see that with them Mayakovsky had found a haven. "For a long time Mayakovsky had been buffeted and tossed around . . . Everyone shoved the poet, everyone wounded him . . . But now, finally, he had a home and a contract with Brik: half a ruble per line, forever, and tomorrow he would publish."

It was also obvious that Mayakovsky had fallen in love, and even though Shklovsky was always to feel a little uncomfortable with Lili, he could see what it was that had attracted Mayakovsky. "She knew how to be sad, feminine, capricious, proud, shallow, fickle, in love, clever, and any way you like. Thus Shakespeare described woman in his comedy." In two sentences—it could even be from the diary he kept at the time—Shklovsky noted his first impression of her. "Her eyes are hazel-brown. She has a large head; she is beautiful, red-haired, graceful, and wants to be a dancer." Of her effect on Mayakovsky he said simply, "And so he fell in love with her at first sight, and, actually, forever—till the very loss of weight. So he began writing verses for her."

With the Briks, Mayakovsky had finally found a home. In the apartment Osip put up an unpainted wooden bookshelf to hold the books of the Futurists. The first one placed on it was "The Cloud" in its regular orange cover, and then Lili's special copy with its blue binding. The shelf symbolized their belief in him as an artist. Soon afterward Lili and Mayakovsky exchanged rings that symbolized their love. The ring she gave him was a heavy gold signet ring with his initials. His to her was a golden circle with her initials, L.Yu.B., which form in Russian the words "I love."

The poem that changed all of their lives was the first of Mayakovsky's longer poems to suggest the originality and intensity of his poetic genius, and it is a powerful and arresting poem. It is also a modern poem. Despite the clutter and strain of the Futurist language, particularly in the introduction, he was able to open the poem out into a more personal expression that was convincingly genuine in its emotional directness. It was a poem he'd labored over for more than a year; possibly the prologue was written even earlier, at a point when he still was straining to shock people. Certainly once past the prologue, "The Cloud in Trousers" develops its fresher and more lyric directions.

It is, however, a complicated piece and it sometimes seems impenetrable. The entire poem is tightly concentrated, developing in circling thematic movements that give it coherence, but also make it difficult to perceive the immediate image and concentrate on the overall outline.

It is a poem composed to be read aloud, and in a reading of it there is no misunderstanding of the larger perspectives. It was Mayakovsky's own presentation of his poetry that won him his audience, and for many people the printed poem served only as a reminder of the power of his performance. Certainly with "The Cloud" it's necessary to read it with the awareness of the clarification that the voice could give it through shifts of emphasis, repetition of tone to sustain the unity of longer sections, and a continued variation of rhythm to clarify which points in the poem are part of its larger themes and which are subordinate to them.

It is also possible to sense the larger dimensions of the poem in its original title, "The Thirteenth Apostle." That title, along with large sections of the text, was taken away by the censor, who found it irreligious. The censor asked Mayakovsky, "Do you want to get hard labor for the poem?" and Volodya answered that he didn't like the idea very much. As he said later, " 'The Cloud' proved feathery. The censor blew right through it: six pages full of . . . Since then I hate dots, and commas too." The poem was mutilated by the censor in its first printing, but his friends wrote the deleted parts into their copies by hand. Lili remembered that Mayakovsky took Khlebnikov's copy away from him, afraid he'd leave it on a park bench in his forgetfulness and get Mayakovsky in trouble.

Perhaps censorship worked to Mayakovsky's advantage in the title itself. "The Cloud in Trousers" is much more effective than his original title, which has overtones of the old Symbolist movement and doesn't suggest the poem's modernity. The new title was intriguing, while the original was dated and obvious, and when Mayakovsky got the chance to publish the first complete edition of the poem in 1918, he decided not to restore the old title.

Much of the imagery of the poem, however, was concerned with the religious motif that the original title expressed. Mayakovsky's choice of the name Maria for all the girls he loved in the poem had, of course, biblical overtones, and he was even more explicit in the foreword he wrote to the later edition, where he explained that he considered the poem "a catechism for the art of today." Its four parts were "four rallying cries" against "your love, your art, your society, and your religion."

As before, in his play *Vladimir Mayakovsky: A Tragedy*, he railed against the unjust, wrathful God who had allowed pain and suffering to dominate the world. The violent outpouring of his emotions in the first part of "The Cloud in Trousers" was expressed in some of Mayakovsky's most powerful images. After "Maria" has refused to love him, he compares himself to a volcano.

But remember!
When Vesuvius was mocked
Pompeii perished! . . .

I feel
my "I"
is a good bit too little for me.
A body stubbornly wants to burst out of me.

Hello!
Who is speaking?
Mamma?
Mamma!
Your son is wonderfully ill!

Mamma!
His heart is on fire.
Tell his sisters, Ludya and Olya,
he has nowhere to go.

In the second part of the poem Mayakovsky predicts a revolution, when "hungry hordes" will tear apart the corruption and decay that complacent citizens refused to face.

I,
mocked by my contemporaries
like a prolonged
dirty joke,
I see someone through the mountain of time
whom nobody sees.

Where men's eyes stop short,
there, at the head of hungry hordes,
a year will come
in the thorny crown of revolutions.

But by defying God and glorifying man—"Sinews and muscles are surer than prayers"—the poet just antagonizes common people, who shout that he must be crucified for his blasphemy. In the final section of the poem, Mayakovsky, pushed beyond endurance by the pain of unrequited love and the suffering of all mankind, confronts God and the angels in heaven and forces them to face their colossal stupidity in creating an imperfect world.

Almighty, you concocted a pair of hands,
arranged
for everyone to have a head;
but why didn't you see to it
that one could without torture
kiss and kiss and kiss?!

The entire poem, like all his longer works, is a dense thicket of suggestion and allusion, but it has consistent thematic unities. The major themes of "The Cloud in Trousers" are resolved by the poet's final vision. As in *Vladimir Mayakovsky: A Tragedy*, the hero sees himself martyred in a hostile world, his voice thundering up to heaven, challenging the universe to silence him.

> You won't stop me.
> Whether I'm wrong
> or right,
> I'm as calm as can be.
> Look—
> again they've beheaded the stars
> and bloodied the sky with slaughter!

Mayakovsky had found his voice as a poet before he met the Briks, and his love for Lili was to strengthen his vision of himself as a martyr in "The Cloud in Trousers" and *Vladimir Mayakovsky: A Tragedy*. Martyrdom was the only possible end for his emotional condition, since his need for love was apparently insatiable. Swept along by his feelings as by an irresistible undertow, he turned to Lili. Whether or not she was interested in accepting the role, he cast her as the perfect woman to play opposite him as the romantic rebel, defying heaven and hell in his search for the ultimate love.

In the early winter of 1915, another friend whom Mayakovsky had met in Moscow, the young poet Boris Pasternak, came to Petrograd. He found Mayakovsky transfigured. Before Mayakovsky introduced him to the Briks, they walked the streets of the city in the snowy twilight, talking excitedly. In Moscow Pasternak had been fascinated by Mayakovsky's iron determination to make himself into a poet, but underneath his friend's public posing, his bouts of sullen rudeness and shouting exhibitionism in front of audiences, Pasternak had also detected a deep melancholy, "a wild shyness, and beneath his pretended freedom hid an apprehensive lack of freedom." In Petrograd it seemed to Pasternak that Mayakovsky had at last found friends, the Briks, who understood him.

Mayakovsky and I walked down the Liteynoy; he trampled miles of roadway under his great strides, and as always I was astounded by the gift he had for seeming the perfect frame for any landscape. In this he set off Petrograd even better than Moscow.

This was the time of "The Backbone Flute" and the first drafts of "War and the Universe." "The Cloud" had just come out in an orange cover. He was telling me about the new friends to whom he was taking me, about his acquaintance with Gorky, about how the social theme was taking an increasing part in his projects and allowing him to work in a new way, spending fixed times over allotted tasks. And it was then that I went to see the Briks for the first time.

5

Drawing of Lili Brik by Mayakovsky, 1916

Tobacco smoke gnawed the air.
The room—
a chapter in Kruchenyk's hell.
Remember—
behind this window
the first time
I, frenzied, was stroking your legs.
Today you're sitting there
heart in iron.
Another day—
perhaps
I'll be driven out cursed.
In the bleary hall the hand broken with trembling
can't get into the sleeve.
I'll run out,
I'll throw my body into the street.
Wild,
I'll go mad.
Chopped by despair.
Don't,
Dear,
Sweet,
Let's say goodbye now . . .
Tomorrow you'll forget
that I crowned you,
that I burned out with love a blossoming soul,
And the whirling carnival of restless days
will scatter pages of my books . . .
Could the dry leaves of my words,
greedily breathing,
make you stop?
Let them at least
carpet with last tenderness
your departing step.

"LILI DEAR! INSTEAD OF A LETTER"

FROM THE BEGINNING LILI AND MAYAKOVSKY MADE no effort to conceal their love affair. Even if they'd tried, the poetry he wrote to her over the next months would have made any attempt at concealment futile. But there were still occasional brushes with reality. At first the poem "Lili Dear! Instead of a Letter" couldn't be published, and when Mayakovsky first read it to Lili, with its description of his stroking her legs, they agreed that "legs" would have to be changed to "hands." The poem's mood of despair reflected the reality of his efforts to deal with Lili's moods and capriciousness. She sent him into storms of jealousy by being less than excited to see him, or by treating him with a sudden indifference. She loved him, but she refused to let him possess her completely, and with her willful temperament she subtly dominated the relationship. It was as if they had definitions of love that didn't quite coincide and there were moments when this was more than Mayakovsky, with his overpowering need to possess her, could accept. Sometimes he found her bewitching, sometimes he found her maddening, and in their early months together he sometimes found her both of these things at the same time.

He was also emotionally demanding, but in a different way. He responded to her moods with an adolescent fervor. If she was warm and responsive he was in raptures; if she had something else on her mind he was hopelessly despondent. Everything for him was a transcendent experience calling into question the very nature of their love—of love itself. Sometimes, in the middle of his outbursts, he seemed to be consciously watching himself performing the role of the despairing lover. Certainly he did it well, even with the theatricality of some of his images.

Could the dry leaves of my words,
greedily breathing,
make you stop?
Let them at least
carpet with last tenderness
your departing step.

He had to be the center of a swirling drama, and he tended to project his life in these terms. As Pasternak understood, to Mayakovsky "the poet is not the author, but the subject of a lyric, facing the world in the first person."

At the same time, and this was at the heart of Lili and Mayakovsky's complicated relationship, they had a strong bond between them, what Pasternak recognized as a "natural friendship" that would last all their lives. As much as Lili loved him as a man, she loved him as a poet, and this both pleased and upset him. As Brik said:

Mayakovsky understood love this way: if you love me, you are with me, for me, always, everywhere, in all circumstances. You can't be against me at any time, no matter how unjust or cruel I am. The least vacillation or change is treason. Love must be constant, like a law of nature which knows no exclusions . . . According to Mayakovsky, love was not an act of will, but the condition of life, like gravity. Were there women who loved him like that? Yes. Did he love them? No, he took them for granted.

Did he love anyone that way? Yes—but he was a genius. His genius was stronger than the force of gravity. When he read his poems the ground rose toward him to hear better. Of course, if one could find a planet impervious to poetry . . . But there wasn't a planet like that.

Since Lili never let him feel that love, for her, was "a condition of life," he tried to change his way of living to please her. She made him cut his hair, ordered him to take baths and go to the dentist. She hated his decayed teeth; when she dreamed about him, she dreamed about his "bad teeth." She got him to stop wearing his Futurist costumes by buying him well-tailored new clothes. In return, he taught her to love poetry and not be afraid of animals. The first time she went to visit his room, the caretaker's little black dog rushed at her and Lili was so frightened that Mayakovsky roared with laughter. "A grown-up woman afraid of a little black mongrel!"

With the money Brik was giving him for his new poems Mayakovsky decorated his room with flowers for her and bought her favorite cakes. Lili remembered the ceremonial quality of her visits to his room, the careful preparations he made for their afternoons together. It was early autumn, the days were still long, a warmth in the September air when he began writing the long poem to her called "The Backbone Flute."

Late in the fall of 1915 they had their picture taken together, and the change in his appearance is startling. He has become "half tamed." Instead of the exaggerations of his Futurist costumes, with either the homemade yellow blouse or the embroidered evening clothes, he's wearing a shirt and tie, a fashionable tweed overcoat, and he has on a cloth cap. In the picture she is wearing a tight black hat that matches her eyes, and her face is set in a soft half smile. They look young and happy and very much in love. It is his head that leans to touch hers, and in most of the photographs that were to be taken of them in the next fifteen years, it was Mayakovsky who leaned to her, rather than Lili to him.

These first months of their life together, the days of what Mayakovsky called "the body's festival," may have been as self-absorbed and idyllic as she remembered, but the poem he wrote at the time is instead filled with his own pain. It was first titled "Verses to Her," but for the sake of discretion the title was changed to "The Backbone Flute" and the poem was simply dedicated to her. In it is all the exaggeration and the straining for effect that was part of his own moods, and as it goes on and on—the poem is more than three hundred lines long—the jealousy that he felt sometimes seems to be lost in the flood of rhetoric. At one point he even says of her:

If someone suddenly came on tiptoe to the bedroom door
and blessed the quilted blanket covering you,
I know
there would be a stench of burning wool,
and in sulphurous fumes the devil's body would rise up.

In much of the poem he is obsessed by the feeling that she
doesn't love him as much as he loves her. Frantically he cries out:

I see many signs of boredom.
In my soul look for your youth.
Invite your heart to the body's festival.

In their long afternoons together their physical contact was
never completely satisfying for Lili. She loved the beginning of
physical intimacy, but for her "the prologue was more important than
the finale," and she never felt fulfilled after their hours making love.
She could always, however, respond to his new lines of poetry, and then
she would go back to Brik relieved because he made no physical
demands on her. Mayakovsky always came to the apartment later
himself, but Lili's eagerness to return to her husband drove him into
new attacks of jealousy.

Doors
banged.
He came in,
sprayed with the gaiety of the streets.
I,
as if split in half with a wail,
cried out to him,
"All right,
I'll go,
all right!
She'll stay yours.

Dress her up in fine rags
and let shy wings grow fat in silks.
Watch out so she doesn't float away.
Like a stone around your wife's neck
hang a necklace of pearls!"

There were also the hours when he was completely alone, with
most of his friends left behind in Moscow, when he complained that
he was nearly suffocated by his loneliness. He brooded over his
suspicion that Lili was wearying of their affair, yearning for her love
with a terrible need to be consoled and caressed. This was what
motivated the poem, giving it a sense of helpless, almost suicidal
urgency.

Today just as I came in
I sensed—
something wrong in the house.
You had concealed something in your silk dress,
and the smell of incense expanded in the air.
Are you glad to see me?
A cold
"Very."
Reason's fence breaks with agitation.
Burning and feverish, I heap on despair . . .

Lips you gave.
How rude you were with them.
At a touch I froze.
As if with repentant lips I kissed
a monastery hacked into cold rocks.

As in "The Cloud in Trousers," he reached out to heaven and
eternity to locate the ultimate cause of his suffering. He suspected
that God was teaching him a lesson because he had blasphemed
in his previous poetry:

I have blasphemed
and screamed that there is no god;
but from the depths of hell
god led out a woman to make
the mountain tremble and shudder, and ordered,
love her!

Instead of opening out to give a sense of cosmic resolution of his suffering, "The Backbone Flute" has a more limited range. As the poet, Mayakovsky was playing on his own backbone as a flute, composing a tirade about his capricious mistress on the bare bones of his spinal column, yet at the same time that he despaired of what was happening to him—the poem begins with him thinking about ending his life "with a bullet"—he also exulted in his despair. The poetry becomes such an extravagant performance that it's difficult not to think that Lili's presence was the strongest influence on its composition. She was coming to his hotel room every day to make love and hear him recite new lines, so he wrote a poem that would flatter her and fulfill her expectations.

The poem he'd written earlier, "The Cloud," had also been filled with hyperbole and a certain straining after effect, but he'd worked on it for a long time, polishing it and expanding its themes. He spoke as the same anguished lover in "The Backbone Flute," although the new verses hadn't the earlier poem's freshness or profundity. Considering the circumstances under which the poem was written in the first months of his love affair with Lili, its extravagances become clearer, and Lili shrugged off the poem's implications that she didn't love him. As far as she was concerned, his tormented jealousy arose because "he needed a subject for his poetry."

Mayakovsky brought all his Moscow friends to the apartment, and everyone took turns reading verses after drinking tea. Lili was most taken by Pasternak, who impressed her in their first meeting as a brilliant musician when he talked to her of Scriabin and "improvised wonderfully" on the piano. Mayakovsky often recited lines of his friends' poetry to the Briks, and Lili had noticed that he quoted Pasternak most frequently, so she wanted to hear more of his verses.

I met Pasternak for the first time in Petrograd before the Revolution.

Pasternak read some poems at our place, and Mayakovsky recited "The Backbone Flute" for the first time. Pasternak loved it. He was in love with Mayakovsky as a personality. There was nothing homosexual between them—both loved women. But their friendship was like a "romance" because it changed all the time. Before the Revolution it was calm and they were evenly in love with each other, but later Pasternak was indignant when Mayakovsky wrote revolutionary poems. He didn't like them and he didn't want to understand them, and here their "romance" became a relationship where Pasternak played the role of a woman. He was jealous, he wrote letters, sometimes he was close to Mayakovsky and sometimes he drew back. But Mayakovsky was constant. He loved Pasternak's poetry.

The small apartment became too crowded with all the visitors. The Briks couldn't move to another building, since Osip was technically a war deserter and he'd have to register with the police if he changed his address, but when a six-room apartment became vacant one floor below in the same building at 7 Zhukovsky Street, they moved downstairs. Their furniture didn't fill the rooms, but they didn't bother to send for their things in storage in Moscow. Osip called one room the library—as usual he'd accumulated a lot of books, including the ones he was publishing himself—and the largest room became a studio for Lili, who wanted to take ballet lessons. She found a teacher in Petrograd who had been trained by Nijinsky, and along with a few friends who also wanted to take lessons, she decorated the studio with photographs of Nijinsky and Diaghilev, sewed curtains of tulle and ribbons, and wore a tutu practicing in front of the mirror. The lessons continued for nearly two years, until

October 1917, when, as Lili said, "There was no time to think about dancing."

Ballet lessons at the Brik apartment before a long mirror draped with tulle, Mayakovsky leaning on his heavy cane in the open doorway, smoking cigarettes and watching Lili and her girl friends in their pink tutus practicing at the bar. He'd come a long way from his poor provincial childhood and his teenage politics. And where was Burliuk's protégé, with his embroidered red tuxedo and the advertising placard for his calling card? How could they keep the jumbled pieces of their reality so far apart? As Shklovsky tried to explain later, "many of us felt that revolution was imminent, but we also thought that we were outside space, that we had established our own kingdom of time and that we were not expected to know what millennium it was outside."

At Christmas there was a celebration to welcome the New Year, a Futurist fancy-dress party with all of Mayakovsky's friends from Moscow. The Briks decorated the apartment with a Christmas tree hung upside down in the corner, a gesture symbolizing their disrespect for tradition. Osip glued cards together to make small black pants, each filled with a cotton cloud as "the cloud in trousers" to hang on the tree. Candles were placed on small paper saucers, and nearly everyone dressed in costume. Brik wore a turban and an Uzbek coat, Mayakovsky put a red scarf around his neck, Shklovsky was a sailor with rouged lips. Vassily Kamensky sewed patches of different colors on his jacket and painted his face: dark-blue penciled eyebrows, a bluebird on his cheek, one blond mustache, the other black. David Burliuk and Velimir Khlebnikov wore their ordinary clothes, but Burliuk peered at everyone with his lorgnette and Khlebnikov sat at the table squeezed against the wall, looking—as Elsa remembered—bent and pale as a large sick bird.

Elsa was still studying in Moscow, but she came to the party dressed as Pierrot, her hair swept up and decorated with peacock feathers that almost touched the ceiling. Lili wore red stockings and a short Scottish kilt, and over her bare shoulders she wrapped a shiny silk Russian shawl, trying to look like a Scottish gypsy. She'd been able to find 95 percent alcohol on the black market, which she mixed with cherry syrup, and the party was a great success. In the candlelight Kamensky got so carried away that he proposed marriage to Elsa, and when she refused he dedicated a poem to her. The war intruded into the party once, when Kamensky lifted his glass and shouted, "Cursed be this war! We're guilty of not understanding it and ashamed of having held on to the tail of General Skobelev's horse."

The Briks hung a sheet of paper on one wall of the apartment for everyone to decorate. Mayakovsky wrote a poem about the Futurist Boris Kushner: "The hippopotamus dived into the water/when he saw Kushner." Burliuk painted skyscrapers and three nude women. Kamensky pasted birds of paradise cut out of colored paper. Shklovsky wrote aphorisms. Lili painted animals with big udders and wrote underneath, in a parody of Pushkin, "What can possibly interest you in my udders?"

It wasn't only in the apartment that Lili and Osip gave Mayakovsky support and encouragement. Just before the Christmas party in December 1915, he wanted to put on a gala Futurist evening of poetry and art, and they chose the largest apartment they knew of, the studio of the painter Lubavina. The studio was decorated with a large poster hung from a pillar, a Suprematist drawing by Malevich of a huge black circle underlined by a thick black stroke, and above it in big bold letters a quote from Gorky's speech the previous February praising the Futurists: "They've got something!" M. Gorky.

For days Mayakovsky worked on his speech about Futurism. Gorky was invited to the studio as the guest of honor, and he appeared in a military crew cut, dressed in a long coat, accompanied by his friend, the editor and publisher Nikolai Tikhonov. Over thirty people gathered for the event, including Shklovsky, the Briks, Professor Nikolai Kulbin, the writer Nathan Vengerov—and all were favorably disposed toward the Futurists. Gorky stood in the corner, leaning on a grand piano, as Mayakovsky made a dramatic entrance into the room and placed himself in front of the huge window running the length of the studio wall. The Briks sat with the others.

It was immediately obvious that something was wrong. Mayakovsky clenched a cigarette tightly in his mouth, nervously squeezing the pages of his manuscript. His voice was much too loud as he called out, "Gracious ladies and gentlemen!" He tried to continue, making a conscious effort to lower his voice, but nobody could understand what he was saying, an incoherent mumble denouncing poets who wrote on expensive paper in their luxurious country estates. After only a few phrases he broke off again. Finally, after a tense pause, he cried out, "I can't!" and turned his back on the audience.

The hostess, Lubavina, invited everybody to drink tea in an adjoining room, and after the guests had left them alone, she went over to Mayakovsky, who was drawing something with his fingernail on the frosty window. He had tears in his eyes. After tea he regained control of himself and tried to explain what had happened: "I'm used to rotten apples and bottles being thrown on the platform, while here I feel tucked up in cotton wool. Lack of resistance." Then he began to read "The Backbone Flute," and this time he continued to the end.

In February 1916 Brik published "The Backbone Flute" in an edition of six hundred copies, another small book for their shelf of Futurist poetry. The books were distributed in Petrograd bookshops and among their friends. That winter, as Lili remembered, she and Mayakovsky "were never apart." During the afternoons they took walks together, his tall figure exaggerated by a top hat. In striking contrast, Lili wore a large black hat with feathers, and they strolled arm in arm among the shops on Nevsky Prospect doing errands for Osip and playing tricks on people.

With a mysterious expression on his face, Mayakovsky would ask a salesgirl, "Mademoiselle, will you please give us a pencil—can you imagine—so strange that it's red on one end and blue on the other," and the salesgirl would give a startled glance at Lili, who enjoyed the game as much as Mayakovsky. In the evenings they rode the streetcar to the broad stone embankment of the Petrograd river front to see the water shining in the harbor. The streets were poorly lit, and in the murkiness it looked as if sparks were coming out of the ships' funnels without smoke. Mayakovsky told Lili, "They don't dare smoke in your presence."

When "The Backbone Flute" was finished, he began writing another long poem on the theme of unrequited love titled "Don Juan," but this time without showing it to Lili line by line as he worked on it. One afternoon when they were walking together he unexpectedly recited it to her from beginning to end from memory. He still, however, hadn't learned how to anticipate her moods. Instead of being flattered that he'd written another poem about her, she was exasperated at the whole idea. "I lost my temper because again it was about love—the same old thing!" In his dejection he jerked the manuscript out of his pocket and tore it into small pieces, which the wind blew along Zhukovsky Street.

Like any other poet Mayakovsky kept copies of everything he liked that he'd written, and it's possible that some of the lines from the "Don Juan" poem found their way into verses of other poems, but a period of his creative life was coming to a close. There wasn't any reason for him to go on writing about unrequited love. Whatever unhappiness he felt at Lili's willfulness and unpredictable moods, she was now giving him and his work her unwavering attention. Once he'd told her that Burliuk used to tease him by saying, "I'll only recognize you as a great poet when you've published a book of your work so thick that there will be room for your long name across the spine." When Gorky published a slim volume of Mayakovsky's poems in the fall of 1916, a selection of early work titled *Simple as Mooing*, Lili had a copy bound in luxurious brown leather, and across the spine she had printed in gold, in tiny but distinct letters, "Vladimir Mayakovsky." She remembered, "Volodya was terribly surprised—and terribly happy."

6

Mayakovsky and Lili Brik, Moscow, 1918

—Passer-by,
is this Zhukovsky Street?

He looks at me
the way a child looks at a skeleton,
eyes this big,
tries to get past.

—It's been Mayakovsky Street for thousands of years:
he shot himself here at his beloved's door.

"MAN"

IN ONLY A FEW SHORT MONTHS THE BRIKS' APARTMENT became a literary salon for the Futurists. The war drummed on in the background, but it affected their lives only peripherally, and they went on with their arguments and enthusiasms as if nothing else that was happening was of any importance. Brik was now more than Mayakovsky's publisher. He was part of the discussions that went on interminably in their apartment, and he was supporting the Futurists with his first critical writings, which were as stridently opinionated as his own personal manner was quiet and absorbed. With Gorky's assistance Mayakovsky had found a place in the army as a draftsman in the Petrograd automobile school. He'd had no drafting experience but a friend helped him at night and he managed to get by with the job during the day. He had to wear a uniform and he was subject to restrictions that controlled some of his activities when he was off duty, but he'd lost his first enthusiasm for service at the front, and he gave as little time as possible to his job.

Lili let Mayakovsky and the others take over the apartment, and the walls were soon festooned with drawings, paintings, poems. In the excitement she began to talk about continuing with the sculpture she'd given up before her marriage. It was a new life for her as much as it was for Brik. Suddenly their apartment was filled with the sound of voices, the smell of cigarette smoke, and the clatter of visitors on the stairs.

Apart from Lili's ballet lessons, she didn't have anything to do, and she found that acting as a hostess for Mayakovsky and his friends suited her perfectly. She'd always liked attention, and the young writers who were part of the Futurist group were pleased to find an attractive woman who was interested in listening to them. Like Mayakovsky, she was bored when she was alone. She shone in company, not because in those first months she had read or knew much, but because she had a great talent for listening, for concentrating on her guests' ideas for new poems or projects, and then making spontaneous comments. She loved to wrap soft cashmere shawls or expensive silk scarves around her shoulders, and she carefully rouged her lips and plucked her eyebrows to emphasize her fair skin and shining eyes. She was very much "the lady of the house," as Shklovsky described her in the early days, hunching her shoulders under the colorful shawls, smiling her radiant smile, and looking at Mayakovsky "as if he were a not quite tamed lightning." Early in the winter he brought another young writer, Nikolai Aseyev, to meet the Briks, and Aseyev could immediately see what had brought Mayakovsky close to them.

Through Mayakovsky I came to an apartment that wasn't like any other, flowering with hand-painted wallpaper, echoing with newly written or recently recited poems, and the hostess with expressive burning eyes, who convinced and surprised with her original opinions, her own, that she hadn't borrowed from any authority or picked up on the street. We—that is I, Shklovsky, and Kamensky too—were captured by those eyes and her pronouncements, which never forced us but always hit the nail on the head in discussions. That was Lili Brik, who was the chief figure in Mayakovsky's poetry.

Osip Brik, in his turn, was direct and disarming. He didn't talk so much but had a sharp intellect. He didn't draw attention to himself right away, certainly not at first glance. When he said something, however, everyone listened with special attention . . . So these were the people Mayakovsky became friends with in 1915 . . . How were they different from other friends and acquaintances? Above all, because they had wide knowledge in both artistic and social questions. The new and unknown in poetry were just as dear to them as something new and unknown in science, in life . . . Art was for them a law of life, a spiritual and material law. And if "the relationship between art and life" was theoretical for them, Mayakovsky personified the real value in this relationship.

Another of their visitors was Kornei Chukovsky, Volodya's friend from Kuokkala, who encouraged them to start their own magazine. Mayakovsky titled it *Seized*, joking to Lili that he'd "wanted to call something that for a long time, either a dog or a cat or a magazine." Despite his joke, the word actually referred to the leading sentence in an article he wrote for the magazine, "Futurism has SEIZED Russia in a mortal grip." Most of the people involved in the journal had already been part of Burliuk's Moscow group, but by now Mayakovsky had become the dominant personality. As Lili said,

> Mayakovsky, Brik, Burliuk, Pasternak, Aseyev, Khlebnikov, and Shklovsky contributed to *Seized*, but Mayakovsky decided what kind of magazine it was to be. Before Brik met Mayakovsky he'd never published, but he liked "The Cloud in Trousers" so much he not only wanted to publish it as a separate book but also to include it in a magazine. It's nonsense to say that Brik made Mayakovsky a Futurist, as some Russian critics have stated. It's just the opposite—Mayakovsky made a Futurist out of Brik. At that time they didn't have any aesthetic philosophy. It was a *direction*. Futurism was the art of the future.

Brik had thought of writing earlier, but that had been when he was a student, before he married Lili. He and two friends had collaborated on a detective novel they called *King of the Fighters*, which they thought they could sell in installments, like the Pinkerton and Nick Carter series then very popular in Russia. The first booklet sold very well; the second came out after a little delay and didn't do so well; and the third was delivered to the newspaper vendors so late that nobody wanted to buy it.

After meeting Mayakovsky, Brik thought of writing again, and *Seized* gave him the chance to publish his first article. In the introduction, setting the tone of the magazine, Mayakovsky managed to suggest that Futurism was simultaneously beginning and ending at the same time. No longer "the idea of the chosen few," he claimed it was maturing as a social force to carry the weight of "the bronze of a sermon." Brik's "sermon" in *Seized* was a rousing description of the book he'd just published, and he expressed himself in a prose style Lili admired as being "simple and violent."

BREAD!

"If they have no bread, let them eat cake." We ate cake because nobody gave us any bread. And what muck the enterprising confectioners gave us. "Cakes! fresh, sugared, melt in the mouth. Take some! Blok's candy sticks, Balmont's delicious éclairs, no ounce of caramels comes without 'Acme' filling from the new Gumilev factory, formerly salesman for the firm V. Bryusov and Brothers. The factory is equipped up to the minute; all the machinery is imported. Highly recommended." And finally the confectioners' absolute highest achievement, "lilac ice cream."

We sucked, munched and chewed, licked the sugared food, rubbed fingers and soul in syrup. Then we rolled around weakly: how do you get rid of the nausea?

Rejoice, cry louder, we have bread again! Don't trust the servants, go yourself and stand in line and buy Mayakovsky's book "The Cloud in Trousers." Cut the pages carefully so you—like a starving person who doesn't want to lose a single crumb—won't lose a single letter in this bread-book.

But if you're so poisoned that food like this can't cure you, then you might as well die—die of your own diabetes!

The cover of *Seized* was made of rough wrapping paper, with the title printed in poster letters. When the magazine came back from the printers, the letters on the cover were so indistinct they could hardly be seen against the rough surface of the paper. For hours Lili sat at the dining-room table with hundreds of copies of the magazine piled around her, lettering the cover with a brush by hand.

She remembered their involvement with poetry during these months before the Revolution as being an all-absorbing passion.

> We loved poetry. We drank poetry like drunkards and were obsessed with analyzing it. We knew all of Volodya's poems by heart. We asked each other, how did Pushkin make verses? Why are they the work of a genius? How shall we solve this enigma? Then Osya began endlessly to unwind Pushkin and Lermontov. He covered masses of paper with different vowel signs. Afterwards he analyzed sound repetition. We called his signs "gnats." After he finished with sound repetitions he began working on an article on rhythmically syntactic figures. He talked with Roman Yakobson, Shklovsky, Polivanov and Yakobinsky. Yakobinsky was a lecturer in Russian Literature in the Cadet Corps, and Polivanov was a professor at the University of Petrograd.

> Scholars came to us to discuss all kinds of subjects. They read their articles aloud in our apartment and published a volume on the theory of poetic language. It is interesting that in their research there's not a single reference or quotation from Mayakovsky's poems—they only mention his name in passing. The members of this group studying poetic language liked Mayakovsky's poetry, but they didn't touch it in their theoretical work. But Volodya would listen to their discussions for hours. He kept asking Osya, "Have you found anything?"

The group—named OPOYAZ from the Russian for Society for the Study of Poetic Language—was to continue for some years and become a shaping influence on the Formalist literary movement of the twenties. Brik published a book of their theoretical analysis, including his own article on "Sound Repetition," in an edition of a few hundred copies. The imprint for his publications was OMB, his own initials. He'd now found his role, not only as a publisher, but also as an organizer and scholar, and his small, quiet face, with its serious expression, small mustache, and rimless glasses, appeared more often in photographs of Futurist gatherings.

Mayakovsky was still seeing the artist Tonya Gumilina, who'd been part of the composite portrait of Maria in "The Cloud," although he'd broken off his affair with her. She'd become involved with a German artist named Schieman who made his living creating batik scarves with Kandinsky-like designs. She was hopelessly in love with Mayakovsky and made him the subject of all her paintings—he played the role of Christ in "The Last Supper" and was pictured as a satyr in a painting of her bedroom. Cruelly Mayakovsky began to gamble at cards with Schieman, laughing at him when he lost, playing with him for scarves when he ran out of money. Elsa was staying at the Briks' apartment one evening when Mayakovsky came back with one of the scarves, purple with pink flowers, trimmed with silver fox. He bowed and presented it to Lili, saying, "I've brought you his scalp!" Lili gave the scarf to Elsa, who couldn't understand Mayakovsky's brutal treatment of Tonya. The young artist later committed suicide by throwing herself out of a window.

Often callously selfish in his behavior toward women he wasn't interested in, Mayakovsky hadn't found any way to possess Lili. He was helplessly in love with her and he forced both of them through all the unhappy excesses of adolescent love. One time when they were together he demanded that she tell him about her wedding night with Brik. She refused, but he kept insisting, until finally she gave in and told him about the things her mother had put in their bedroom in their Moscow apartment. She knew it was probably a mistake to tell him, but she was tired of his pestering and she didn't think he could be jealous of something that had happened years before they'd met. Hearing her describe her wedding night—even when he'd forced her to tell him about it—drove him out into the street sobbing. As with nearly everything else in the beginning of their affair, the moment found its way into a poem, a frighteningly incoherent poem called "To Everything" that even had some of the things she told him included in its chaotic lines.

No,
It's not true.
No,
You too,
Beloved.
Why?
What for?
All right—
I came,
I brought flowers,
But I didn't steal your silver spoons.
Pale-faced
I tottered down from the fifth floor,
The wind burned my cheeks,
The street was laughing, screaming, neighing
Lecherously the horns climbed one on the other.
Over the city's tumult
I raised the heavy brow of the ancient icons.
On your body like a deathbed
My heart finished living.
You didn't soil your hands with a brutal murder,
You merely dropped
"In a soft bed, he—
Fruit,
Wine on the palm of the night table."
Love,
Only in my
fevered
brain you lived,
Stop the course of this crazy comedy . . .

In his most despairing moments Mayakovsky often threatened to commit suicide. Lili refused to take his threats seriously, but once in 1916 he awakened her early in the morning with a telephone call. She picked up the receiver to hear his voice, toneless and low, announce, "I'm going to shoot myself. Goodbye, Lilik." It was so unexpected that she cried, "No, wait for me," threw on a robe, dashed down the stairs, and found a cab. When she arrived at his room, Mayakovsky opened the door for her, explaining that his pistol had misfired and he hadn't the courage to try a second time. Lili was terribly frightened. She remembered, "He gave me the bullet, and at first I thought he did it to convince me, to buy me—but I was already all bought."

After another quarrel she wouldn't listen to his suicide threats, and it was Elsa that he turned to in his desperation. Elsa was living with her mother in Moscow, studying architecture, when Mayakovsky wrote her on December 19, 1916, that she was "now the only person" whom he regarded with love. Elsa felt that the situation was serious. She rushed to a friend, crying, "We must save Volodya!" But her friend just laughed at her, insisting that Mayakovsky felt insulted only because nobody would go to the movies with him. Elsa was sure she understood him better and that he was close to suicide. She was still a teenager and had never gone anywhere without her mother's permission, but that day, without giving any reason, she said that she was leaving for Petrograd. Later she wrote:

> My memory has only fragments of this trip. A half-darkened room . . . There was a sofa, a chair, a table, wine on the table . . . Volodya is sitting at the table, walking up and down in the room, keeping silent . . . I am in the corner on the sofa. I am waiting. He is silent, drinking, sits down, walks . . . Hour after hour . . . And now the legs of *my* nerves begin to buckle! How long will this torture continue? Why did I come? I can't help him in anything. He doesn't need me at all. I jumped to my feet and began to leave. Downstairs near the front door, another Vladimir, my friend Vladimir Ivanovich, had promised to wait for me, and he must have been waiting a long time.
> "Where are you going?"
> "I'm leaving."
> "Don't go."

"Don't tell me 'don't.' "

We argued. Volodya in his fury held me by force. I broke away. "I'd rather die than stay here." I dashed to the door, pushed it open, clutching my fur coat. I descended the staircase when Volodya thundered past me. "Pardon, madame," and he tipped his hat.

When I got to the street, Volodya was already sitting in the sledge with Vladimir Ivanovich. Without ceremony, Maya-kovsky announced haughtily that he would spend the evening with us. Right then, on that spot, he began to make jokes and make fun of Vladimir Ivanovich. My friend couldn't compete in this business with Mayakovsky, and in fact the three of us really spent the evening together. We had dinner and saw some program . . . Both laughter and tears. But what a hard and difficult man Mayakovsky was!

Through all the torrents of emotion, Mayakovsky was continuing to write. He was publishing poems in *The New Satiricon*, and he and Shklovsky were both contributing to Gorky's journal, *The Chronicle*. After leaving Moscow he didn't see so much of Burliuk, but he was still close to Boris Pasternak, who had come to Petrograd to be part of the Futurist group. While Pasternak had already published two volumes of verses, they were in a more conventional style. The brilliant poems in *My Sister Life* were written during the summer of 1917.

As his friends recognized, Mayakovsky was in full stride as a poet, immersed in long, complicated poems as well as in short lyrics. His most successful project, the long poem "Man," had a new tone. The influence was another revolutionary poet of large dimensions and great emotional power, Walt Whitman, who was just being published in extended Russian translations. The year before when Chukovsky was preparing a new Russian translation of *Leaves of Grass*, Mayakovsky had read Whitman and felt a great sympathy for him. Whitman impressed him as being, like himself, a forerunner in the history of world poetry as a destroyer of philistine literary traditions. Mayakovsky had been very critical of his friend's translations, which he thought were too smooth and polite. He couldn't read Whitman in English, but Chukovsky felt that Mayakovsky's intuitive responses to the spirit of the poetry were much closer to the original than his translations.

There had been suggestions of Whitman in earlier poems, but "Man" often seemed to be echoing specific passages from Whitman's "Song of Myself."

> How then
> can I not sing of myself
> when I'm throughout—
> such a wonder-thing,
> when my every movement—
> is a huge
> inexplicable miracle.

The swaggering egotism of the earlier poems often was transmuted by the kind of simple wonder that Whitman had developed in his longer poem, even if Mayakovsky still retained his own characteristic toss at the end.

> Go around both sides.
> On each side—
> marvel at the five rays.
> They're called "hands."
> A pair of beautiful hands!
> Note:
> I can move them from right to left
> and left to right.
> Note:
> The finest neck
> I can select
> and twine myself around it.

Open the jewel box of my skull—
the most precious mind
will glitter.
Is there anything
I can't do!
Maybe you want me
to invent
a new animal.
It will walk around
two-tailed
or three-legged.
Whoever has kissed me
will say
if there's
any juice sweeter than my spit.

The theme of "Man" is more Mayakovsky than Whitman, with
the poet as the angry rebel tragically succumbing to his fate as the
sacrificial innocent. The long poem chronicled "the thousand-paged
Gospel of the days of my love"—"Mayakovsky's Nativity," "The Life
of Mayakovsky," "The Passions of Mayakovsky," "The Ascension of
Mayakovsky," "Mayakovsky in Heaven," "Mayakovsky's Return,"
"Mayakovsky to the Ages." The sections of the poem didn't intercon-
nect into the linked structure that made "The Cloud in Trousers"
so effective, but in the section "Mayakovsky to the Ages" the poem
suddenly shook free of rhetoric and soared with a description of his
anguished love for Lili. In all the despair that he poured out in poem
after poem to her, there was never a deeper sadness than the verses
where he imagined returning after his suicide to her apartment on
Zhukovsky Street.

The street lights were set into the middle
of the street in the same way.
The houses were similar.
Likewise,

the carving
of a horse's head
from a niche.

—Passer-by,
is this Zhukovsky Street?

He looks at me
the way a child looks at a skeleton,
eyes this big,
tries to get past.

"It's been Mayakovsky Street for thousands of years:
he shot himself here at his beloved's door."

The poet finds his way to Lili's room and gets inside through
the window, but an engineer named Nikolaev lives in the apartment
now, and Mayakovsky imagines himself standing next to Nikolaev's
wife, who is lying naked and terrified in the bed.

High.
Further upward I passed
floor after floor.
She has put herself behind a curtain.
I look behind the silk—
everything's the same,
the same bedroom.

She's passed through thousands of years and still looks young.
You lie there,
your hair made blue by the moon.
Wait a minute . . .

The lights came on.
Two eyes open wide.
"Who are you?"
"I'm Nikolaev,

an engineer.
This is my apartment.
But who are you?
Why are you pestering my wife?"

A strange room.
The morning shook.
A strange woman,
with the corners of her lips trembling,
stripped stark naked.

I run.

Like a shadow torn to pieces,
large,
shaggy,
I sneak along the wall
flooded by the moon.
The tenants run out,
wrapping their nightgowns around them.
I thunder against the slabs.
I drive the doorman into a corner with my blows.

"From Number 42,
what's become of her?"—
"There's a legend:
she jumped
to him
from the window.
They were scattered about
on top of each other."

Where to now?
Wherever the eyes
look.
To the fields?
Let it be to the fields!

Tra-la-la, dzin-dza
tra-la-la, dzin-dza
tra-la-la-la-la-la-la-la!

In "Man," Mayakovsky gave poignant expression to his desperate
need for love, imagining his own suicide and predicting with a heroic
flourish that Lili would also sacrifice herself to love, the supreme
power which remained triumphant after the end of all living things.

Everything will perish.
It will all come down to nothing.
And the one
who moves life
will burn out of the last suns
the last ray
over the darkness of the planets.
And only
my pain
is sharper—
I stand,
entwined in fire,
on the inextinguishable bonfire
of inconceivable love.

In many ways "Man" was the crowning point of Mayakovsky's
pre-revolutionary poetry, the culmination of his obsessive concern with
himself and his tragic fate. It was mostly written during the period
between the February and October revolutions, but unlike the long
poem "War and the Universe," which he had started in 1916, shortly
after he met the Briks, "Man" didn't prophesy a bright time in the
future when mankind would live in harmony. In "War and the
Universe" Mayakovsky allowed himself a brief vision of peace and
happiness with Lili:

Your eyes are full of blossoms
like two green meadows.
And I tumble around in them
a happy boy.

Years later in his autobiography Mayakovsky spoke of writing
"War and the Universe" with his "head" while he conceived "Man"
with his "heart." The two sides of Mayakovsky alternated in his work
between great bursts of optimism and deep despair, both moods
always in precarious balance. Whatever his mood, his poetry was
always autobiographical, and in 1917 in "Man," his pessimism had
grown to the dimensions of cosmic alienation. With the poem he had
written everything he could about the love he had found with Lili.
He needed a new subject, a new turbulence in his life.

7

Mayakovsky, Osip Brik, Boris Pasternak, S. Tretyakov, V. Shklovsky,
Elsa, Lili, and Rose Kushner, 1925

Our cause—Art—must mean in the future state the right of free determination for all creative artists . . . My motto, and that of everybody, is—long live the political life of Russia and long live art free from politics!

MAYAKOVSKY
AT THE MIKHAIL THEATER,
MARCH 1917

THE REVOLUTION THAT CAME AT THE END OF FEBRU-
ary 1917 was jumbled, disorganized, and inevitable. The
war had become hopeless, yet still the slaughter went on.
Even in the upper levels of the government there was a
rising mood of anger and despair, with the vague hope that the
Tsar might be forced to abdicate and that the Duma would take over.
At the same time, Petrograd was going through one of its worst
winters. In January temperatures dropped to 40 degrees below zero;
the weather stopped the trains carrying food for the city and supplies
for the army. Most of what happened took place in what is now
March by the new calendar, but it was in the last weeks of February
by the old calendar, and it has always been known as the February
Revolution.

There were demonstrations and strikes against bread rationing
when the Revolution began on March 1. Mobs took to the streets
and found that for once there was only token resistance from the
police and the army. The Tsar considered the disturbance so unimportant that he left Petrograd to go to his army headquarters more
than four hundred miles away. The street demonstrations grew as
workers crossed from their neighborhoods on the north banks of the
Neva into the center of the city. The government tried to hold the
bridges, but the ice was thick enough to walk on and the numbers
of people milling along the Nevsky Prospect swelled.

On March 8 there was a women's march, demanding bread, and
the shadow of violence hung over the city. Most of the political
groups stayed aloof, and even the Bolsheviks opposed what was
happening in the first days. They were confused and disorganized,
suspicious that the police were letting the situation become more
openly anarchic so that they could sweep in and destroy the leadership. The city was a scene of gesturing crowds in their heavy winter

coats and thick scarves, streaming along the gray streets, their mood more and more assertive as the government failed to move decisively. Finally, on the night of March 11, the first army unit mutinied. On March 12 power had shifted to two groups from the Duma, one a "Soviet" like the group that had been formed in the 1905 revolution, and the other, more to the right and still conciliatory to the monarchy, the Emergency Committee of the Duma. The two groups were distrustful of each other and unable to resolve their differences, leading to the helpless drift of the next several months.

The Tsar, who'd refused to take the disturbance seriously until too late, abdicated on the night of March 15, turning power over to his brother. The rush of events made that move almost meaningless, and his brother announced that he would take power only if asked by an elected constituent assembly. The situation was hopelessly confused, but the people in the streets had swept away the Tsar. There was no coherent program for the future, but the Provisional Government stubbornly insisted on continuing the war, the disastrous war that had brought the collapse of the autocracy. At the distant fronts Russian soldiers began streaming away from their entrenchments in mass acts of disobedience. To hurry the end, the Germans—hoping to force Russia out of the war and leave their armies free to swing around against the French and the English—made contact with the one Russian political figure they felt could bring it about, Lenin, who was in exile in Switzerland. He was smuggled across Germany in a sealed train, and then made his way to Petrograd through Sweden and Finland, reaching the city late in the day on April 16. For the next few months the Revolution hung in the balance as Lenin confronted the liberal socialist lawyer, Alexander Kerensky, who had emerged as leader of the Duma group.

Mayakovsky threw himself into the turmoil of the streets with wild excitement. Shklovsky hurried to the Briks' apartment to find him, but he was following the sea of people as it surged through the city. As Shklovsky said, he "entered the Revolution as he would his own home." At dawn, another friend met Volodya on the streets, bareheaded, his overcoat unbuttoned, rushing toward the sound of shooting in the direction of the railroad station.

"Where are you going?" the friend cried.

"Why, they're shooting over there!" called Volodya.

"But you're not armed!"

"I've been running all night to where the shooting is."

"What for?"

"I don't know! Let's run!"

Lili was swept along with the excitement, but she didn't have Volodya's taste for violence. She went out into the streets one afternoon with friends, but when they heard shots fired close by they hurried back to the apartment.

When the street fighting ended they went out together, often to the old Stray Dog Café, which had opened again as The Comedians' Shelter. Sometimes Mayakovsky read poetry, sometimes he met his friends and sat talking. A new world was opening up for him out of the turmoil.

One night Shklovsky saw him leave with Lili and then hurry back a few moments later to recover a handbag she'd forgotten. His hair was cut short—he shaved his head whenever he was happy—and he had so much vitality that everyone turned to look at him. Also in the café was the talented young journalist Larisa Reisner, another contributor to Gorky's journal. She was infatuated with Mayakovsky. She looked up at him, squinting her eyes as if looking into the sun, and said, "Now you've found your love's handbag and you'll go on carrying it." "Yes," Volodya agreed, "I'll carry it in my teeth."

The Revolution brought an end to the literary salon in the Briks' apartment, but there were more people than ever climbing the stairs to visit them and discuss politics. The first mood of enthusiasm in February and March 1917 was to dissipate in the coup by Lenin's group eight months later, but for a moment it was as if a door had been thrown open, and for the brief time that it was open, a bright light streamed in. Mayakovsky, like nearly every other writer and intellectual in Russian society, rushed out into the light. He immediately involved himself in the aesthetic and political struggles that were going on, but he was too inexperienced to have much effect, and his own ideas were too individualistic for him to join any of the groups that were rapidly forming.

Tirelessly he declared the role of the Futurists in the new society. He was as loudly self-assertive as he'd always been, and as adolescent in his behavior, but at the same time he had a talent for public speaking, a gift for expressing the artists' urgent desire for a political climate that would free them of censorship and control. He immediately came into conflict with Gorky, who was trying to prevent the destruction of works of art and libraries that had followed in the wake of the peasant uprisings in the countryside. Only nine days after the Tsar's downfall, Gorky issued an appeal against the worst excesses of the looters. "Citizens! The old managers have departed, leaving behind them a great inheritance which now belongs to the entire people. Citizens, protect that inheritance . . ."

To Mayakovsky, who was committed to the Futurist idea that the heritage of the past should be destroyed, the effort to preserve paintings and books was infuriating. What did a revolution mean if it didn't mean destroying the past? The Provisional Government established a Commissariat for the Protection of Art Treasures, which included Gorky, and at the same time the government proposed to set up a Ministry of Fine Arts to take the place of the ministry which had controlled the arts under the Tsar.

A group of young artists immediately rejected the idea. Calling themselves the Freedom for Art Association, they protested against the new proposals, saying that under present conditions it was impossible to organize the arts in Russia until there could be a constituent assembly of "all persons active in the arts," and that would be impossible until the war was over. The group was opposed to "the undemocratic attempts of certain groups to obtain control of the arts" and called a protest meeting to be held at the Mikhail Theater four days later. Among the artists signing the statement were Mayakovsky, the young composer Serge Prokofiev, and the stage director V. E. Meyerhold.

Considering his later role as a propagandist for the Bolshevik dictatorship, Mayakovsky's speech in the theater meeting has an ironic ring. It was a noisy meeting, with everyone trying to speak at once, most of them gathering for the first time in a burst of clamoring self-assertion. Mayakovsky made himself heard because he had a strong voice, a commanding physical presence, and a deep relish for the aggressive give-and-take of erupting argument that had characterized all his appearances with the Futurists. His speech was garbled in transcription, but among the things he shouted was his repeated insistence that politics must not be imposed upon art.

> Our cause—Art—must mean in the future state the right of free determination for all creative artists . . . I am against a ministry. I regard it as essential that art not be concentrated in one definite place. My motto, and that of everybody, is—long live the political life of Russia and long live art free from politics!

When another speaker objected, asking why cab drivers and shoemakers could take part in politics and not artists, Mayakovsky interrupted him to say, "I do not withdraw from politics, only in the sphere of art there should be no politics."

As if to make his point even more emphatically, Mayakovsky refused to join any of the groups that were trying to organize against the chaos. He went on insisting that the only artists who represented the Revolution were himself, Burliuk, and the other Futurists. He stormed into meetings, often still in his army uniform with the shoulder tabs removed, he harangued people who disagreed with him, he demanded over and over again that the Revolution should do away with all past art. Others tried to bring him into some kind of front that would represent all the artists on the left, but he answered by saying that the Futurists were the *only* artists on the left.

Within a few weeks after the collapse of the Tsar's government, the ideological disputes that were to open the way for Lenin's group were already festering. Mayakovsky was too much of a poet to be a politician, and he was too immature to understand group movements. He somehow believed, with a naïve optimism, that the arts could stay free of political control. It was this stubborn individualism that was his greatest strength as a writer, even if it meant that he was continually in conflict with all authorities.

A few of the writers close to him were disturbed by the state of near-anarchy that the society was drifting toward. While Mayakovsky was in Moscow for a meeting at the Hermitage Theater, Boris Pasternak came to his room to wake him up one morning. As Mayakovsky dressed, he read parts of his long poem "War and the Universe," the poem describing the horrors of world war in Europe and predicting the glories of the Revolution. Mayakovsky once more dramatized himself as a martyr for his prophetic vision of the ideal world to come:

All right!
Shoot me.
Tie me to a post!
I won't flinch!
If you like
I'll paste an ace on my forehead
so the target will burn brighter.

Pasternak didn't like the poem at all. "I made no attempt to enlarge on my impressions. He read them in my eyes. And besides, he knew the extent of his influence on me. I started talking about Futurism and said it would be wonderful if he would send it all to the devil now, publicly. Laughing, he almost agreed with me."

It was only a brief moment in a small room as Mayakovsky was hurrying on to another meeting, but it was a deeply significant moment for both men, who as poets were to go in different directions. Pasternak had admired Mayakovsky, accepting the excesses and adolescent outbursts, the sullenness and the desperate need for adulation as part of the other poet's youth and immense talent, but at that moment he took his first steps away from Mayakovsky. He began to look at him with the beginning of what was to be a measuring objectivity, and he recognized that his friend had made a fatal error. It was not so much Mayakovsky himself he suddenly questioned but the overblown concept of the poet as romantic hero that was at the center of Futurist art. Pasternak later wrote:

> In the poet who imagines himself the measure of life and pays for this with his life, the Romantic conception manifests itself brilliantly and irrefutably in his symbolism . . . But outside the legend, the Romantic scheme is false. The poet who is its foundation is inconceivable without the non-poets who must bring it into relief, because this poet is not a living personality absorbed in the study of moral knowledge, but a visual-biographical "emblem," demanding a background to make his contours visible . . . Romanticism always needs philistinism and with the disappearance of the petty bourgeoisie loses half its poetical content.

Pasternak sensed the duality in Mayakovsky's character as warring factions, and he could see that his friend had taken on a role that demanded self-destruction; it was as obvious in his poetry as it was implicit in his public insistence on his own dynamic and unique function in the new society. If the ideal Communism he was clamoring for ever came into existence, Mayakovsky would have no subject as a poet—"Romanticism always needs philistinism." And to Pasternak there was an even more ominous threat when poetry put itself at the service of politics: the state could decree that the poet was no longer useful when it decided that society no longer benefited from his rhetoric.

When Mayakovsky returned to the Briks in Petrograd, he found more streams of people going in and out of their apartment. There were still endless games of cards—sometimes with Gorky among the rest—and the same clouds of cigarette smoke and arguing voices and political debate. But the mood had changed. It wasn't the Futurist salon; the ideas being discussed were more immediate. Volodya still had his shabby room, and his affair with Lili was as intense as it had been for the past two years, but he was also passionately involved with the tides rising and falling in the streets.

In April 1917 he quickly put together what he called a "verse-chronicle," titled "Revolution," for Gorky's magazine, *New Life*. Lili was sympathetic to the Revolution—this was a point on which she, Osip, and Volodya were in complete agreement—but her own life took place in the apartment, and her name at this point doesn't appear as part of the groups that were gathering and breaking apart. For the first weeks Brik's name wasn't there either, but since his only published piece had been his review of "The Cloud in Trousers" in his own small magazine, he wouldn't have been included in any committee of writers and artists.

Brik, however, in his less obvious way, was making himself useful. When Gorky began publishing *New Life* on April 19, 1917, both Mayakovsky and Brik were among the contributors. Two months later Brik was considered for the job of editor of a journal to be published in the summer, a satirical magazine called *Wheelbarrow*. Behind its publication was Anatoly Lunacharsky, a Russian man of letters and a leading Bolshevik. In the next years his relationship with Mayakovsky and Brik was to be of crucial importance to them.

Mayakovsky was still in the army, and as the Provisional Government persisted in its efforts to continue the war, the situation within the military became more confused. Kerensky had launched a hopelessly ill-advised summer offensive; its complete failure led to mass desertions and a deepening mood of disillusionment with and distrust of his weak government. In August Mayakovsky was taken from the rolls of the Automobile School and transferred to the Petrograd district military command for a three-month sick leave, and then suddenly, a few weeks later, he borrowed money so that he could go to Moscow. He must "disappear from Petrograd at once, today," because of a disagreement with the commander of his military unit.

On the twenty-fifth of September, 1917, Mayakovsky wrote to the Briks from his mother's apartment in Moscow, the first of many letters he was to write them, and the first time he was to ask them, "Write me"—a theme that persisted through nearly all of the letters until the end of his life.

DEAR LICHIKA, DEAR OSKA!

I kiss you at the very beginning of the letter, instead of the end, where it is usually done. How are you? Those lucky people who visited the fairy tale country . . . "at your house," those scoundrels told me nothing more than the classical phrase, "Lili is Lili."

Yesterday I did a reading. It was a full house. But, unfortunately, full not of money but of good friends. I could have begun my lecture not with a cool "Citizens," but with a tender "Dear Elsa, Abram, and Liova."

I live in Presnia. Mama and my sisters feed me and go on tiptoe. The first is good, the second worst. A family genius. A little bit like Averchenko.

I don't know if I can arrange a trip to the country. There is my friend here, Nika.

My sweet kids, do write me.

Kiss your putting on weight

VOLODYA

The reading was at the Polytechnic Museum in Moscow, where he read a lecture titled "Bolsheviks of Art" and sections from "War and the Universe." In his letter he enclosed a ticket for Lili as a souvenir—the first row, the first seat.

Early in October, Mayakovsky returned to Petrograd, and he was in the Smolny Institute on October 25, 1917, when the storm that had been rising through the spring and summer finally broke and Lenin's group seized power. Lenin's hold was still so tenuous that in the first weeks it was vital for him to gather support by convincing other groups to join his party. But, in contrast with the enthusiasm of the previous spring, the first attempts of the Bolsheviks to attract the writers and artists were met with suspicion. A week after the October coup the Soviet authorities appealed to people engaged in cultural work to come to the Smolny in order to organize, but there was so much distrust that on the evening of the meeting only a small group assembled, among them Mayakovsky, Alexander Blok, Meyerhold, and Larisa Reisner. There was enough room on one sofa for them all to sit.

For Mayakovsky there had never been a question of choice. As he said later in his autobiography: "October 1917. To accept or not to accept? For me (as for the other Moscow Futurists) this question never arose. My Revolution. Went to Smolny. Worked. Did everything that came my way. Meetings began to be held." For Lili there was also no hesitation. "We immediately voted for the Bolsheviks in 1917. We were of the same opinion, we were for revolution." In a typically impulsive gesture she brought her maid Paula with her to the polls so there would be an extra vote for the Bolsheviks. The election, already scheduled by the Provisional Government, was held in November to set up a new Constituent Assembly. It was the last relatively free election to be held in the Soviet Union. The Bolsheviks got only 25 percent of the vote, and though they permitted the Assembly to convene for one day in January, it was dispersed and abolished as a counter-revolutionary body.

On the thirtieth of October, Mayakovsky was officially released from the army by the Committee of Doctors. Lili remembered there were dental and medical problems. A short time later he wrote his mother that he planned to stay in Petrograd for two or three months to have his teeth fixed and his nose looked at, and "then I will come to Moscow for a bit, and later intend to go South for a final recuperation."

If the tone of his letter to his mother was calm, it didn't reflect his situation in Petrograd, where he had thrown himself into new committees and meetings, immediately finding himself in conflict with Lunacharsky, who had become Commissar of the Arts under the new Bolshevik government. As Brik described it, Mayakovsky was too "arch-revolutionary" for Lunacharsky. Volodya was still insisting, as he had the previous spring, on the same program the Futurists had announced in their 1912 manifesto and in the 1915 magazine *Seized*—"Throw the old greats overboard from the ship of contemporaneity"—burn the old masterpieces in the museums, ban Pushkin, look only to the Futurists for the new art of the people.

Lunacharsky recognized that Mayakovsky was "a very talented near-giant, bursting with energy," but thought him too immature to have any immediate function in the reorganization of museums and culture. Without Lunacharsky's support, there was nothing for Mayakovsky to do in Petrograd. He found himself without a role in the emerging action groups and without any source of income.

Brik, who'd had a more doctrinaire political education, was useful to Lunacharsky, and he began working with the new government. His money from his father had stopped, but he had a small salary, so he and Lili could go on living at the apartment. Mayakovsky unhappily turned to his Moscow friends Burliuk and Kamensky, who had started a literary café. On December 8, 1917, he joined them in Moscow, leaving Lili behind with Osip for what he thought would be a very short separation, necessitated, as Burliuk said, because of "the problem of the empty stomach."

When Mayakovsky first saw the Poets Café in Moscow, he wrote Lili that it reminded him of the Stray Dog in Petrograd. Burliuk and Kamensky had modeled it on another literary café, then the most popular in Moscow, called Pegasus Stall, which had as its motto a quotation from Sergei Esenin scrawled on the wall in large letters: "Spit, O Wind, with an armful of leaves, I am a hooligan like you." Burliuk drew "Poets Café" in crooked letters on the outside wall beside the steps leading down to the door of a former laundry in the basement; inside he and Kamensky painted the walls red and black and hung Futurist canvases and banners with slogans from Mayakovsky's and Khlebnikov's poetry. There was sawdust on the floor, wooden tables and chairs, and a small platform stage crowded at one end of the room. Food was served out of a tiny kitchen, heat came from primus stoves, and during the bitter winter nights, when the dark, snow-covered Moscow streets were patrolled by the Red Guard, who—as Pasternak remembered—"opened fire enthusiastically from their revolvers," the lights and noisy laughter from the café seemed like a welcome refuge from the darkness.

What Mayakovsky did in the Poets Café was a Futurist nightclub act. He and his two friends dressed in costumes, and after songs or recitations by other performers who happened to be present, they began to recite. Often Burliuk would taunt the audience until there was an uproar and Mayakovsky would have to shout down the people in the club, telling them that they had to be "quiet like anemones." For a few weeks he was excited by all of it. In mid-December he wrote to the Briks:

> DEAR, DEAR LILI!
> SWEET, SWEET OSIK!
>
> > "Where are you, my best beloved,
> > where, respond . . ."
>
> Having put all the grief of a young soul into the epigraph, I move on to facts.
>
> Moscow, as the saying goes, presents itself as a succulent, juicy fruit, which is being zealously picked by Dodia [Burliuk], Kamensky, and me. The main place of the picking is the Poets Café.
>
> The café for the time being is a very gay establishment (like the Stray Dog in its early times for gaiety). It's packed with people. On the floor is sawdust. On the stage is we. (Now just me. Dodia and Vassia left before Christmas.) We send the public to hell. Money is distributed at midnight. And that's all.
>
> Futurism is in great favor . . .

At the same time that Mayakovsky had been forced to leave Petrograd to find work at the Poets Café, Brik had continued to expand in the new role he'd found for himself with the Bolsheviks. On

December 5, 1917, he published a letter in Gorky's journal *New Life* concerning his decision to serve in the Duma on the voting list of one of the Bolshevik groups. He said in the letter that he disagreed with certain aspects of the Bolsheviks' cultural program, but then went on to say, in an ominously suggestive tone, that he considered "any sabotage, any refusal to participate in active cultural work, is a crime before culture."

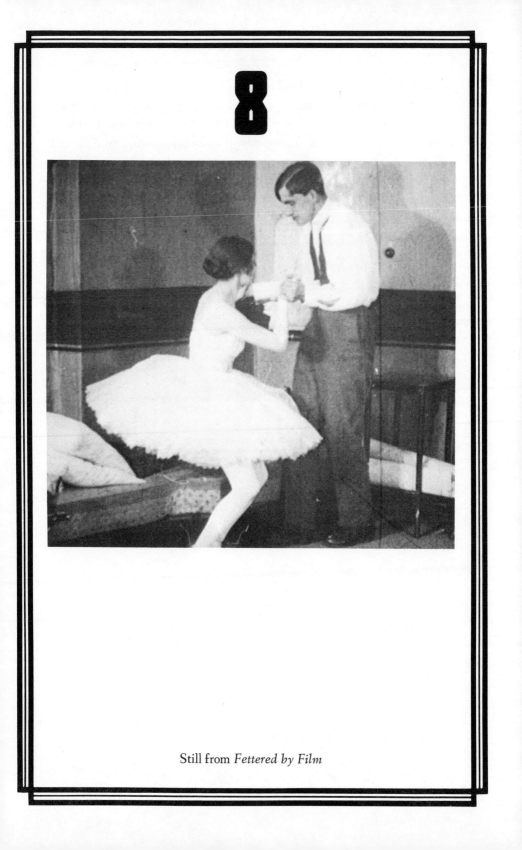

Still from *Fettered by Film*

Dear Lilik, who is hardly kind to me!

Why don't you write a word to me? I sent you three letters and didn't receive a line in answer . . . Don't do it, little one. It doesn't suit you. Write, please. Every day I wake up in distress "How is Lilia?"

Don't forget that except for you, nothing is interesting and I don't need anything or anyone. I love you . . .

MAYAKOVSKY TO LILI
APRIL 1918

MAYAKOVSKY WAS SEPARATED FROM LILI FOR nearly five months in 1918, and during that time he barraged her with letters, pleading for news about what she and Osip were doing, kissing them "a hundred times," begging them to write him. As Mayakovsky knew, there was always time for Osip to talk to him at the apartment, but somehow there was never a free moment to write letters. Besides, writing didn't come easily to Brik; he would much rather formulate his ideas in theoretical discussions than refine them on paper. He left the letter writing to Lili, who hated to write. When Mayakovsky stubbornly insisted on letters, she assured him that she continued to think about him after he'd left for Moscow, but she'd always defined her love for him in her own way, and her way didn't include writing letters as often as he wanted them.

Lili had planned to go to Moscow so that she and Mayakovsky wouldn't be separated for the entire winter, but she hurt her knee and couldn't join him. He began to miss her intensely. In mid-January 1918, a month after he'd left Petrograd, he wrote the Briks to complain that they hadn't come to Moscow. His mood was still fairly good, despite his disenchantment with the Futurist nightclub act he was doing.

DEAR DEAR DEAR LILIK,
SWEET SWEET SWEET OSSYUKHA:

Until the 7th I had been waiting for you (I was smart enough not to go to the railroad station). So you won't come . . . What's happened to you, darling? Write, please. I am also a human being.

There's nothing new with me. I live like a gypsy romance:

in the daytime I lounge about, at night I soothe the ear. The café is repulsive to me. It's a small bughouse . . .

I talked too much at the "Futurists' Christmas" at the Polytechnic Museum. Crowds of people, like at a Soviet demonstration. By the beginning of the evening it was clear that of the four people announced on the poster, Burliuk and Kamensky wouldn't show up—and Holzschmidt refused to perform. I had to grind the organ myself. I shudder to think about it. I recited at the Circus too. It's strange. They whistled at Henkine, but they listened to me, and how! At the end of January I recite "Man" at the Polytechnic.

I have a brisk trade with books. "The Cloud in Trousers," ten rubles. "The Backbone Flute," five rubles. "War and the Universe" sold by auction, 140 rubles. Considering the prices for wine, it's not enough to pay for the hotel.

All the women love me. All the men respect me. All the women are sticky and boring. All the men are rascals . . .

To the Sooouth.

Write!

How is Lili's knee?

I kiss all of you a hundred times.

YOUR VOLODYA

Away from the Briks, Mayakovsky was less involved in politics. He was once again under Burliuk's influence, and sometimes in all their posturing it seemed as though the years that had passed since they'd been closely associated had never happened. However, the world had changed around them. The Bolsheviks were involved in a civil war, fighting with desperate ferocity to hold on to the power they had seized. Lenin was negotiating a surrender to the Germans so he could turn his attention to the tumult within the country, and the winter months were filled with uncertainty and hardship.

Mayakovsky borrowed money from friends and managed to publish two books in his first weeks in Moscow, plowing through the snow-filled streets as he hurried from the printers to the Poets Café. One of the books was the original "The Cloud in Trousers," with all the blank lines that the censor had forced him to delete restored to the text. The other was "Man." Part of his rush to get something published was his desire to have more copies of his own books to sell. Brik had ceased publishing when the money from his father ran out, but even if the funds had been available, he was so involved in his new political activities that there was little time for anything else.

However bored Mayakovsky was with the Poets Café, he'd again become involved with Burliuk's projects. With Kamensky they decided to do a *Futurist Gazette*, a newspaper espousing the principles of Futurism. It was a single sheet the size of an ordinary newspaper page printed on both sides, proclaiming on the front page, in a manifesto entitled "Decree Number One on the Democratization of Art," that a wave of Futurism was to sweep over Moscow on the day of publication, March 15, 1918.

Mayakovsky, Burliuk, and Kamensky went through Moscow pasting up copies of the *Gazette*, all three of them overlooking the fact that since the Revolution the fences and walls in the streets of Moscow were already covered with announcements and proclamations telling people of new plans and changes of the government. Everyone knew the magic word "decree," which usually had come to mean a further prohibition of some kind. The young writer Ilya Ehrenburg, who had become friends with the group, described a street scene when a crowd gathered to read a copy of the *Gazette* that Kamensky had pasted up on a wall.

> Someone was reading it aloud: "From this day forward, with the abolition of tsardom, the *domicile of art* in the closets and sheds of human genius—palaces, galleries, salons, libraries, theaters—*is abrogated*." An old woman shrieked, "All saints have mercy, now they are taking sheds away!" The man in spectacles who was reading the decree aloud explained, "There is nothing here about sheds, but they will close libraries and, of course, theaters . . ."

The *Futurist Gazette* was very much involved with the old poses of 1912, which seemed bizarre in the spring of 1918. Part of the decree was that ". . . the Free Word of creative personality be written on the corner of walls, fences, roofs, the streets of our cities and villages." To carry out this part of the program, Burliuk borrowed a ladder and nailed some of his paintings to a wall, with jeering advice from a crowd that gathered to watch. Mayakovsky had written an "Open Letter to the Workers," insisting again that the art and poetry of earlier periods was of no use to the present. As he said flatly, "Only the outburst of the Revolution of the Spirit will rid us of the rags of old art."

Events in Moscow were keeping Mayakovsky away from Lili, but he was expecting almost weekly to get back to her or hoping that she would join him there. After the dancing lessons had stopped, she'd picked up her old interest in sculpture, and she was beginning to work in the apartment on counter-reliefs, first painting a surface and then introducing iron and plaster until the flat surface of the picture disappeared and several intersecting metal planes, variously bent, seemed to be suspended in the air.

It would have been easier for him if she hadn't been writing letters to anyone in Moscow, but, as always, she was making it clear that she wasn't dependent on him. She wrote to her mother and her sister, but to make it worse, she wrote most often to a wealthy friend who worked in films, Lev Grinkrug. At the beginning of March Volodya sent her a drawing of Grinkrug's smiling face and another of his own unhappy scowl. In the letter he went on, "Do write, Lilionok! I feel disgusted enough without that. I'm bored with myself. I'm sick. I'm angry . . ." His pleading finally had some effect, and in the middle of March Lili sent him a notebook and a letter calling him a puppy, a term he took up as a symbol for himself and their relationship.

DEAR BELOVED, FRIGHTFULLY SWEET LILI!
From now on, nobody can reproach me with my insufficient reading—all the time I'm reading your letter . . .

If I am to be looked upon as your puppy, then I can tell you straight that I don't envy you—you have a poor puppy: a rib sticking out, fur in tufts of course, and near my red eye there is a long molted ear that has grown there especially to flick away tears.

Naturalists affirm that puppies always look that way if they are given into other people's unloving hands.

I don't go anywhere.

I sit three or four chairs apart from women, so they won't breathe anything bad for my health into me . . .

During these months Mayakovsky often saw Elsa, who was still in Moscow, living at home with her mother, although she was now engaged to a French officer named André Triolet. It was a period of change and confusion, but it seemed to be suited to Mayakovsky's volatile temperament. He suddenly wrote Lili that he'd begun a new career as a movie actor. "My only entertainment (I should like you to see it, you'd have a lot of fun) is that I'm playing in a kinemo. I wrote the script myself. I have the main role."

Mayakovsky's word for films was "kinemo," a coinage crossing "film" with "cinema." He'd always been fascinated by film, and when he was approached by the Neptune Studio with an offer to write a scenario and star in it himself, he accepted immediately. The Neptune Studio was a private film company managed by a family named Antik, who thought that Mayakovsky's name as the starring personality at the Poets Café was good publicity. For his first film he cast himself in the role of the hero in a scenario he titled *Not Born for Money*, his adaptation of Jack London's novel *Martin Eden*.

Not Born for Money was begun in March 1918, on an early spring morning when melting snow covered the film pavilion, and it was finished two weeks later. With only the skimpiest budget everything had to be done at top speed. The film looked so promising to the Antik family that they signed Mayakovsky for another production, this time based on a sentimental novel by the leftist Italian writer Edmondo De Amicis, entitled *The Workers' Teacher*. Maya-

kovsky named his scenario *The Young Lady and the Hooligan* and
he starred again as a tramp hero. This film was very successful for
the Neptune Studio, and it was so widely distributed (it was still
being shown on May Day 1919 in Moscow and Leningrad) that
prints of it still survive.

Mayakovsky disliked adapting novels for the screen, and with
his usual burst of energy he began to rough out an original scenario
even as he worked on the second film. He mentioned it to Lili in a
a letter at the end of March 1918. "In the summer I'd like to play in
a movie with you. I'd like to write a script for you. I'll develop this
plan when I come [to Petrograd]. For some reason or other, I'm sure
you'll consent." Although Lili never bothered to reply, Mayakovsky
went ahead with his idea, and in May 1918 she arrived in Moscow
for the filming.

Little remains of *Fettered by Film*, the title of the script Mayakovsky wrote for Lili, and he was bitterly disappointed when it
wasn't successful. "Having familiarized myself with the technical
aspects of filmmaking, I wrote a scenario on a level with our innova-
tive literary works. The production by Neptune made a shameful
mess of it." He felt that the fault lay with the Antik family, who
wouldn't let him direct the film, giving the job to Nikander Turkin,
who was unsympathetic to Mayakovsky's "futurist" effects.

Lili salvaged some segments of *Fettered by Film* that were cut
out during the editing, and from this footage she and Mayakovsky can
be glimpsed as they acted out their roles in 1918. In her ballet tutu
Lili has a fragile beauty, her long hair pulled back like a dancer
except for a few curls escaping at the sides. Her oval face is very
pale, and despite her strong jaw she looks small and vulnerable,
totally dependent on Mayakovsky's direction, following him with her
large dark eyes as he helps her strike different attitudes on the set. In
a long, loose overcoat and business suit he looks very tall—Lili barely
comes up to his shoulder—and he walks clumsily, like an adolescent,
rushing from his bed to a table, back to a chair, then up to a wall,
smiling tightly at her while the action lurches along almost as if he

were pulling strings. Yet the difference between them is striking. Lili was an amateur who never forgot the camera was there, while Mayakovsky was a natural performer, totally absorbed in his role.

From the outline of the scenario and the few minutes of it that have survived on film, it is clear that he tried to show not only what Lili's beauty meant to him but, on a symbolic level, the emotional effect of their love affair. At the same time, he wanted to use the film as a medium for Futurist visual experiments. It seemed as though he'd thrown together all the separate pieces of his confused life and tried to make something coherent out of them. Most of the trick shots he wanted to use, like unexpected dissolves and sudden cross-cutting, had already been developed by directors like the French experimentalist Georges Méliès, but Mayakovsky tried to use them in a love story. It was another expression of his theme of hopeless love for an unobtainable woman.

Fettered by Film opened with a complicated sequence of the artist (Mayakovsky again playing himself) finding that his life has become materialistic and empty. Instead of a heart his wife has pots and pans—with visual effects to make the point; his best friend's heart is only a deck of cards and a bottle. The artist tries to paint a portrait of a gypsy woman, but instead of a heart she has coins. In despair he rushes out of the house, goes to a movie theater, and in the middle of a pastiche of scenes from other films called *The Heart of the Screen* is a ballerina—Lili—and he immediately falls in love with her frail beauty.

When *The Heart of the Screen* ends, the artist stays in the theater, applauding, and the ballerina suddenly appears again, steps out from the screen, and joins him. Overjoyed, he tries to take her home, but the rush of traffic on the street frightens her and she disappears back into the theater, leaving him outside banging desperately on the door.

Up to this point the scenario has the feeling of a stylized vignette, with overtones of other films of the period. But there is already a suggestion of his first feelings for Lili, that she was a beautiful vision he'd been able to take away with him for only a moment. The artist returns from the movie theater so unhappy with what has happened that he has to go to bed, feverish and sick.

A doctor comes, writes a prescription, and the maid goes out to get the medicine. On her way home the wrapping paper around the bottle tears, and the maid picks up a torn film poster of *The Heart of the Screen,* with Lili's picture on it, and wraps it around the medicine. In the artist's bedroom the dancer comes alive again, steps out of the poster, and sits next to the bed. The artist is so happy to see her that he feels better immediately. He says he'll take her to his country house, where they can be alone.

But the ballerina cannot live very long without her screen. The artist tries to amuse her by giving her a new dress and beautiful pearls, he prepares lunch—but she misses the screen and tears the cloth off the table to hang on the wall, leaning against it as if it were a screen. She begs him to get her a real one, and he rushes back to the city.

While he's away, the jealous gypsy woman stabs the dancer in the artist's garden. As the knife goes through the ballerina's heart, she turns into a poster again, this time with a knife through it. When the painter returns, the gypsy confesses her crime, but the artist pushes her aside to embrace the film poster. At the bottom of the poster, in very small print, he reads the name of the studio where the film was made: "Lyublandia," the land of love. The final scene in *Fettered by Film* shows the artist on a train, traveling to the magical studio in the hope of finding the ballerina once more.

The film was a visualization of Mayakovsky's deepest emotions, and as Lili said, it continued the themes of his poetry. The scenes of the artist trying to keep the ballerina amused so she won't leave certainly reflected the situation of Lili's and his first afternoons together in his hotel room: he read her poetry, they made love, she had tea and her favorite things to eat, and at the end of the afternoon she put on her clothes and went back to her husband.

Mayakovsky planned a sequel to the film in which the artist finds

"Lyublandia" and meets different screen characters in his search for the ballerina, but it was never produced.

Before the filming had started with Lili, the Poets Café had already run into difficulties. The situation in Moscow had deteriorated until even the Red Guard and armed soldiers were hard-pressed to maintain law and order. Corruption was widespread, and one night the three poets arrived to find that their café had been sold without their knowledge to a profiteer. Mayakovsky was so angry that he refused to read poetry, and when it was his turn to perform, he made a speech instead attacking profiteers in art. Burliuk and Kamensky were not discouraged. With the backing of the Filipov family, they began to set up a new café, the Pittoresque, which Mayakovsky thought too "exquisitely" Futuristic. Finally, on April 14, 1918, during the filming of *Not Born for Money*, the Poets Café officially closed.

With the pressures of his film work, Mayakovsky had almost ceased writing poetry. There was very little time for him to write anything, and the people working in the film studio didn't take him very seriously as a poet. Once, riding in a cab on the way to the Pittoresque Café with the actress Alexandra Rebikova, he presented her with his little book "The Cloud in Trousers." She opened it, read some lines, and said she didn't understand them. She was laughing, but Mayakovsky's reply was a grim smile. "You don't understand anything," he told her. "I am the greatest modern poet. One day you will realize this." He took the book out of her hands, tore it to shreds, and threw the bits of paper out of the cab window.

Eugene Slavinsky, the cameraman for Neptune Studios, once asked Mayakovsky when he found time to write his poems. He answered that when he felt like writing he'd find the time and nothing could stop him. At a crucial moment in the production of *Fettered by Film*, when Mayakovsky was needed in every scene, he didn't show up at the studio. People were sent to look for him in his room, in his friends' rooms, and at the Pittoresque Café, but he couldn't be found. The actors gathered the next morning at the studio, but again no Mayakovsky. All work stopped and everyone wandered about with nothing to do. Finally Volodya reappeared, ready to continue filming. "Where have you been, Vladimir Vladimirovich? What were you doing?" Mayakovsky replied, "I was working. I wanted to write a poem, so I found the time. I warned you, remember?"

The poem was "Be Good to Horses," and Mayakovsky found time to write it because he had a deadline to meet. He wrote poems to order, and this one was for Gorky's magazine *New Life*. Although it was to be one of his best-known short poems, at the studio it only made him the object of a joke:

"In one respect you're like your ballet dancer, Vladimir Vladimirovich!"

"How's that?"

"Just like your heroine, you disappear from the picture."

9

Mayakovsky and Lili Brik, Moscow, 1919

Who am I?
I'm of no class,
no nation,
no tribe.
I've seen the Thirtieth
and the Fortieth Century.
I'm simply a man
from the Future . . .

MYSTERY-BOUFFE

A T THE BEGINNING OF THE SUMMER OF 1918, WHEN
Fettered by Film was finished, Lili and Mayakovsky went
back to Petrograd together, and they went to live with
Brik in a country hotel, just outside the city, in Levashova.
There Mayakovsky wrote his play *Mystery-Bouffe*.

To the other guests in the Levashova hotel they must have
looked a little strange, the beautiful, dark-eyed, red-haired woman
with her slight, bespectacled husband, and the tall, brooding younger
man with them. They had separate rooms, but there was no longer
any pretense about their living together openly, something they
hadn't done before. Elsa was surprised at the new arrangement when
she visited them in Levashova on her way to France to marry Triolet.
She didn't even see Osip with the other two in the country. Probably
there were many days when he stayed in town for his job in Lunacharsky's department and Lili and Mayakovsky were left entirely alone.

Before leaving Petrograd in July 1918, Elsa and her mother,
Yelena Yuryevna, visited the Briks' apartment, only to be told by the
maid that Lili and Mayakovsky had gone off together to Levashova for
the summer. Yelena Yuryevna hadn't been aware of her daughter's
complicated life, and she was deeply shocked. She was angry enough
to want to leave for France without saying goodbye to Lili, but Elsa
insisted on seeing her sister. The scene at the hotel in Levashova
made a deep impression on her.

It was very hot. Lilichka, very sunburned and blistered,
was lying in a half-darkened room; Volodya was silently walking
to and fro. I don't remember what we spoke about, how we said
goodbye . . . My deepest conviction that someone's personal
life is something inviolate didn't allow me to ask what would

happen in the future, or even to show that I noticed a new situation between them.

Elsa stayed the night at the hotel, and the next day she and Lili went back to Petrograd together. Mayakovsky didn't come, because Yelena Yuryevna had made it very clear that she didn't want to see him, but Lili accompanied her mother and sister to the pier. Elsa remembered the heavy, cloying smell of the oppressive summer heat as she stood on board ship waving goodbye to Lili, who seemed a very small figure waiting on the pier in her thin sandals between puddles of dirty water and mountains of rotting fruit.

After his experience in Moscow, Mayakovsky had learned that although Burliuk and Kamensky could conceive new creative projects on what they called a "cosmic scale," they were as helpless as he was in finding a secure foothold in the rushing current of events. In Petrograd it was Brik who had found temporary security. His job in Lunacharsky's Commissariat of Enlightenment had none of the exalted pretentions of Burliuk and Kamensky's projects, but at this moment he was much more useful to Mayakovsky than the Moscow Futurists, who found themselves left behind in the turbulence.

In Levashova they walked in the woods, lay in the sun, played cards, and talked together. Mayakovsky painted landscapes of the groves of spruce trees. Late in the summer, as the season began to change, they went into the forest to pick mushrooms, which they dried for food during the winter or cooked to vary their monotonous diet of salt fish and peas. All this time Mayakovsky was working on a new play he called *Mystery-Bouffe*, writing it very quickly and reading it aloud as each scene was finished, first to Lili and then to both the Briks. By the end of the summer, as with his other works, they knew it by heart.

In August, when they could no longer afford to stay at the hotel, they moved back to Petrograd with the immediate problem of money. Brik had his job in Lunacharsky's commissariat, but Mayakovsky hadn't earned anything since he'd finished the film. As a family, they shared their finances. At that time Lili's way of contributing to the household was to sell her clothes and jewelry, and when they were gone, she sold the oil painting she liked so much, the large portrait of her by Boris Grigoryev. An art dealer named Brodsky took it before she had time to photograph it, and when she asked him about it years later, he denied ever having bought it from her. The only expensive things that she couldn't bring herself to part with were the diamond ring she'd been given by Brik's grandmother, and the gold ring engraved with her initials spelling out "I Love."

In Petrograd Mayakovsky rented a room at 7 Zhukovsky Street on the same floor as the Briks; he'd given up his old room when he left for Moscow months before. He furnished it with a low divan and a big mirror with a pink velvet frame which he'd borrowed from friends, and it was in this room that he and Lili would meet.

The government was planning a festive first-year anniversary of the Revolution on November 7, 1918, and Mayakovsky decided that his new play should be part of the celebration. He approached Lunacharsky, encouraged because early in August both he and Osip had been asked to work within the commissariat's Department of Fine Arts by David Shterenberg, the well-known artist, who'd visited them in Levashova.

On a warm day in late August Brik asked Lunacharsky and Shterenberg to come to the Petrograd apartment to hear Mayakovsky read his new play, *Mystery-Bouffe*. There were other friends too, and everyone shared Lili and Osip's excitement at the reading. Meyerhold immediately offered to direct the play and Lunacharsky ordered it to be produced at the Alexandrinsky Theater. But, once outside the circle of his friends, Mayakovsky ran into trouble.

His difficulties began when he brought *Mystery-Bouffe* to the Actors' Union for a reading, and the actors complained that it was a "Futurist" play—the adjective applied to anything they couldn't understand. Specifically, they protested that the action was hard to follow, the characters weren't developed, and the humor was too farcical for the dignified event it was to commemorate. Finally, the chairman of the meeting rephrased their objections by saying tactfully, while Mayakovsky smiled ironically, that his traditional theater company wouldn't do justice to such a modern play. He advised Mayakovsky to find younger actors, and as for a theater—he was sorry that none was available at that time. This was Mayakovsky's first attempt to work within the bureaucracy of the new state; the obstacles and hostility he encountered trying to get his play produced were to be repeated with maddening variations for the rest of his life.

After the delay in finding a theater, there was very little time left for rehearsals. On October 12, 1918, less than a month before the November celebration, Brik, Mayakovsky, Meyerhold, the artist Malevich, and others issued a typically peremptory announcement recruiting actors:

> Comrade Actors! It is your duty to celebrate the great day of the Revolution with a revolutionary show. You should perform *Mystery-Bouffe*—the heroic, epic, and satiric picture of our era written by Vladimir Mayakovsky. Let all come on Sunday, October 13, to the concert hall at the Tenishev School. The author will read *Mystery*; the director will present his production ideas; the designer will show the sketches; and those of you who are attracted to this work will act in it . . . Time is precious! We ask only those comrades who would wish to take part in the production to come. Seating is limited.

It was harder than he'd expected. In his inexperience as a playwright Mayakovsky had conceived of a workers' theater that had little relation to the practical demands of theater production. The complex verse form of *Mystery-Bouffe* was tricky enough for the amateur actors, but the total production design was equally formidable. The spectacle required over sixty roles (actors could double, of course), as well as complicated visual effects and stage settings. As Mayakovsky boasted in the prologue, his play was no simple melodrama. In his theater the audience would find miracles, not humdrum Chekhovian situations like

> Uncle Vanya
> and Auntie Manya
> parked on a sofa as they chatter.
> But we don't care
> about uncles or aunts:
> you can find them at home—or anywhere!
> We, too, will show you life that's real—
> very!
> But life transformed by the theater into a
> spectacle most extraordinary!

The complicated visual effects made the play difficult for audiences to follow at first. Mayakovsky began by transforming the stage into a terrestrial globe covered with rope ladders representing the parallels and meridians. Between two walruses supporting the world, an Eskimo hunter stands with his finger stuck into the earth. He's noticed that the world is leaking and he asks his friend, an Eskimo fisherman, to help. Suddenly they're joined by a German, two Australians, Lloyd George and Clemenceau, the Negus of Abyssinia, a Chinese, a Persian, a Turkish pasha, an Indian rajah, a Russian priest, a Menshevik, a diplomat, an intellectual, and a lady with several hatboxes—all these characters are the Clean, the bourgeoisie who've fled the flood of revolution threatening to submerge he earth. The Clean are soon joined by seven pairs of workers, the Unclean. (One of the difficulties with the play is that the Unclean are the heroes; despite the broad satire it takes a while for the audience to understand.)

Before the flood submerges the North Pole, everyone builds a Noah's ark together and scrambles aboard. But the revolution is relentless and pursues them onto the ark after the bourgeoisie cheat the workers out of their food. The Unclean seize control and sail the ark to hell, where they deposit the Clean. The ark then goes to heaven, which disgusts the workers, since they can't fill their empty bellies with cloud milk and cloud bread, and they're deeply offended by the laziness of the angels. They steal God's thunderbolts for later use in electrification projects before proceeding to the land of Chaos, where they mill about in confusion, starving and afraid: "What can we do?"

Suddenly they catch a glimpse of a Man of the Future, and at first they're suspicious, convinced he's sent to them by God. The Blacksmith says,

God has oranges,
cherries,
and apples;
He can make spring leaf out seven times a day.
But from us He's always turned away.
And now He's sent Christ here to snare us.

Instead of Christ, a "most ordinary young man" urges the workers to take up revolutionary action in a monologue that Mayakovsky tried to give to one of his amateur actors, but no one could deliver the lines the way he wanted. Finally he performed the role himself. A Man of the Future was a spokesman for Mayakovsky, the revolutionary ecstatically welcoming a utopian socialist future.

Who am I?
I'm of no class,
no nation,
no tribe.
I've seen the Thirtieth
and the Fortieth Century.
I'm simply a man
from the Future.
I've come to blow
in the forges of souls,

for I know
how hard it is to try to live.
Listen!
A new
Sermon
on the Mount!
Are you waiting for Ararats?
There are no Ararats.
They're only in dreams . . .

In the final act the workers' struggles are triumphant when they realize the Millennium—the Commune—and the "Things" of the world, tools and machines, food and drink, come to life and promise to obey the Unclean forever. The workers are elated at their power to create a luminous future. In the finale the locomotive engineer shouts to his comrades:

Never have I seen such light!
It's not the earth,
but
a blazing meteorite with a tail of trains.
Why did we bellow like oxen under the yoke?
We waited
and waited
and waited for years,
and never once did we notice
such a blessing right under our noses.
Why do people go to museums, anyway?
All around us, treasures are heaped up high!
What's that—the sky or a piece of fustian?
If this is the work of our own hands,
then what doors will not open before us?
We are the architects of earths,
the decorators of planets.
We're miracle workers . . .

The rehearsals for *Mystery-Bouffe* were long and arduous. There were so many difficulties in the theater that they suspected sabotage: the theater administration locked entrance doors and kept nails for the sets under lock and key. Posters arrived only on the day of the opening, incompletely painted. Lili had helped with the sketches for costume designs, and she finished coloring the posters. She sent her maid out on the streets to put them up wherever she could, but in her inexperience the maid didn't fasten them securely and they were immediately blown away by the wind.

Lili was objective enough to see that despite all the work there hadn't been enough time to rehearse the play properly.

Mayakovsky enjoyed hearing the actors recite his words. He thought they all read well, but in reality it wasn't true. It was a mediocre performance. He was grateful to them all, though. During the performance Meyerhold and Mayakovsky were simply in love with each other. Mayakovsky carried out every direction of Meyerhold's with enthusiasm, and Meyerhold adored every sentence of Mayakovsky's. But actually they interfered with each other's work. The words of Mayakovsky's play didn't reach the public in the production; it was too fragmented. Meyerhold's genius blinded Mayakovsky, and Mayakovsky's genius interfered with Meyerhold's work.

The Music Drama Theater was full for the première of *Mystery-Bouffe*, with Commissar Lunacharsky in the official box and Alexander Blok in the audience. But the actors' voices didn't carry and most people were bewildered by the play. Blok liked it—he thought it a work of genius—and Nikolai Punin, a critic supporting the Futurists, recognized the emergence of a new Mayakovsky, an event of great significance in the context of the new art of the Revolution.

The most interesting thing about *Mystery-Bouffe* is that Mayakovsky, after all his street rhetoric, has now placed himself in a square like a monument and, as the first among Futurist poets, has clearly said "we." At that moment he ceased to be a romantic and became a classic. In the future, no matter how much he would like to, Mayakovsky will not be able to bring himself to such ungovernable rebellion as before . . .

Mayakovsky's play was one of the poetic attempts to create an "art of the commune" immediately after the Revolution. All of his friends were swept up into it, even Lili with her sculpture at the apartment. Every artist in Russia had been invited to take part in the celebration of the first anniversary, and in the streets of the larger cities there were colorful decorations like Burliuk had been struggling to achieve a few months earlier, with his canvases nailed up on a Moscow house front. But it wasn't the spontaneous avant-garde rush of freedom that Burliuk had envisioned. Nothing was so simple right after the Revolution—there was a short burst of freedom, but mostly chaos prevailed. The majority of the artists who participated in the anniversary were conservative, and they had only slight leanings toward the new experiments in the arts. Of the ninety artists who worked on the decorations in Petrograd, only ten were avant-garde or Futurist. The resulting turmoil centered around Nathan Altman, one of Lunacharsky's artists, who took for himself the job of decorating the square in front of the Winter Palace, Petrograd's most important public place. He hung the buildings around the square with thousands of yards of canvas painted in semi-abstract designs, and he covered the Alexander column in the center with large abstract sculptures leaping out of a Futurist construction that ringed the base. There was an immediate and horrified protest against his radical designs, and the figures on the monument became so notorious that they were mentioned in the attacks on Futurist art for several years. The popular reaction against Altman's designs and Mayakovsky's play was so strong that the Futurists were banned from taking part in the decorations for May Day the next spring in Petrograd, and a planned outdoor performance of *Mystery-Bouffe* was canceled.

There was also the problem of intrigue and rivalry within the group of avant-garde artists themselves. Brik later wrote that "any reason was good enough to spark off a flare-up: a proposed exhibition site, the purchase of works of art, the composition of a competition jury, etc." He was now working under David Shterenberg and called himself "the Revolution's doorman." He said that he had opened the door for the Revolution, and understandably his friends entered first. When a huge exhibition was planned inside the Winter Palace filling all the rooms, among canvases by Repin and Chagall were Lili's sculptured reliefs and a chandelier she'd worked in tin. Despite the controversy *Mystery-Bouffe* had stirred, Brik and Mayakovsky had come close to grasping real political power in cultural matters.

There was a new tension in the unending discussions back at the apartment on Zhukovsky Street. In the first months of Bolshevik rule the new cultural policies were dominated by a handful of avant-garde artists and writers who only a short time before had found it difficult to have their paintings hung or their poems printed. If October 1917 was to be a revolution of the Russian proletariat, how could they be culturally represented by a group of intellectuals whose inspiration came largely from the experimental art being created in Italy, France, and Germany? Somehow for a short time it happened, despite the almost total hostility to their work and a mounting protest at their role in the government.

Within weeks of Lenin's coup Lunacharsky had tried to bring the artists into a Commissariat of the Arts. He specifically approached the Artists' Union that had been founded in March 1917, but the union, fearing that they would be under governmental control, refused to join, and at the meeting with Lunacharsky it was only Mayakovsky who even responded to the commissar's proposal. The rejection by writers and artists of every school was so total that it was finally only the avant-garde that Lunacharsky could turn to.

Since he couldn't persuade the Artists' Union to join him, he set up two departments of the arts within what was called the Commissariat of Enlightenment: the Department of Fine Arts (IZO), which was directly involved with the building of a new cultural policy, and the Department of Museums and the Protection of Monuments of the Past, which was concerned with the preservation of older works of art and the establishment of new museums that would bring culture more broadly to the people. It was through the agencies that Lunacharsky had set up that the avant-garde artists— the Futurists among them—were able, momentarily, to seize power.

On paper at least, the position of the Department of Fine Arts looked powerful, and there was an immediate outcry from writers everywhere in Russia against their "dictatorship." There were to be two cultural newspapers, *Art of the Commune*, edited in Petrograd, and *Art*, edited in Moscow, and there was to be a publishing house associated with them. The editors of *Art of the Commune* were Brik, Altman, and Punin. Mayakovsky wasn't named as an editor, but he was one of the dominating figures among the contributors. His poems were used as editorials in seven of the paper's nineteen issues, and he did most of the physical work involved in preparing the newspaper for the printers, so much of it that the editors didn't even see the first issue until it came out.

Lili completely accepted Mayakovsky's new role of working for the government. It didn't seem to her that he was stifling his voice as a poet. "It was different from Volodya's way of life when we were first together, but everything was changing." Brik's explanation was more political. He said that by joining the committee of the Department of Fine Arts, Mayakovsky had "realized that the struggle for new art could only be waged from within the Soviet institutional framework." Whatever Mayakovsky's motivation might have been, Lunacharsky immediately discharged any debt he might have felt he owed the poet for joining the government by giving him permission to publish *Mystery-Bouffe* and a small Futurist anthology entitled *Rye Word*.

Living conditions were hard. As the winter came on, Lili was forced to cut up heavy drapes to use as material for her dresses. Mayakovsky and Brik began organizing readings at factories and schools, trying to sell copies of the new books and newspapers and interest the workers in performing *Mystery-Bouffe,* usually reading something from it during the lectures. It was raw and cold in the drafty buildings, and the workers often didn't seem to know how they were supposed to respond to work that was mostly incomprehensible to them, but Mayakovsky went on with it with all his intense energy, a gesticulating, aggressive figure who could shout loudly enough to be heard everywhere in the crowd. When he wasn't busy with the lectures, he was working with the papers, and he billed IZO for 481 rubles, 20 kopeks for his services as a proofreader and general amanuensis for the first two numbers of *Art of the Commune.*

The first issue of the paper was published on December 5, 1918, and one of its most controversial articles was by Brik, who continued his attack on artists who weren't committed to the new political position. When these writers had been given less food under the new rationing system, they'd complained. Scornfully Osip replied that only the proletarians should get larger rations, for, "The answer is very clear. The proletarianization of all labor, including artistic labor, is a cultural necessity . . . and no amount of tears shed for their supposedly vanished creative freedom will help in the matter."

Futurism had changed after the Revolution to become part of the new political reality. Brik's position from the period only a year and a half before when he was publishing Futurist poems had decisively veered even more than Mayakovsky's, whose contribution to the magazine was a poem, the first of his "Orders to the Army of the Arts."

They planned the issues of the magazine at the apartment, where the rooms were bitterly cold. Mayakovsky insisted on taking off his overcoat "to boost the morale," but Osip and the rest of the editorial board huddled under sweaters and coats, while Lili draped layers of shawls and blankets around her heavy dresses and stayed at the table beside the samovar. They had a clear realization of how close they were to power, but they had little idea of how to use it or even to hold on to it longer. Instead of trying to reach out and form some alliances or bridge some of the gaps that separated them from other groups of artists, they continued stubbornly with the same kind of separation they'd been insisting on since the old Futurist manifesto of 1912. On December 15, 1918, in the second issue of the journal, they published Mayakovsky's poem "It's Too Early to Rejoice," and it roused even more protest than *Mystery-Bouffe*.

This time the difficulty was the Futurist theme of the necessity of doing away with the influence of the old culture. Instead of the poem's appearing as a street manifesto or as a pamphlet by a struggling avant-garde group, it was published in the official paper the new government had established for the arts. In his poem Mayakovsky's style was as "simple and violent" as Brik's editorials.

> We line up machine guns
> in the forest clearing,
> we're deaf to the appeals of the White Guard,
> so why don't we execute Pushkin
> and other classic generals?
> We guard the old junk that we call art—
> has the tooth of revolutions dulled against crowns?
> Hurry up!

Pushkin was not only Russia's national poet, but because of his covert resistance to Alexander I, he was also considered a revolutionary figure. This time the public protest was so strong that Lunacharsky was forced to defend Mayakovsky, and even Blok tried to write to him pointing out that the destruction he advocated was in itself a carryover from the past. The letter, however, was never sent.

Mayakovsky and Brik hadn't grasped the reality of their situation, which was that they and the other avant-gardists had been given what power they had to work for the consolidation of the new regime, not for their own program. They were fumbling toward a concept of control in the arts, but they hadn't understood, as Pasternak and many other writers had, that the controls would also apply to them. At this point Brik and Mayakovsky were willing to accept a cultural dictatorship—if they were the dictators.

As the winter passed, civil war raged on throughout the country, and the shortages of food, of wood to burn, shortages of almost everything, became even more acute. As if Brik and Mayakovsky could feel their power slipping through their fingers, they made another attempt to strengthen their position, and after meetings at the Viborg District of the Communist Party on January 13, 1919, they organized a "Communist-Futurist" commune to be known as Komfut, which was intended to be a collective of artists that would control creative expression in the Soviet Union through its collective publishing house and schools. They made extensive plans to publish manifestos and booklets, elected officers, and agreed on organizational statutes. But they still had to function within the Party, and when they applied for permission to form their collective, the Party committee, probably at Lunacharsky's suggestion, refused their request.

The opposition to Komfut centered largely around their near-dictatorial control of the arts and their "cultural elitism"; despite defensive articles by Punin in *Art of the Commune*, Mayakovsky and Brik and their associates were exposed on both counts. They used official journals largely to propagandize their own positions. The contributors were almost entirely themselves and their supporters. Even in the visual arts they had tried to impose avant-garde ideology on Russian art. They were especially vulnerable to attack from an organization called Proletcult, which insisted that only the workers themselves could create their own culture. This group had had its beginnings some years before, but it formally organized the week before Lenin's coup in October 1917.

At some points there were grounds for agreement between the two, since both of them wanted to do away with the heritage from the Tsarist past and create a new culture. Their reasons differed, however. The Proletcultists argued that the older works were tainted by their bourgeois background and that they had to be replaced by a body of work that was pure in its proletarian identity. The struggle between the two groups was prolonged and bitter, and both were to lose out to Lenin, who insisted on complete control of Marxist ideology. But Proletcult was able to establish a broad popular base, something that had always eluded the Futurists, however stridently they insisted that they were the art of the future. By the end of 1919 Proletcult had grown to 80,000 active members and 400,000 passive members in three hundred local organizations, which had twenty publications.

In the face of the attacks on the Futurists and their role in IZO, Lunacharsky gave way. *Art of the Commune* was discontinued in April 1919, after only nineteen issues. The Moscow paper *Art* attempted to defend the Futurists with an issue on April 1 that included a poem of Mayakovsky's as an editorial. After the issue, which only intensified the criticism, the journal experienced sudden difficulties, and supposedly because of a paper shortage, the next issue didn't appear until July 8. It ceased publication shortly after.

By this time the Briks and Mayakovsky were out of the struggle themselves. Packing a few trunks in the apartment on Zhukovsky Street, the three of them left Petrograd to follow the government to the new capital in Moscow.

Mayakovsky, Boris Pasternak, Lili Brik, Sergei Eisenstein, 1924

Will the eye of the eagle fade?
Will we stare back toward the old?
Proletarian fingers
the world's throat
still tighter hold!
Chests out! Shoulders straight!
With flags glue over the sky!
Who's marching there with the right?
Left!
Left!
Left!

"LEFT MARCH"

THE MOVE TO MOSCOW HAD TO BE MADE HURRIEDLY. In the tense months of the civil war there was little time to prepare accommodations, and the people from Petrograd who moved to the new capital had to be crowded into whatever empty space could be found in a city that was already jammed. It was still the last month of winter and there were shortages of everything in Moscow. When Mayakovsky and the Briks were moved early in March 1919, they gave their apartment on Zhukovsky Street to Shklovsky, with all their books and furniture and the landscapes that Mayakovsky had painted in Levashova the summer before. When Shklovsky later left Petrograd, the Red Guardists who moved in fed all the books, magazines, and papers into the iron stove standing in the middle of one room. Mayakovsky's landscapes disappeared at the same time, probably along with everything else, into the belly of the stove.

In Moscow the IZO members were crowded together into rooms, the Briks assigned to the same apartment as the painter David Shterenberg and his family, and a professor whose wife had an artist lover. The apartment was on Polyektovy Alley, their own quarters a single room about ten and a half by twelve feet in area. Although the room was assigned to the Briks, this time Mayakovsky openly moved in with them. Lili remembered:

> In our one room we had two beds, and a third you could pull out and unfold. Later our puppy Sjen slept in this bed at Mayakovsky's feet. We were four in one room because we were so very cold. We hung carpets on the walls to make it warmer. There was an open fire and a stove, and we burned old newspapers which had remained behind from the people who had lived there and emigrated.

The Moscow Housing Council had assigned Mayakovsky to a small, narrow room—Shklovsky later described it as looking like a "blunt-nosed boat"—on Lyubyansky Passage. It was close to the publishing offices and it was in the same building as the Moscow Linguistic Circle, so Mayakovsky sometimes stayed there when he worked late, but most of the time he was able to get back to the Briks' room. Even with their stove it was still cold, and often there was so little fuel to burn that they huddled in heavy coats in the small space. To decorate the wall above her bed, Lili hung a tapestry with a duck made out of beads, a present from Mayakovsky that amused her.

The government was still functioning, although wages were irregular and shortages of materials made it difficult for the Commissariat of Enlightenment to keep going. Brik worked there with Shterenberg, but Mayakovsky—after contributing to the April issue of *Art* in defense of the Futurists—was no longer with the Department of Fine Arts, although he continued to get support from the new government. He spent most of the spring traveling back and forth to Petrograd supervising the publication of his books by a publishing house known as IMO, which had been established within the commissariat. Despite shortages of paper and printing facilities, he was able to get three small books through the press: a second edition of "War and the Universe," a collection of his poetry entitled *Everything Written by Vladimir Mayakovsky*, and a second edition of *Mystery-Bouffe*.

The mood that gripped them all in Moscow was a kind of desperate exhilaration. For the artists whom Lunacharsky had collected in the Commissariat of Enlightenment, Mayakovsky among them, there was a release of energies that had been throttled in the tumult immediately after the Revolution. One of the typical projects of this time, the short period later called the years of "heroic Communism," was a new "Soviet Alphabet" for the Red Army which Mayakovsky drew in September 1919.

It was difficult to find a printer, but Mayakovsky discovered one that nobody was using, transferred the drawings to the lithograph stones himself, and worked the press by hand. With Lili's help he rounded up friends to put together five thousand copies of a small booklet. They laid out the printed sheets at home and poured paints into soup plates, working night and day on what Lili called "the conveyor-belt principle"—one person painted strokes of red, another yellow, a third green. It was all done in a rush in an attempt to get the booklets ready for a ceremony in the Kremlin for the officer candidates who were going to the front; the new "Soviet Alphabet" was to be a present for them. The books were still damp when Mayakovsky took them to the Kremlin and gave them out to the soldiers.

There was determined opposition to the avant-gardists, as they had found in their struggles with *Art of the Commune*, but the artists and writers had an opportunity to do work that was seen and read, and their enthusiasm led to a vivid, chaotic outburst of artistic activity. In Moscow Marc Chagall was painting his friezes for the State Jewish Theater and directing the School of Art. The Suprematist painters—Malevich and younger disciples like El Lissitzky and Alexander Rodchenko—were designing signs, cafés, and exhibitions. For the center of the new capital Vladimir Tatlin was proposing a revolving tower, constructed out of glass and iron, that would be taller than the Eiffel Tower, issuing constant news bulletins, proclamations, and manifestos by means of telegraph, telephone, and loudspeaker. He envisioned at night an open-air screen on the tower showing news films, while in cloudy weather a projector would throw words on the sky displaying the motto of the day.

Six months after Mayakovsky came to Moscow, he found a place for himself creating "slogan art" in the propaganda department of Rosta, the acronym for the Russian Telegraph Agency. The job was to occupy him for more than two years, a time when he gave up lyric poetry almost completely to draw and write propaganda texts. He was moving toward a position he was to take with Brik later, that poetry was a product to be manufactured for the use of the Revolution, and that the poet should produce to fulfill work quotas like any other worker in the society.

During the summer of 1919 Brik had become interested in the

sociological aspect of pictorial art, such problems as art production
and consumption, and supply and demand during the rigorous conditions of civil war. He and Mayakovsky had long discussions about
"the poet's place in the working ranks," and Mayakovsky took up his
position at Rosta with Brik's theoretical ideas supporting him. "Why,"
he argued, "should literature occupy its own corner? Either it should
appear in every newspaper, every day, on every page, or it's totally
useless. The kind of literature that's dished out as dessert can go to
hell."

In these years Mayakovsky did not feel that he was wasting his
talent as a poet. On the contrary, he was proud of his service to the
Revolution, and he enjoyed a vital sense of community with his
fellow workers. Panels of the Rosta posters decorated the walls of his
room on Lyubyansky. His point of view was that art's function was to
serve the Revolution, and his polemical fervor was inexhaustible. He
derived great satisfaction when his immense resources of images
and words flooded Soviet Russia in the form of the caricatures and
verses on his Rosta posters.

Rosta had been started in the summer heat of August 1919 as
an attempt to rally support against the heavy military offensives that
had been launched against the Red Army. There was little newsprint
for daily newspapers, and even if they could be printed, it was almost
impossible to get them distributed. The news over the telegraph was
disjointed and fragmentary, and in addition to the confusion, the
shops of the city were depressingly empty and dark. There wasn't
anything to sell except the produce the peasants themselves brought
and sold in the open markets.

To decorate the shop windows, the director of Rosta allowed
the artist Mikhail Cheremnykh to put up propaganda drawings.
Called "Windows of Satire," they were loose groupings of separate
satirical drawings with verses on different topics, usually related to
news about the civil-war military campaigns.

When Mayakovsky saw the first windows, he was immediately
drawn to the possibilities of the idiom. He suggested that instead of
random drawings they should work the ideas for slogans into some-

thing like comic strips with a single theme and a linking rhymed commentary. Mayakovsky was hired from October 1919 to February 1922 to produce posters, and he arranged a job for Lili to work beside him, coloring his drawings. When Shklovsky came to Moscow from Petrograd he found them both completely immersed in turning out Rosta posters, and he was very surprised to see Lili working so hard: "She knows how to work when she wants to."

Lili painted alongside Mayakovsky until she left in the evenings to join Osip at the apartment on Polyektovy Alley, but often Mayakovsky stayed into the night, covering dozens of pieces of rough paper with charcoal sketches for the next day's posters. He sometimes signed them with a small drawing of a puppy in the margins where they'd be hidden when the poster was displayed, a message to Lili, who often returned the next day to color the posters in bold red, yellow, and black. In the morning she heated buckets of glue and paint on the stove, whose smoke settled just above eye level. Mayakovsky usually worked on the floor, out of the smoke, and when he couldn't straighten his back after he was finished, he painfully stretched out on the floor to sleep, with a block of wood for a pillow.

All the materials were of the poorest quality. They took any paint, mixing it with saliva, and worked with rolls of paper that were rejects from the printing presses, with holes and uneven edges. They cut the paper to size, sometimes gluing the uneven margins. If they made a mistake drawing a poster, they just glued another piece of paper over it, and all scraps of paper were carefully saved for the metal stove, which burned so inefficiently that Lili kept warm by wearing a dress made from a green ribbed velvet drape, lined with squirrel fur.

It was grueling work. In addition to his sleepless nights and the primitive conditions of the Rosta workroom, Mayakovsky was under enormous pressure to create as many as eighty new lines of rhymed poetry every day for the posters. As he described it, "A machine-like quickness was demanded of us. Sometimes the telegraph gave news of a victory at the front, and in forty minutes to an hour it was already posted in the street as a picturesque slogan."

In the early months he took charge of the posters himself, organizing the department to include people who prepared stencils by cutting out cardboard according to a design, and others who used the stencils to make copies so posters could be shown in many store windows. In the years that he worked at Rosta his energy gave a continuity and direction to the project as it developed from the first simple ideas.

Rosta's activities were extended to other cities, and soon nearly every local artist in sympathy with the government was employed by the agency, but Mayakovsky continued to be a dominant influence through the sheer quantity of his work. He scrutinized the teletype messages, chose the ones most useful for posters, wrote the rhymed texts, drew the pictures, and distributed the copying and coloring work to others. He created more than fifteen hundred posters, each of them with several drawings and accompanying verse.

For Lili one of the most satisfying events in the arduous schedule of their work was when they were paid.

The number of paintings on each poster varied from two to sixteen frames, and we were paid according to the complexity of the finished work. The pressure from the artists at Rosta for money was so high that the Director of Finances put a boy at his door to warn them when the artists were coming. When this boy saw Mayakovsky and the others marching in geese fashion, one behind the other, toward the Department of Finance, he always cried out loudly, "The artists are coming!" and the director would quickly disappear through another door in his office. The settlement of wages was negotiated through the union. Mayakovsky and Cheremnykh went to the union and showed them poster models, the most complicated ones, of course, so they'd get the most money possible.

Occasionally Lili and Mayakovsky worked late together after the others had left Rosta. Once the phone rang when they were alone, and Mayakovsky went to answer it. The voice on the telephone asked, "Who is speaking?" Mayakovsky answered, "Nobody." The voice asked, "But the director, is he there?" "No." "Who is substituting for him?" "Nobody." "That means there's nobody there at all?" "Nobody." The voice said, "Well, I must say!" Mayakovsky said, "Who's talking?" The voice said, "Lenin," and hung up. Lili remembered that he put down the receiver and turned to her, totally silent.

The work at Rosta refined Mayakovsky's skills as a propaganda poet, but earlier he had already shown the direction his work was to take with poems like "Left March" that were to become popular political rallying cries. He dedicated this poem to the Red Marines, who were fighting the British and other interventionist armies then attacking the young Soviet state, and he read it at a meeting he addressed with Brik at the Mastrosky Theater on December 17, 1918, before they moved to Moscow.

With "Left March" he had found his tone as a revolutionary poet—the sudden swaggering assurance, the brilliance of the short, staccato images like "You/have the floor,/Comrade Mauser" and the rhythmic emphasis of the thundering "Left!/Left!/Left!" The political setting and direction of the poem were immediately clear, channeling the brutal force of the stanzas into a patriotic call to action. As a propaganda poem it was startlingly effective, and it was with work of this individuality that Mayakovsky served the Revolution.

> Rally the ranks into a march!
> Now's no time to quibble or browse there.
> Silence, you orators!
> You
> have the floor,
> Comrade Mauser.
> Enough of living by laws
> that Adam and Eve have left.
> Hustle history's old horse.
> Left!
> Left!
> Left!

As a performer he was in great demand, addressing boisterous audiences of soldiers and sailors with such skill that he usually had no trouble getting them to listen to him read at patriotic assemblies before they went off to fight at the front. Twenty-seven years old, he had matured physically; his shoulders had broadened, and he was strong. With his tall, stocky figure—his legs were short in proportion to his long body—he looked more like a prizefighter than a poet, and his booming shout was loud enough to be heard above the din of accordions and the stamping boots of dancers as he stood on platforms in drafty halls and invited the servicemen to hear a poem he'd written "especially" for them.

Mayakovsky was in his element with the crowds at the large public meetings, but Lili sometimes worked behind the scenes to help his appearances before smaller and more reserved audiences, like his performance at the Arts House in Petrograd on December 5, 1920, when he read his new poem "150,000,000" before a group of other writers, including Evgeny Zamyatin and Osip Mandelstam. After he'd finished the long poem, which some listeners found "tiring," Lili came into the room leading a group of applauding schoolchildren whom she'd coached to beg Mayakovsky to continue reading.

"150,000,000" was a long propaganda poem published anonymously as the expression of the entire Soviet population, which at that time was 150 million people. Even though his name wasn't on the title page, the opening lines bore his unmistakable stamp.

150,000,000 is the name of the creator of this poem.
Its rhythms—bullets,
its rhymes—fires from building to building.
150,000,000 speak with my lips . . .
Who can tell the name
of the earth's creator—surely a genius?
And so

of this
my
poem
no one is the author.

Influenced by Brik's research into the old Russian literary forms, Mayakovsky conceived the poem as a parody of the ancient folk epic, the *bylina,* and he tried to create two figures of mock-heroic proportions in "150,000,000": Wilson, the American defender of world capitalism, who was beaten by Ivan, the Russian champion of the oppressed proletariat. As with all of Mayakovsky's propaganda poems, the issue of their duel was a foregone conclusion, the victory of a classless Communist society.

The poem was dedicated to Lili, although the dedication couldn't be included on the title page, since Mayakovsky wanted to publish it anonymously. But when the book was finally printed in April 1920 by the State Publishing House, he arranged for three copies to be printed and bound separately, with a special dedication page to her. The printers never delivered these special copies, and Mayakovsky made them write an official apology. He also sent a copy of the poem to Lenin, with his own signature, and the signatures of the others in the Komfut group. Lenin's response—and the response of others in the Party—was immediately hostile. Lenin wrote a note to Lunacharsky that unmistakably clarified his position toward the Futurists: "Aren't you ashamed of yourself for voting to publish '150,000,000' in five thousand copies? Nonsense, stupidity, double-dyed stupidity and pretentiousness! In my opinion only about one in ten such things should be published, and in editions of not more than one thousand five hundred copies—for libraries and eccentrics."

Trotsky was more sophisticated in understanding the poem as a literary parody, but he thought it brutally heavy-handed and completely unsuccessful: "How out of place and how frivolous do these primitive ballads and fairy tales sound when hurriedly adapted to Chicago mechanics and to the class struggle!"

The official position against Mayakovsky's work was as firm as ever, despite his dedicated service in Rosta. Lunacharsky gave him as much support as he could, but even Lunacharsky distrusted him, sensing the fundamental instability in the poet's character, what he later described as a "double" personality. Beneath his exterior of "metal armor in which the whole world was reflected, there beat a heart that was not only passionate, not only gentle, but fragile and very sensitive to pain." Lunacharsky wrote:

> We can rightfully state that Mayakovsky's coming to the Revolution was an extremely organic arrival, an extremely remarkable arrival. The successes which resulted from Mayakovsky's joining our forces were extremely important to us.
> But Mayakovsky had a double, and this was his misfortune. Why, in Mayakovsky's metallic lines and social poems, do we notice a seeming lack of concreteness, as if he is afraid of the concrete, afraid of the individual and is seeking very great and resounding symbols?
> In a way, this can be explained by the fact that Mayakovsky did not approach all this closely enough in general. Just as a city seen from afar appears as a colossus in a blue haze or a great electric glow, but you cannot make out the streets, the houses, or especially the people, so did Mayakovsky approach the city of socialism, the city of Revolution, in his own way, seeing it, welcoming it, and describing it, but never walking its streets.

Without support from the leading intellectuals of the Party, Mayakovsky depended increasingly on the Briks for advice and encouragement.

Living conditions in Moscow steadily deteriorated. When Lili worked at Rosta she ate with Mayakovsky in dining rooms reserved for government employees; otherwise the food was strictly rationed. Most people lived on an oat mash they made by steaming the oats in pots, grinding the puffed-up grains, and then putting them through a sieve and adding water. When potatoes could be found they were usually frozen, and when they were cooked they were badly flavored. There were few spices to add to the boiled grains or potatoes, and the diet was dangerously low on fresh vegetables.

During the heavy winter of 1919–20 Moscow was filled with snowdrifts, which further hampered food distribution. On a trip from Petrograd to Moscow, Shklovsky noticed that the only thing to eat in the railway station was bright red and yellow gelatin. The cold seemed to seep in everywhere, and anything combustible was fed into the little stoves and fireplaces in the drafty apartments. Mayakovsky and Lili were paid regularly for their Rosta work, and with Mayakovsky's tireless output they did very well, but the money often bought nothing.

Lili fell sick after months of the bad diet, and Mayakovsky tried desperately to take care of her. She had scurvy from the lack of fresh vegetables, and she had developed a bad eye infection aggravated by the work at Rosta. In those months vegetables were more precious than diamonds, and Mayakovsky, half out of his mind with anxiety, scoured the city and managed to find only two carrots. In 1927, in the poem "Good!" written to celebrate the tenth anniversary of the Revolution, he described the long winter in Moscow and his distress when Lili became ill.

> If
>   I've
>   written anything at all,
> If
>   I've
>   told you something,
> That's the doing
>   of those heavenly eyes,
> My
>   lover's
>   eyes.

Round and
            hazel-brown
Hot
     almost burning.
The telephone
                went raving mad,
Thundered,
            struck my ear like a club:
Brown
        eyes
Smothered, swollen,
Hunger and no vitamins.

The doctor told me—
To make those eyes
                        see
You need
            vegetables,
You need
            warmth.
Not home to make soup
But to go to
            my love
I'm dragging
            two
                    small carrots
By their small tails . . .
Greens
        and love
Cured her eyes.
Bigger
        than saucers
They are eyeing
Our Revolution.

II

Lili Brik and Sjen, 1920

I yelled at the sun:
"Go down!
Don't just crawl down into that hole!"
I yelled at the sun:
"You lazy lump!
The clouds caress you
while—winter and summer—
I have to sit and draw these posters!"
I yelled at the sun:
"Now wait!
Listen, goldenbrow,
instead of going down,
why not come down to tea
with me!"

"A MOST EXTRAORDINARY ADVENTURE . . ."

THE WINTER DRAGGED PAST, AND IN THE FIRST FEW weeks of spring 1920 they managed to find a dacha in Pushkino, about fifty miles outside of Moscow. The income from their government jobs made it possible for them to live in comparative comfort, and it was a relief to move for the summer out of the crowded room on Polyektovy Alley, where they had very little privacy. Mayakovsky still had to work nearly every day at Rosta, but there was train service from the country. Their cook Annushka was with them, and the worst of the desperate shortages of food were over, although Lili remembered that for most of the summer they lived on mushrooms. "As appetizers, cold slices of marinated mushrooms; then mushroom soup, sometimes with piroshki made of rye flour with mushroom fillings, and finally the main course, boiled mushrooms."

The summer of 1920 was one of their most tranquil times. As a propagandist for Rosta, Mayakovsky had found a way to serve the Revolution that suited his talents. No one could accuse him of Futurist obscurism in such Rosta jingles as

Prayers to heaven,
                on God to call
for help in a famine
                is no use at all.

Although his creative energy was poured into his poster texts, at the dacha he also found time to write one of his most well-known poems, "A Most Extraordinary Adventure Which Befell Vladimir Mayakovsky in a Summer Cottage." In it he was a lyric poet again, but he shifted away from the intensely fragmented clusters of images that had marked his early Futurist work. Instead, he developed a long narrative flow that was in itself as startling and imaginative as the most fevered similes of his first poems. "A Most Extraordinary Adventure" was nothing less than a meeting with the sun, which came to drink tea with him in his summer dacha. As he described in the opening lines, he often sat watching the sunset in Pushkino.

> The sunset had the power of a hundred and forty suns,
> and summer turned into July;
> Terrific heat
> the heat swam—
> and this was out at the dacha.
> Pushkino, a little hill, had as a hump
> Akula, a big hill,
> and at the foot of the hill
> stood a village
> with crooked roofs like old bark.
> Beyond the village
> gaped a hole
> and it was probably into this hole
> that the sun crept down
> slowly and punctually.
> And day after day
> the sun would rise up purple
> to flood the world
> all over again.

Finally the sun's lazy circling was too much for Mayakovsky as he sat exhausted after a stifling day turning out posters, and he yelled at it to come down for a cup of tea. To his astonishment the sun joined him, squeezing into the dacha's tiny room.

> . . . . drawing a breath
> he spoke in a deep bass:
> "I'm coming back along my shining way
> for the first time since creation.

You called me?
Come on with the tea,
come on, poet, give me some jam."
Tears were streaming from my eyes—
I was crazy with the heat,
but pointing to the samovar
I said:
"Well, sit down,
you big star!"

Once they began talking, they found that they had much in common, and at the end of their conversation they were slapping each other on the back, agreeing that each of them would keep shining.

"Come on, poet,
let's poemify
and lightify
the world's grisly trash.
I'll pour out my sunny beams
and you—your own—
in poems."

The poem's last lines were one of Mayakovsky's most personally optimistic passages. He could write decisively and positively about Revolution, but his writing about himself had so often been desperate and defeated. The sudden expression of joy in the poem's last lines seemed to reflect his new mood of happiness.

To shine all the time,
Shine everywhere,
to the very bottom of the last day,
shine—
and no bones about it!
That will be my motto—
and the sun's!

People who visited them in Pushkino and Moscow during these months were often surprised by the relationship between Lili and Mayakovsky. A young medical student named Rita Rait, who began to work at Rosta after the summer holidays, couldn't believe her first sight of them in the office. She had admired his poems so much that she'd tried to translate them into German, and she phoned Mayakovsky to show him the translations.

> Although I was warned by people who knew Mayakovsky more in his poetry than in life that he could be very aggressive, very rough, I heard a very soft and beautiful voice tell me, "All right, come over to Rosta—you know where it is?" I said yes, I do. "And bring your translations with you."
>
> I ran from the university to Rosta, which was about fifteen minutes away, at a trot. Then I came to a closed door and knocked, and I heard the same voice say, "Come in." I opened the door, petrified. But I saw a small, very beautiful red-headed woman scolding—not scolding, but reprimanding—a very big fellow with a shorn head and big brown eyes who was saying to her, like a small boy who'd been naughty, "Well, Lili, please don't be angry, well . . ." It looked so different from the way I'd pictured Mayakovsky that I just opened my eyes and stood there.
>
> He was glad of the interruption. He said, "Well, well, come in. Are you Rita the translator?" I said yes. They laughed, since I looked so young. Although I was twenty-one, I must have looked fifteen with my long braids and startled eyes.
>
> Mayakovsky said, "I don't know any German, but Lili knows it very well." I read some lines, and Lili said, "Well, it's all right, but you know, Volodya has just written a poem about a young girl—you read it to Rita." That was the first time I heard Mayakovsky.

After being lovers for five years, Lili and Mayakovsky made no effort to hide their intimacy, and it was clear to everyone around them that he adored her and that she dominated him effortlessly. He was always courting girls—Rita was startled when Lili told her that "Mayakovsky adores young girls"—but Lili treated his momentary infatuations as the mischievous behavior of a small boy. However, her moods were mercurial; everyone close to her periodically went through periods of displeasure, when she was very critical of them, but she never criticized Mayakovsky's poetry. She treasured every scrap of paper he touched.

Rita had never met anyone like Lili before, and at first she was puzzled. "For all of us Mayakovsky was immortal. But for me, Lili wasn't merely a simple mortal. She seemed a person from another planet, utterly unique." Lili was always outspoken, always quick to give a personal opinion. Yet she seemed to have two faces, one that could be cold, distant, and critical, and a second that was responsive and beautiful when she smiled, with a sensitive mouth and shining dark eyes. It was impossible to predict her mood, but Rita felt the smiling face was the true Lili. Rita, who was short and intense, was so eager to be Lili's friend that Mayakovsky drew a caricature of her as a little terrier. She became Lili's confidante because she decided, "It was so hard to understand Lili, you've just got to love her. Lili never lived like we all do. She was always herself, she never pretended. Although sometimes I wished she'd keep her bad moods more to herself."

Lili had refused to have a child with Mayakovsky, as she'd refused with Brik, but she and Mayakovsky had come to the point in their relationship where they were ready to extend their family. One afternoon during the summer, when they were at Pushkino, they found an abandoned puppy, dirty and starving, which they promptly adopted. Years later, when Lili reminisced about their life together, it was this summer and the puppy Sjen that she loved to describe.

As more people took over the work at Rosta, Lili wasn't needed to color the posters, and she could accompany Mayakovsky on some of his readings outside Moscow. They traveled together to Petrograd, the two of them taking a crowded train and staying in a hotel together. They always reserved two rooms. Lili never slept the entire night with Mayakovsky; she said he was so big that it wasn't comfortable lying beside him and she joked, "Better a single coffin than a double bed." Their physical relationship hadn't improved. Mayakovsky continued having many "small affairs" which he usually told Lili about after they were over. In her dissatisfaction she also tried other lovers, but she always found them disappointing and returned to Volodya, who knew nothing of her involvements.

Mayakovsky was, as always, working hard, turning out short plays, poems, and rewriting *Mystery-Bouffe*. Although stung by its failure two years before, he'd also realized that there were clumsinesses in his own writing that had hampered the production. But his name still aroused as much hostility from the Soviet authorities as before, despite the success of his propaganda work for Rosta. After a reading of the revised play for Meyerhold, it was accepted for production, but then abruptly canceled.

With his usual determination Mayakovsky organized his friends into a new Communist-Futurist collective, to try to get his play produced. They had their first meeting at the apartment on January 13, 1921, with Lili officially designated as secretary. Then a few weeks later he had an unexpected official endorsement, and the pressures against him were suddenly eased when Lenin himself praised one of his poems at a meeting of the important Metal Workers' Conference. The pages of the Party's official journal *Izvestia* had been closed to Mayakovsky because of the opposition of the editor to his work as a Futurist, but one of the younger members of the staff took advantage of the editor's absence from the office to include one of the poems Mayakovsky was writing about the new bureaucracy. The poem "Lost in Conference" was published in *Izvestia* on March 5, 1921. It was an effective satirical piece, and like many of his poems on the subject, it was bitingly funny.

In the poem Mayakovsky tries to see someone in an office, saying he's "been there since once upon a time," but the official is tied up in conference. Even the younger members of the office staff disappear for a conference of the Young Communist League. When they come back he still is kept waiting, and at the end of the day he's told that the man is still in conference.

> ... Furious
> I throw myself like an avalanche
> into a meeting
> throwing out wild curses on my way.
> And I see:
> halves of people sitting.
> Oh the Devil!
> But where are the other halves?
> "They've been slain!"
> "They've been killed!"
> I run on shouting.
> This terrible picture has driven me mad.
> And I hear
> the calmest little voice of the secretary:
> "They're at two meetings at the same time.
> We have to get to
> about twenty conferences
> in a single day.
> Whether you want to or not you have to split yourself in two.
> Down to the waist is here,
> and the rest
> there."
>
> Can't sleep for worry.
> Early morning.
> I meet the early dawn with a dream:
> "Oh, just
> one
> more conference
> concerning the extermination of all conferences!"

Lenin, speaking to the workers' group, said, "Yesterday, quite by chance, I read in *Izvestia* a poem by Mayakovsky. I don't count myself among the admirers of his poetic talent, although I frankly admit my incompetence in that sphere. But it is a long time since I experienced such pleasure from the political and administrative standpoint. In this poem he laughs at conferences and makes fun of Communists because they are always in meetings and conferences. I don't know about the poetry, but as for the politics, I can vouch for it that he is absolutely right."

Lenin's casual mention of the poem was enough to open the pages of *Izvestia* to Mayakovsky, with all the official backing this implied. Lenin never lost his distrust of the Futurists, but when "150,000,000" was read at propaganda meetings he no longer protested openly. More important, the new version of *Mystery-Bouffe* was finally presented for the May Day celebrations in Moscow in 1921. Despite some adverse criticism and struggles within the Commissariat of Enlightenment by people who couldn't bring themselves to accept Mayakovsky's work, it ran for more than a hundred performances. This time it was put on by professionals with a brilliant stage design, and its success was a vindication for Mayakovsky and the Briks of their belief in the play.

With the spring there was a new feeling of ease at the apartment. In a photograph of Lili outside on the steps with Sjen she's in a coat with a fur collar and a stylish hat, looking as fashionable as ever, the rhetoric of the new social equality lying somewhere beyond her own interests. Mayakovsky's new success and Brik's work for the government meant money and an increasingly privileged way of life for all three of them, but their way of living began to put a strain on some of Mayakovsky's friendships. Both he and Brik were employed by the government, and guests at the apartment included members of the Cheka, the secret police, giving rise to rumors that Brik did more than work with the Commissariat of Enlightenment. He was now employed in a department of the Cheka that investigated speculators. After 1921, when he was deprived of his Party card in one of Lenin's purges of bourgeois elements in the government, his job in the Cheka was officially over, but his association with members of the secret police continued. Some of his old friends began to feel a little uncomfortable, though it was difficult for them to say what it was that disturbed them. In 1922 Pasternak told the writer Mikhail Kuzmin that he "didn't like the rumors he'd heard about the people around Mayakovsky." Kuzmin is said to have answered Pasternak, "Well, who knows? It's dangerous to visit their apartment, so be careful. But perhaps it's good for you, Pasternak, to have friends among the secret police."

Brik's Party card had been important to him, and when it was taken away he grew cynical, but for Lili these changes were simply part of the policies of the Bolshevik government, which she accepted without question. "If it's done it must be right, and I don't want to talk about it." She'd never been political, except to endorse the Party. There were things she was beginning to find confining in her life, but they involved her sense of independence and her relationship with Mayakovsky.

Part of the isolation Mayakovsky began to feel was the result of the confusions of the period and the loss of his closest friends. David Burliuk had been forced to flee Moscow with his wife and two young sons in the spring of 1918 to avoid imprisonment for speculation. While living in Siberia, Burliuk supported himself by lecturing on Futurist poetry. Civil war had divided the country into segments, and once in White territory he was unable to cross back into the Red zone. Fearing persecution from the Whites as a radical and a Futurist, Burliuk went to Japan in 1920. In August 1922, he and his family left Kobe via Canada for the United States.

During the Briks' and Mayakovsky's second summer in Pushkino in August 1921, Alexander Blok died after a lingering illness. As a young poet Mayakovsky had loved Blok, respecting him as an "incorruptible knight." In an obituary for Blok in the newspaper *Agit-Rosta* he tried to define their different approaches toward the Revolution.

Blok approached our great Revolution honestly and enthusiastically; it was not possible, however, for the subtle, refined words of a Symbolist to carry its most real and brutal images. In his most famous poem, "The Twelve," which has been translated into many languages, Blok overreached himself.

I remember how, in the early days of the Revolution, I passed a thin, stooping figure in a soldier's coat, warming himself by the fire near the Winter Palace. He called after me. It was Blok . . . I asked him, "Do you like it?" "It's beautiful," Blok replied. And then he added, "They've burnt my library in the country."

Despite Mayakovsky's love for most of Blok's work, he had never been able to accept Blok's religious references, and the famous last lines of "The Twelve," Blok's masterpiece about a Red Guard patrol on the streets of Petrograd, especially exasperated him. Blok ends the poem saying that the patrol is led through the night snowstorm by the figure of Jesus Christ.

> In a wreath of white roses
> Goes Jesus Christ before them.

But Mayakovsky always read the last lines as:

> In a wreath of white roses
> Lunacharsky, Commissar of Enlightenment.

Mayakovsky was still close to Pasternak and continued to respect him as a poet, though after 1920 they saw each other only occasionally, since Pasternak had begun moving away from him politically. After 1924 they steadily disagreed.

But he couldn't avoid meetings with the self-proclaimed "peasant poet" Sergei Esenin, who was his most serious competition for the Russian audience. When they were put on platforms to read together, the audience usually took it as a contest between them. Mayakovsky responded to Esenin's poetry, but the pose was more than he could accept. Esenin had come into Petrograd in 1915 wearing tarred boots and an embroidered blouse and reading deceptively simple poems that were filled with nostalgia for the life of the Russian countryside. Esenin was obstinately suspicious of the Bolshevik regime, insisting on his independence in stanzas like

> I see everything
> and understand clearly
> this new era is
> not a pound of raisins to you,
> that the name of Lenin
> resounds like the wind
>
> about the world,
> generating thoughts
> like the sails of a windmill.
>
> Turn, turn, dear sails!
> A benefit is promised you . . .
> Come on, Esenin,
> let's sit quietly at our Marx,
> guessing at the wisdom
> of his boring lines.

Often at public meetings Esenin was forced to defend his position against Mayakovsky, who argued just as loudly for Futurism. Esenin's work was loved by Russians on every level despite the notoriety of his personal life. Once Mayakovsky arranged to meet Lili in a café, and he arrived late to find her flirting with Esenin, who sat with his arm around her. Jokingly he asked Mayakovsky if Lili could be his "little Beatrice" too, or was she exclusively Mayakovsky's poetic inspiration? Mayakovsky was furious, and he left with Lili right away. There were many quarrels, but Esenin was correct when he shouted at Mayakovsky in one of their exchanges, "Russia is mine, understand, mine, and you . . . you're American." To which Mayakovsky is said to have contemptuously replied, "Take her, please. Butter your bread with her!"

For Khlebnikov the new era was impossible to assimilate. He lived in a series of poor rooms, hurrying to the Briks to ask for advice about problems with publication. One winter day when he arrived at the apartment blue with cold, Lili took him to buy winter clothes, and he chose an old-fashioned coat trimmed with a collar made out of skunk fur. She left him in the store, but she gave him three rubles to buy a warm hat. Instead he used the money to buy her a package of fancy Japanese paper napkins. Khlebnikov was an eccentric in every way. Reading his poems aloud bored him, so he used to begin reading and then, after a few lines, break off with "And so on." Despite his brilliant intellect, he kept losing his manuscripts, stuffing them into pillowcases. He always completely rewrote his proofs, and he seemed to have less and less relationship to what was going on around him. He died destitute and sick in his sister's house in a remote village far from his Moscow friends in the summer of 1922.

In his increasing politicization, Mayakovsky drew even further away from poets like Anna Akhmatova, Osip Mandelstam, and Marina Tsvetayeva, although they were intensely conscious of his presence on the literary scene. He often saw Tsvetayeva, and when a false rumor of Akhmatova's suicide swept through the Moscow literary world, Tsvetayeva wrote Akhmatova in August 1921 that her only friend—" 'friend' means action!"—turned out to be Mayakovsky. At the Rosta office he cabled Petrograd for more information about Akhmatova, and he brought the news to Tsvetayeva that the rumor had been false.

In Petrograd Mandelstam was writing criticism, as well as his own poetry, and in one of his articles on Mayakovsky's work he described—with another poet's perception—the aesthetic corner Maya-kovsky had backed himself into by asserting with Brik that poetry was superfluous unless it served the Revolution. Mayakovsky wanted to write poems that were so simple they would be understandable to everyone, intellectual, bureaucrat, and proletariat alike, and to do it he had to strip his poems of the kind of cultural basis that gave them their power of image and suggestion. And at the same time he was writing poems that were vitally concerned with culture. Mandelstam's own reaction was to feel sorry for Mayakovsky as an artist: ". . . [he] has absolutely no business impoverishing himself." Once in conversation Mayakovsky referred to Mandelstam as a "marble fly," probably knowing his criticism.

The poet in Mayakovsky must have felt a conflict, however he denied it publicly. To friends he confided, after hearing Pasternak read, "Oh, happy Pasternak, what lyrics he writes! I probably won't ever again . . ." and he broke off. While at the same time, in poems like "Order Number Two to the Army of the Arts," he was demanding that his contemporary poets join him in abandoning "trifles" like lyrical verse.

> I—
> genius or not—
> who have forsaken trifles
> and work in Rosta—
> I order you—
> before they disperse you with rifle butts:
> give it up . . .
>
> Who's interested now
> in—"Ah, wretched soul!
> How he loved,
> how he suffered . . ."?
>
> . . . Comrades,
> give us a new form of art—
> an art
> that will pull the republic out of the mud.

In 1921 Mayakovsky's commitment to being a spokesman for the Revolution didn't leave him much time to question what he was writing. Of course the Briks completely supported his poetry, but Shklovsky felt he was overworking himself at Rosta and slyly suggested that he was beginning to be manipulated by Brik. "Meanwhile, Osip Brik was drawing theoretical conclusions about everything that was happening, including the necessity to write too many lines and not to write narrative poems. For everything he found a justification as precise as it was incorrect." Shklovsky was less and less in sympathy with the difficulties of the period, and within a year, when he was warned he might be arrested, he abruptly left the Soviet Union to live in Berlin as an émigré.

Lili didn't work at Rosta after the summer of 1921, and for a while she'd given up her attempts at sculpture, dissatisfied with what she felt was her small talent. Her enthusiasms came and went, and unlike Brik and Mayakovsky, she was uninterested in a career; she felt she shared their careers. There had been a special sense of closeness working together with Mayakovsky at Rosta, and when this was over she found herself bored at home.

There was another problem. As a beautiful woman nearing her thirtieth birthday, she began to feel a little panic at the thought of growing old. Mayakovsky was two years younger, but he shared her feelings—he told her that he wanted to live until he was thirty and no longer. He tried to joke her out of her depression when she complained that old women weren't beautiful with wrinkles and rounded backs; he told her, "You, Lili, are not a woman. You are an exception." "But," she asked, "what about you? Aren't you an exception, too?" He didn't answer.

In the summer of 1921 their friend Rita Rait was invited to Pushkino after translating *Mystery-Bouffe* into German, and for the first time she became part of the household. Lili found her very sympathetic. She told Rita, "We've shared the same nursery," meaning they were from the same social class. Rita's father had been a physician and she also had been brought up with governesses and language tutors and a sense of order in the house. Rita was impressed by the way Lili organized the household: Annushka cleaned the rooms and served the meals at definite times, and Lili expected everyone to be punctual.

But during Rita's first days at Pushkino she found it difficult to understand the relationships. Once she said impulsively to Lili, "Osya seems like a son to you and Volodya." Lili answered, "No, Volodya is like a son to Osya and me." Rita understood this to mean that Lili dominated Mayakovsky because he needed the sense of discipline that she imposed. As much as she loved Mayakovsky, however, Lili was even more attached to Brik, forming all her own judgments about literature and politics from what "Osya says."

Rita admired Lili's beauty, and she was often invited to watch her take a bath in a portable folding rubber tub, with water heated in the samovar. Lili always made her a glass of strong, hot, sweet imitation coffee. The first time she helped Lili dry her back and get into her light cotton flowered pajamas, Rita exclaimed over the luxury of bathing in a tub of warm water instead of a washbasin, and Lili said with a smile, "In my soul I am Communist, but in my body I am terribly bourgeois."

Her life was in some ways too still. She and Mayakovsky had been lovers for six years and she felt their relationship was not as intense as it had been. He was as absorbed in his career as ever; there were the flurries with the Komfut meetings and the successful productions of *Mystery-Bouffe*, and Brik had arranged for them to be moved into a larger apartment on Vodopyany Lane, but she felt increasingly restless. She didn't see herself as the plump wife of a Party official; in fact, as food became more available, she began rigorously to diet and exercise to maintain her slim figure.

Subtly, and then openly, she began to change things for herself. Her mother had taken a job in London with the Soviet Commercial Trade Commission and sent Lili silk stockings, perfumes, and cosmetics, none of which were available in Moscow. Lili decided to visit her mother in London to get away from the restraints of her life. Lenin's retreat to a kind of modified capitalism in the New Economic Policy (NEP) had opened the borders of the Soviet Union to limited foreign trade. She knew she couldn't get a visa to England in Moscow, but she might be able to in Riga, a port city on the Baltic coast in the independent state of Lithuania.

In October 1921 she left Moscow, traveling alone by train. As a present to Rita, who was going to stay at the dacha with Brik and Mayakovsky, Lili bought a thick notebook with a sturdy brown binding. Quietly she took Rita aside and said, "You should write down everything Volodya says. He's a genius, he'll last. Later on every word will be interesting." Rita was startled, but it was impossible to refuse Lili, who went happily on her way to Riga, leaving Mayakovsky behind without her.

12

Lili Brik, Riga, 1922

You came—
businesslike,
because of my roaring,
because of my height;
having looked,
you recognized a mere boy.
You took,
seized my heart
and simply
began to play with it—
like a little girl with a ball.

"I LOVE"

D URING THE WEEKS THAT LILI WAS IN RIGA WAITING for a visa, Mayakovsky bombarded her with letters, even though he could never be sure that the letters he was writing her were getting through. He stayed with Brik in their new apartment on Vodopyany Lane, sometimes alone in his own room on Lyubyansky. For some weeks they were at the dacha at Pushkino, where Rita stayed with them. Rita tried to write down everything he said, but he never said anything "genius-like," so she put away her notebook. Mayakovsky was continuing his usual habit of writing lines of his poems when he was taking walks alone and revising the verses in his room later, and he didn't talk to Rita very much. She didn't mind, because she was waiting for Pasternak to come and walk in the woods with her. They went off together, Pasternak telling long stories about his university days and the philosophy he'd studied in Germany. Rita didn't understand most of what he said, but she was in love with him, and when she got back to her room she scribbled his stories down in her notebook.

Rita had been in love with Pasternak for months, and Mayakovsky often teased her about it. Once in Pushkino, he found her chewing on a piece of grass, which upset him because of his feelings about cleanliness, and he demanded to know why she was doing it, why she was always chewing on grass stems, didn't she know that they were unclean. She answered, "No, I take them from where no human foot ever stepped." Immediately recognizing the line from Pasternak's poem, Mayakovsky smiled condescendingly and recited the original text, "In the suburb where no human foot ever stepped." Then he went on, "There's a Pasternak soul for you."

In the quiet evenings at the dacha it was still warm enough to sit outside on the wide terrace overlooking the hill that sloped down to the river where they had bathed with their dog Sjen. Usually Brik read a book, and Mayakovsky tried to interest Rita in games. She didn't know how to play cards or Mah-Jongg and refused to learn, but she offered to teach him checkers. It was the first and last game they played together. Since Rita had no money, they played for "penalties"—Volodya insisted that even his first game of checkers had to have stakes to make it interesting. She won the first game and was awarded a chocolate bar. He won the next two, and then they stopped playing. Her first penalty was washing out his shaving brush. The second was more complicated; she was to greet their guests the following Sunday by kneeling on the floor and touching her head to the ground three times while repeating the words, "Dear God, forgive me for daring to challenge Volodya." By the time Sunday came, Rita thought that Mayakovsky had forgotten her penalty and dressed in a clean white skirt and blouse, but when the guests arrived, he called out to her, "Rita, come and repent," and she had to kneel on the floor and repeat her lines to Mayakovsky while he and the others roared with laughter.

Rita remembered that he was in high spirits most of the time they were in Pushkino in 1921–22; he was young and full of jokes and quick to respond to pretty girls. Rita had a friend named Tamara who was staying in a dacha in Pushkino with her lawyer husband and baby daughter. Tamara was studying acting at Meyerhold's studio, and Rita asked to bring her along when Osip and Mayakovsky went to the theater in Moscow one evening. When Rita introduced Tamara to Mayakovsky, he thought she was so pretty that he said, "Oh, Rita, hiding such a friend from us!" After the theater it was too late to catch a train back to Pushkino, so they arranged to sleep over in Moscow, Osip and Mayakovsky on Vodopyany and the two girls at Tamara's apartment in the suburbs. Brik left them, saying he was tired, and Mayakovsky took Rita and Tamara home. Rita excused herself and went to bed, while Mayakovsky and Tamara sat up together. The next morning the two girls overslept and were an hour late for their appointment to meet Mayakovsky and Brik on Vodopyany. They'd just left Tamara's apartment when Mayakovsky pulled up in a cab, furious at them for not being punctual. "I thought your throats had been cut!" he shouted, and he was so sullen toward them that Osip had to joke him out of his mood.

Mayakovsky saw Tamara many times after this while Lili was away in Riga. Once when Rita tagged along with them on a boat ride, she wanted to sit next to Tamara, unaware of what was going on between her friend and Mayakovsky, but he told her, "Rita, stop sticking like a burr." Months later, when Lili came back from her trip, Mayakovsky pretended he'd never even been introduced to Tamara when they met again in Pushkino.

There were so many guests at the dacha during this time that the cook, Annushka, later complained to Lili. When Lili was home she was very strict; there were no parties and no overnight guests, the dacha was to be kept very quiet so Mayakovsky could rest. With Lili away, Mayakovsky invited friends to Pushkino for Sunday parties, apologetically asking Annushka to prepare extra cutlets, which made her grumble, since she felt Lili's orders were being disobeyed. Aseyev came with his wife, Oxana, who flirted with Brik on the sofa while the others played cards—Osip's stories made her giggle—and she brought her younger sister along as company for Mayakovsky, who was totally bored with her. Another evening a theater director and his wife came to the dacha with several bottles of vodka. They got drunk, and the lady was very disorderly. After they left the next day, Rita, who'd never seen a drunken woman, said to Mayakovsky, "Imagine Lili acting that way!" Mayakovsky was astonished. "Lili? But Lili is God Almighty."

Regardless of what Mayakovsky was doing while Lili was away, in his first letters to her he gave a laconic description of his activities. On October 17, 1921, he wrote:

DEAR SWEET, MARVELOUS KISSA,

Thank you for the letter and the presents. But if you keep sending so much, you'll be left with nothing. That's why we categorically forbid you to do it.

My life is monotonous and boring. Thursday I was at

Liova's, Friday at Menshoy's (it went well), Saturday and Sunday I stayed home because friends were at our house. Sunday they had dinner here.

I'm very glad that you miss Moscow.

Write. I kiss you terribly.

YOUR SJEN

Three days later he wrote again, telling her that there was to be a dog show at the zoo and that he was thinking of looking for a puppy to take the place of Sjen, who had disappeared from their Moscow apartment—they suspected he'd been poisoned by jealous neighbors. Every three or four days there was another letter. He usually signed himself Sjen and drew a sad little dog who was crying at the thought of how far Lili was from him. To amuse her, he made up endless nicknames playing on the simple "Lili" that she preferred. She was Lissik (which meant "little fox"), Lilik, Liliatik, Lichik, Lisyok, Liyok, Lilyok, Lisyonysh, Lilyonok, Lilyonochek, and Lilyochek. Sometimes she was simply Kiss, Kissa, or Kissik—"little kitten"—to his mournful Sjen, "little doggy."

He complained over and over again that she wasn't writing him. "During the whole day only one thought is in my mind—whether it will be soon, whether your letter will be soon," he wrote on November 6. A few days later he described how he spent her birthday trying to focus a telescope on Riga. When he did get a letter, the mails were so irregular that she'd be complaining about not hearing from him, and the weeks would pass in hopeless confusion as letters groped toward each other across the distance from Moscow to Riga.

As he missed her more intensely, he became increasingly emotional. He began to kiss her—186 times, 150 million times, 32 million times a minute. His letter of October 26 was typical of the extravagance of his feelings.

MY DEAR, MY SWEET, MY DARLING, MY ADORABLE LISSIK!

I profit from Vinokour's trip to write you a real letter. I miss you, I long for you—if you only knew how much—I don't know what to do with myself and I think only of you. I don't go anywhere, I drift from one corner to another looking at your empty wardrobe, there is nothing in the world more dreary than a life without you. Don't forget me, for god's sake. I love you a million times more than all the rest of the people together. I don't take any interest in seeing anyone or talking to anyone but you. The most joyful day in my life will be your return. Do love me, little one. Take care of yourself, have a rest—write if you need anything. Kiss Kiss Kiss Kiss Kiss Kiss Kiss Kiss Kiss Kiss Kiss Kiss Kiss Kiss Kiss Kiss.

YOUR SJEN

If you don't tell me something about yourself, I'll go crazy. Don't forget. Do love.

In Riga it was uncertain whether Lili would be able to get a visa. Mayakovsky was furiously busy with his work and with new writing, but he managed to get a letter off with nearly every courier. He was working on another play for Agitprop, he was writing articles, he was struggling to keep up with his work, and at the same time, on November 22, he wrote Lili, "I am worrying that I shall not be able to write a poem for you before your arrival. I'm trying awfully hard."

As a present for Lili during her absence, he began a long autobiographical poem called "I Love," which traced the role of love in his life with the constant refrain made up of the initials of her name, L.Yu.B. It was one of his most tender poems, and like his "A Most Extraordinary Adventure . . ." it was one of his most mature poems describing himself and his emotions.

In the first lines he wrote about the loneliness and the difficulties of his life before meeting Lili. Remembering himself as a young man, he laughingly described his anguish as he staggered around under the weight of his love, "exhausted by lyricism." He raised his heavy heart and carried it around like a circus strong man, crying out, "Here it is!" to girls who

jumped away from me
like rockets:

"Something tinier would be much nicer;
something like a tango . . ."
I can't carry that burden
but still I go on carrying it.
I'd like to drop it—
but know
I won't!
The ribs can't withstand the pressure.
The thorax creaks under the strain.

In the poem he confronted his own emotional vulnerability, but
it seemed to him that it was something out of his past, before he met
Lili.

But with me
anatomy has gone crazy.
I'm all heart
sounding everywhere within me.

In Lili he had finally found a woman who wasn't frightened
away by his overwhelming need for love.

You came—
businesslike,
because of my roaring,
because of my height;
having looked,
you recognized a mere boy.
You took, seized my heart
and simply
began to play with it—
like a little girl with a ball.
And everyone—
as if stunned by that miracle—

be it a lady
or a miss,
"To love someone like him?
Why he could pounce on you!
She's probably a lion tamer,
probably right from the zoo."
But I'm exulting.
It's gone—
the yoke!
Overwhelmed with joy
I leap about like an Indian
doing a wedding dance,
I feel so gay
and so light.

The poem was free of politics; he had at last found somewhere
to rest his heart.

I can't do it by myself—
I can't carry the grand piano
(much less—
the fireproof safe).
And if not the safe
or the grand piano
then having taken it back
how could *I* bear my heart.
Bankers know:
"We are endlessly rich.
There aren't enough pockets—
we'll put it into the safes."
I have hidden
my love
in you
like riches in iron;
I walk around

rejoicing, a Croesus.
And if
I want to very much
I'll take out a smile,
a half smile,
even less,
and with others reveling,
in half a night expend
about fifteen rubles of lyrical change.

For the first time in his poems to Lili he wasn't jealous, and he rejoiced, including himself among the richest men in the world.

At first, as Lili waited in Riga for her London visa, she busied herself talking with publishers about the possibility of having Russian books and magazines printed there. A month after she arrived, on November 17, 1921, she wrote to Mayakovsky:

> I've talked to the owner of a big publishing house. He agrees and wants very much to publish our books at his expense. It would be possible to publish monographs, collections, illustrated books—with hard covers or in periodical editions. It would also be fine to publish some textbooks . . .
>
> To begin, certain things are necessary: (1) go to the Commissariat of Foreign Trade and find out how to get permission to import books from Riga to Moscow, for money, of course (they will pay in Riga); (2) prepare the materials so completely that it would be possible to put them right into print; (3) send this material via Comrade Granik, working in the press section of the Commissariat of Foreign Affairs, to the editors of the newspaper *The New Way*. It would be wonderful to publish works by Khlebnikov, Pasternak, and others, as fully as possible, and articles collected from *Art of the Commune*, and a book about Russian posters, with an introductory article—in other words, any book however expensive.

Take this very seriously, Volodik. It'll give you the chance
to rest and to write.

She was trying to ease the difficulties he was facing with the
State Publishing Company, since during this period there was
considerable activity in cities like Riga and Berlin, publishing for
Russians whose books were held up by the bureaucratic channels in the
Soviet Union. Mayakovsky answered her immediately with a de-
tailed letter on November 28. With his usual disruptive energy he
had gone directly to the officials whose permission was needed.

DEAR AND SWEET LILYONOK,
Here is a report about publishing.
1. I've spoken to Comrade Vasilev, who is in charge of
importation. He turned out to be an old acquaintance and
promised to do everything possible, but permission depends
also on the Commissariat of Enlightenment (Gosizdat).
2. I went to Lunacharsky, and while I was there he spoke
with Gosizdat. From their side, there were no obstacles, and
Lunacharsky approved the list of books and asked the Commissariat of Foreign Trade for an import permit.
3. The next step will be sending a specific import permit
with each book manuscript to the editor.
4. Here is the list of books proposed for publication:
1. MAF—An illustrated magazine of art. Editors—
Vladimir Mayakovsky and Osip Brik. Contributors—Aseyev,
Arvatov, Kushner, Pasternak, Chuzhak, and others.
2. Mayakovsky—Book of poems.
3. Pasternak—Lyrics.
4. A book about Russian posters.
5. Poetics—A collection of articles on the theory of
poetic language.
6. Khlebnikov—Works.
7. *Art of the Commune*—Collection of articles.
8. Anthology of Recent Literature . . .

With this "business" letter, written on official stationery, he sent a more personal note with a description of himself and Osip facing the days without her:

> . . . Every morning I come to Osya and say, "It's boring, brother Kis, without Lisky," and Osya says, "It's boring, brother Sjen, without Kissi."

Mystery-Bouffe was being presented in Kharkov and he wanted to get to the performances, but it was difficult to arrange transportation. Mayakovsky was able to get away after December 5, and he returned to Moscow on Sunday, December 18, to find two personal letters from Lili and three letters filled with business details. The excitement lasted for a few days, but by the beginning of January he was becoming impatient. She described more complications with the publishing project in Riga, and he wrote her on January 2: "I was sure that by the eve of the New Year you would have come, and now I'm entirely disappointed."

It was now definite that Lili wouldn't get a visa, but she still lingered in Riga. In a mood of high excitement, Mayakovsky expected her to return on January 16, but she didn't arrive. He wrote her on the twenty-second: "I made the room spotless! After that for about five days I would call home every half hour." But there were two letters from her, one offering him a reading tour there, and he accepted without hesitation. "I'll go with pleasure. I'm fed up here. I have nothing to do. For the last two months I haven't drawn even half a poster. Isn't that fine?!" Then finally, in the last days of January, she was back.

But Lili's mood had changed. She realized how much she enjoyed her freedom. After trying to help Mayakovsky find publishers in Riga, she had used her months there to her own advantage. She had met several diplomatic couriers who went back and forth between Riga and European cities. They carried messages between Lili and her mother in London at ARKOS, the Soviet Trade Center, and others brought presents to Moscow from her to Osip and Mayakovsky.

Among the people she saw was a man named "Alf," an official at ARKOS whom she met in Riga, a tall blond man, very quiet, recuperating from tuberculosis. He fell in love with her, and she stayed in contact with him when she returned to Moscow. Determinedly Lili clung to her original resolve to arrange a visa so she could visit London alone. Rita, who had studied English, became her tutor as well as her confidante, and the two of them took long walks in the countryside, speaking English to each other.

In Pushkino in the summer of 1922 Lili met a man named Alexander Krasnoshchokov (Tobinson) who had moved into a nearby dacha. Born in 1880, he was Jewish like the Briks; he'd emigrated to the United States after the unsuccessful revolution of 1905 and then returned to Russia early in 1918. Deeply committed to politics, he'd been appointed by Lenin for a short time as president of the Far Eastern Republic. He was married, with a son named Eugene and a daughter Louellen, but he and his wife were separated. During the summer he fell in love with Lili, whom he nicknamed "Luri," meaning "to lure." He tried to make a joke of his affection for her, but he was entirely serious. Despite his own affairs, Mayakovsky grew dark and unhappy when he saw Lili with Tobinson.

As always, Brik was calm. Rita remembered, "I saw Mayakovsky in rages, I saw Lili in tears, but I never saw Brik lose control." Mayakovsky felt it was perfectly all right for him to have casual love affairs, but he didn't want Lili to become emotionally involved with anyone else. She told him that she had a "light character" to justify her interest in other men. As she said of herself, "I have no capacity for sticking to people like glue. I'm not dependent."

In September 1922, she finally got a visa to visit her mother in London for a few weeks, where Elsa was now living too. Before Lili left she exchanged notes with Tobinson in Pushkino, with Rita acting as a messenger. She called him the "O.B. One," or the "Other Big One." Mayakovsky, of course, was the first "Big One."

In London with her mother and sister, Lili found herself in a society that had not endured the destruction and privation that the Russians had suffered in the previous five years. On September 22, 1922, she wrote Rita a glowing letter about her life there.

MY DARLING RITA,

You write extraordinary letters—write me again quickly! I need so terribly "to talk with you in English," especially after the little note from the "O.B. One."

I'd love to stay in London another two or three months. In the daytime I walk the streets and go to museums, and in the nighttime I go dancing!

For the past several days I've gone to the National Art Gallery. Fell in love again with Titian, Cranach, etc. They are not to be compared with our painters (but don't tell anybody, for God's sake!).

There are no Futurists here, and I'm awfully glad. On the 28th I want to go to Germany, to have a little time before Osya and Volodya come. I want to see Alf for a few days in St. Blasien. His health is improving (in the tuberculosis sanitorium) and he loves me more than ever, I'm sorry to say.

I speak English badly, mostly because I'm shy. But I understand almost everything at the theater.

In the airplane from Moscow to Königsberg, a man fell in love with me, the man who later brought you the little hat I sent you. He went to Andorra, but he promised to send me a visa just for another chance!

This week I'm going to Chinatown one evening. In the next ten days I want to see horse races, a boxing match, three musical revues, and two more museums. Then I can leave— although I don't want to . . .

Going to the zoo—wonderful! I don't take any English lessons—no time now. Don't take riding lessons either—too expensive. Hugging you tightly, little girl.

LOTS OF LOVE,
LILI

When Rita received the letter on October 4, 1922, she telephoned Mayakovsky and Osip at the apartment on Vodopyany to say she'd come over and read it to them after dinner. There was also a photograph of Lili, her mother, and Elsa at the London zoo. Apparently Lili had written to Rita first, and Brik and Mayakovsky wouldn't wait until after dinner. Mayakovsky said, "You're crazy. Wait until dinner? We're coming right away." Fifteen minutes after her phone call, they burst into Rita's room dressed in pink shirts and felt hats that Lili had bought for them in Riga. They wanted to read the letter for themselves, but she insisted it had private things meant for her—she would read it aloud to both of them. She managed to skip over the last part of the opening paragraph about the "O.B. One," but when her voice hesitated picking her way through Lili's comments about the art gallery and the painters, omitting, "There are no Futurists here, and I'm awfully glad," Volodya told her brusquely to read it all. Osip said, "Don't force her," and Mayakovsky answered sadly, "I bet she's happy to be free of us Futurists."

Rita was startled that he guessed the truth, almost verbatim, in the letter. He sensed, too, Lili's interest in other men. Of course, Lili and Elsa didn't go dancing every night in London alone. Lili's escort was a young Russian working in ARKOS. He was a very good dancer who taught her the fox-trot and the tango, and before she left London for Berlin he had become her lover.

13

Lili Brik and Mayakovsky, 1924

Put a heart in me—
                blood—
                          to the uttermost vein.
Knock thought into my skull!
My earthly life I didn't live out,
on earth
          I didn't get love to the very end.

"ABOUT THIS"

O N OCTOBER 8, 1922, MAYAKOVSKY AND BRIK FLEW to Berlin to join Lili. She had come over from London with Elsa, who had recently separated from Triolet and wanted to begin a new life for herself in Berlin. Both women found fault with Mayakovsky when he arrived, since after the excitement of London he seemed tiresome and boorish. Lili had no intention of telling him what she'd been doing and she wrote Rita to keep her letters confidential. Reunited with Mayakovsky in Berlin, Lili was very impatient with him.

I dreamed of showing him all the important sights in Berlin, but he didn't want to see anything. A Moscow friend was staying at our hotel, and Mayakovsky played cards with him day in and day out. They played poker for high stakes in the bedroom. I was terribly angry in the beginning, but I think I joined them later on. In any case, Mayakovsky did not see anything in Berlin. There was inflation in Germany and with our money we seemed like millionaires. I remember that for the equivalent of about one dollar I bought a very nice fur coat and brought it back to Russia for Rita. We changed our money legally in Moscow. Brik was very different from Mayakovsky. Osya not only went all over Berlin, but he knew Germany well. He'd delivered two lectures on Bauhaus art, and he met people who were to the left in art and in politics.

But Mayakovsky was always generous. We had dinners at the most expensive restaurants, where he treated everybody. There were many Russian émigrés in Berlin who had no money at all. Sometimes Mayakovsky invited ten people to dinner. We ate turtle soup, and if he liked the soup or the compote he'd order extra portions because he liked everyone to eat as much

as he wanted. After dinner sometimes we went to a dance hall
or a cabaret, but only Elsa and I would dance—I don't remember
what Mayakovsky did then.

Mayakovsky knew only a few words of German, and Lili quickly
tired of being his interpreter. Besides, she and Elsa were absorbed in
shopping, sightseeing, and dancing, none of which interested him.
Lili had waited until Berlin to go shopping, as she was short of
money in London, but she knew she could rely on his generosity to
buy cosmetics and new clothes. In 1922 inflation had started in
Berlin—Germany had begun to drift into the anarchy and near-
collapse that came a year later—but in the western section of the city
the shops still had luxuries like French perfumes, and Lili knew
where to find them.

Despite what she remembered, Mayakovsky in fact did more in
Berlin than play cards and eat in expensive restaurants. He was
moody when they were together, but after dinner, when Lili and
Elsa went dancing, he met acquaintances like Victor Shklovsky and
Ilya Ehrenburg, who were then living in Berlin. They took him
around to their favorite cafés, especially the Romanisches Café, which
had become the meeting place of so many foreign visitors and émigré
revolutionary artists and writers that Ehrenburg joked that the solid
citizens of Berlin were apprehensive that it was the headquarters of
the world revolution.

In the cafés Mayakovsky passed on the latest Moscow news,
praised Meyerhold's theater to foreigners, and argued belligerently
with anyone who would listen. As always, he was concerned with
earning money. He gave five readings during his month in Berlin, at
the Café Leon, the House of Arts, the Russian Embassy, and Schu-
bert Hall, and he was deeply involved in publishing a collection of
his short lyric poetry, *For the Voice*, which was designed in Berlin
by the artist El Lissitzky, one of Russia's most brilliant Constructivists.
Lissitzky had come to Berlin to mount the exhibition organized by
David Shterenberg in the Van Diemen Gallery, the most compre-
hensive exhibition of Russian abstract art ever seen in the West, a

stunning collection that was the first glimpse of Russian culture
since the blockade of 1917 had isolated the country and its artists.
Included were canvases by Tatlin, Malevich, Lissitzky, Kandinsky,
Chagall, Rodchenko, Archipenko, and the two Burliuk brothers,
among others.

It must have been satisfying for Mayakovsky to be associated
with the success of the Russian art exhibition—he participated in
discussions about it and Shklovsky arranged for a reading of his
poems from *For the Voice* at the Café Nollendorfplatz; it developed,
as Lissitzky remembered, into a "truly uproarious evening." Yet in his
personal life with Lili, Mayakovsky had never been unhappier. When
he was with her, his jealousy expressed itself in sullen withdrawal and
endless games of cards.

He also found it almost impossible to be on good terms with
Elsa, in spite of their long-standing friendship. When she gave a
housewarming party in her new apartment in Berlin, Mayakovsky
showed up with a deck of cards after Elsa had specifically asked him
not to gamble at her party. She refused to let him begin a game, and
they had a brief, ugly quarrel in front of all the guests before Mayakovsky stormed out, swearing he'd never talk to her again. Lili
patched it up, but to her irritation, Mayakovsky made no effort to be
sociable.

The situation eased a little after the Briks returned to Moscow.
Mayakovsky stayed on to work with Lissitzky, and Shklovsky visited
him frequently. He thought that Mayakovsky's hotel room in Berlin
was very modest. "There were quite a few wine bottles; a small amount
had been drunk from each. He felt only curiosity toward wine." One
afternoon they went by themselves to the resort island of Norderney
for a walk on the beach, Mayakovsky, "cheerful and all windblown,"
reminding Shklovsky of a sixteen-year-old boy. Shklovsky was wearing
a fancy light-beige suit, and because he was in love with Elsa (he was
writing a novel about her called *Zoo, or Letters Not about Love*),
Volodya regarded him with an affectionate mixture of "sympathy
and irony."

Together the two men rolled up their trousers and waded in the ocean, running after the waves on the sand, trying to catch the little crabs that scuttled sideways at high tide. They skipped stones in the water, then ran out on the boat dock chasing the waves. Shklovsky tried not to let the salty water splash on his light suit. It grew windy, and when the sea spray on their clothes dried, it left gray edges of salt. Finally they sprinted back to the station to catch the train, Mayakovsky running ahead, Shklovsky following, in his excitement breaking his watch. Later Shklovsky wrote:

> Many things were going on then—rejection in love, and nostalgia, and youth.
> Memory has selected the sea and the wind.
> By that immense, alien sea, with its lip-cutting wind, our youth was ending.

Mayakovsky had been invited by Diaghilev to visit Paris, and when he left Berlin he sent a postcard back to Rita, who'd given him German lessons in Pushkino: "Eh, Rita, Rita— You taught me German, but I'm to talk in French." Once in Paris he had an exuberant seven-day review of French painting: he visited the studios of Picasso, Delaunay, and Léger; he went to countless galleries. In the end, his nationalistic pride in Russian art was satisfied. He wrote: "I went to Paris trembling. I saw everything with a schoolboy's diligence. What if we turn out to be provincial again?" He decided that although the French were superior in painting, the Russians had contributed Constructivism, which he considered the most exciting new movement in art. "Not the kind of constructivism that constructs unnecessary little instruments out of good and necessary wires and sheet metal. But the Constructivism that conceives of the artist's formal work as engineering only, essential for the shaping of our practical lives. Here French artists have something to learn from us . . ."

When he returned to Moscow after Paris, he found Lili still impatient with him. His excitement over Paris led him to arrange a return visit the next spring as an *Izvestia* correspondent, which didn't make her any happier. She'd never been to Paris, and she resented his coming home thinking of himself as an experienced traveler after she had despaired of him as a sightseeing companion in Berlin. Over the years her way of dealing with Mayakovsky had been to take the offensive whenever he irritated her, so she became even more critical. She said he was getting soft and lazy and not working hard on his poetry any more. She challenged his praise of European luxuries like good food, tailored clothes, and expensive cars. She had enjoyed them in London and Berlin, too, but she pointed out that, having taken on the role of spokesman for the Revolution, Mayakovsky had to set a better example.

Her arguments were emotional and inconsistent, but Mayakovsky had no success in quieting her down. Their quarrel flared up in public at a lecture on Berlin he gave just before Christmas 1922. The auditorium was crowded, and Lili sat at the back of the stage while he read his prepared speech, "What Is Berlin Doing?" It was the first of a two-part talk, to be followed by "What Is Paris Doing?" a week later.

Lili had not heard the speech before Mayakovsky read it, but as she listened she realized that some of the experiences he recounted as his own were those Osip had had while Mayakovsky had stayed in his room playing poker. Brik had helped Mayakovsky write the speech, but Mayakovsky described everything in Berlin as if it had happened to him, and Lili began to grow angry. She whispered to Mayakovsky, hissing louder when he paid no attention to her, "Oh, don't lie, don't say things others have told you." She was so furious when Mayakovsky kept talking to the audience, his back to her, that she started to take off her shoe to throw it at him and make him turn around. People in the audience began to watch her, and finally one of the Komsomol officials led her off the stage to avoid a scandal. He said to her: "If you don't understand Mayakovsky, go away."

Lili went back to the apartment alone in a cab, took a sedative, and woke the next morning feeling terrible. Mayakovsky asked her contritely, "Shall I cancel the second lecture?" But it was too late. "As you like." She shrugged, and he lectured on Paris, this time about his own impressions, while Lili stayed at home.

Rita broke in on them after the Paris lecture, unaware they were quarreling. She found Lili in bed with a hot-water bottle, her eyes very red. Lili explained that she had a bad cold, but later Rita realized she had been weeping. Mayakovsky was still in the apartment, standing with his back to Lili, and he didn't turn around when Rita came in. She began to chatter about seeing the proofs of a story she'd translated for a magazine. "Did they pay you well?" asked Lili.

"A little," answered Rita. Lili pressed her. "Why only a little?" She called to Mayakovsky, "Volodya, I think they cheated Rita." He turned around, and Rita saw his eyes were red, too. But his voice was calm. "Let me phone the editor immediately."

Lili shook her head. "Later, Volodya. From your place. Weren't you in a hurry to go?"

So Mayakovsky said goodbye and left, and when they were alone Lili said to Rita, "Volodya was crying," and she began to weep also. She tried to explain why they had been quarreling, but the reasons she gave for the quarrel were less clear than its outcome—they had decided to separate. Later Lili remembered:

> We agreed—I don't remember if it was my initiative or if it was his idea—that we should not meet for two months. It was mostly my idea, and Mayakovsky agreed to it. He would live these two months by himself in his place on Lyubyansky. He said he would not go to our apartment on Vodopyany and we would not meet. We talked chiefly about him, about what he would do, because in any case I felt no one cared about my life, whether it was good or bad, this way or that way. But he was a proletarian poet. He had to be exemplary.
>
> During these two months he wrote a poem "about all this," about love, about jealousy, about drinking tea, about everything.

In the poem he thought in a very literal way that his room was a prison. It seemed to him as if he were sitting in a prison where he'd committed himself voluntarily. He had a hyperbolic attitude toward life—everything had to be exaggerated—and he was doing this to himself here, too. It was his inner emotional condition.

Except once, when he broke his promise not to try to see me, Mayakovsky never came to Vodopyany himself. Instead, he sent me letters and I returned notes. We agreed on the twenty-eighth of February, after exactly two months, we would arrange to meet again.

On the train he read me his poem "About This," and we both wept. This poem left a very deep impression on me too, of course. I thought that even if it had been very hard for him during those two months, it was thanks to those two difficult months that he'd been able to write that great poem. Perhaps he made it too hard for himself by agreeing to a two-month separation, but he wouldn't have been the poet he was without the exaggeration. Everything in Mayakovsky's life was hyperbole.

There has always been confusion about the reasons for their quarrel, and Lili came as close as she wanted to in disclosing its background in her footnote to Mayakovsky's letters, which she edited for a Soviet edition in 1956. There she indicated that she and Mayakovsky "decided, by mutual consent, to part for two months. At the root of the conflict were moral problems and questions regarding personal relations, both of which were very painful and difficult to solve at that time." She later admitted that she didn't keep all his letters, but those she published suggest that he knew of her involvement with other men, when he says that despite his jealousy he would let her be free. It was this understanding that was to govern their lives for the next seven years, just as Brik's "We must never separate" had governed their lives since they had first fallen in love.

Cover of *About This*, 1923 (Rodchenko design)

But in verse I love, and in prose I'm dumb.
You see, I can't say it, I just keep silent.
But where, my beloved,

                     where, my dear,

Where

         —in a song!—

               did I ever betray my love?

                     "ABOUT THIS"

MAYAKOVSKY'S LETTERS TO LILI DURING THE WEEKS of their quarrel are filled with the raw pain he felt when they parted. Even before he shut himself in the "prison" of his room the day after the "What Is Paris Doing?" lecture at the Polytechnic on December 27, 1922, he sat down at a restaurant table minutes after he left Lili and wrote as if she had told him she never wanted to see him again.

Moscow, the end of December

LILIOK,

I see that you have decided firmly. I know that my pestering is painful for you. But, Liliok, what has happened to me today is too terrible for me not to clutch at a last straw, this letter.

It has never been so hard for me—now I have really grown up too much. Before you turned me away from your door, I believed we could still go on meeting. Now I feel that my life is ended and that nothing more will ever happen. There is no life without you. I always said it and always knew it. Now I feel it with all my being. Everything I thought about before with pleasure has no value now—everything's repulsive.

I'm not threatening, not extorting forgiveness. I shall do nothing to myself—I care too much for my mother and sisters . . . I can't promise you anything. I know there is no promise you would believe in. I know there is no way to see you or become reconciled that wouldn't make you suffer.

Yet nevertheless I am unable not to write you, not to beg you to forgive me for everything.

If you've made this decision with difficulty, with a struggle, and if you want to try to believe me once more, you'll forgive me, you'll answer this letter.

But if you don't even answer—only you are in my thoughts. How I loved you seven years ago, the same way I love you this very second. Whatever you want, whatever you order me to do, I'll do it with rapture. How terrible it is to part, knowing that I love you and that I myself am to be blamed for this parting.

I'm sitting in a café and weeping. The waitresses are laughing at me. It's terrible to think that all my life in the future will be like this.

I write only about myself, not about you. It's terrible to think that you are calm and further away from me with every passing second, and soon I'll be entirely forgotten.

If you feel anything besides pain and disgust after this letter, for God's sake answer me, answer me right now. I'm running home. I'll be waiting. If not—a terrible, terrible grief.

I KISS YOU. ALWAYS YOUR

V.

Now it's 10 o'clock. If you don't answer by 11, I'll know—there's nothing to wait for.

The words "terrible, terrible" keep running through the letter; in his pain Mayakovsky took all the blame for the quarrel on himself. "It has never been so hard for me—now I have really grown up too much." Since Lili adamantly insisted on her independence, he had to accept their relationship on her conditions or leave her alone. From the letter it would seem that at first Lili turned him away forever, but after a short time she relented and said that a two months' separation would suffice. Early in January she sent him a brief note, using their friend Aseyev ("Kolya") as a messenger—her maid Annushka brought back Mayakovsky's reply.

Moscow, the beginning of January, 1923

LILIK,

I write you now because in Kolya's presence I couldn't answer you. I must write you now or my joy will prevent me from understanding anything further.

Your letter gives me hopes I don't dare rely on, because any expectation based on your old attitude toward me is wrong. A new attitude toward me can only be created after you know me at present.

My trifling letters to you also mustn't be and can't be taken into consideration, because I can't have any decision about our life together (if such will be) until after February 28. It's absolutely true, because if I had the right to solve this problem this very minute, if I could guarantee an answer you'd find acceptable, you would ask me today and you would resolve the problem. And in a minute I would be a happy man. But you have no guarantee I've really changed, so you insist we wait two months. If you destroy my hope that you'll accept me back, I'll lose all my strength and all my belief in the necessity of bearing all this horror.

With childish, lyrical excitement I jumped at your letter. But you should know that *you'll become acquainted on the 28th with a completely new man. Everything between you and him will consist not of past theories but of new deeds dating from the 28th of February concerning "matters" both yours and his.*

I had to write you this letter right away, because this very minute I'm feeling the same kind of nervous shock I had when I left you.

You understand with what love, with what feeling I'm writing this letter . . .

I ask you and wait for your answer from Annushka downstairs. I cannot live without your answer.

You'll answer me as a friend who tries to "warn" you about a dangerous acquaintance. "Go to hell. It's none of your business—that's the way I like it!"

You said I could write when I really needed to—this "really" is now.

You may wonder, why does he write this? It's clear enough anyhow. If it seems so, fine. Excuse me for writing today when there are guests at your apartment—I don't want anything forced in this letter. And tomorrow, it will be so. This is the most serious letter of my life. It is not even a letter, it is— "existence."

My entire being embraces your little finger.

Sjen

At first Mayakovsky was almost suicidal in his loneliness, but after a short time he hurled himself back into work. He'd stopped drawing Rosta posters, but throughout 1922 and into 1923 he continued to write a series of agitational verses on subjects like the starving peasants in the Volga, as well as contributing poems regularly to *Izvestia* and *Red Virgin Soil*. He composed anti-religious political pamphlets and signed contracts with the publishers Gosizdat and Circle for collections of his poetry. After returning from Paris in December, he gave poems and articles on his trip abroad to the Press Bureau of the Central Committee of the All-Russian Communist Party, which issued special "city-town-and-village" bulletins, copied in huge editions for local newspapers.

His two-month imprisonment in his room was more figurative than literal, since he left Lyubyansky nearly every day to attend meetings and deliver manuscripts to the editorial offices of magazines and publishers. But where Lili was concerned, he felt himself a prisoner. As a lover's gesture he arranged to have birds in cages sent to her every week to remind her of his own imprisonment. And alone in his room during the evenings he wrote her letters and worked on "About This," struggling with his feelings of depression and despair.

Moscow, the middle of January 1923

Dear and beloved Lilyonok:

In the future I forbid myself to write anything to you or reveal my feelings about you—in the evening. This is the time when I'm always feeling out of sorts.

After your notes, I feel a relief of my tension and I want to write you calmly.

At meetings I look terrible. I'm repulsive to myself. Besides, I know that most of all it hurts me. You understand that nobody and nothing needs me in such a state.

Don't worry, my little child. I won't disgrace myself. If I did that I wouldn't dare meet your eyes.

One thing more: don't worry, my beloved sunshine, that I extort messages about your love. I understand that you write them only to spare my feelings. I don't build up any hopes, and of course I don't expect anything because of them.

Take care, little one, of yourself, be satisfied. I hope I'll still be dear to you without any commitments, without any wild tricks. I swear to you on your life, that although I still possess all my jealousies, despite them I'm always glad to know that you are having a good time.

Don't curse me for my letters more than you should.

I kiss you and the birds.

YOUR SJEN

As he worked on "About This," Mayakovsky began to think of himself as Byron's Prisoner of Chillon. Byron's hero had been a political prisoner, ironically a martyr to tyranny. There was no similarity between Mayakovsky's political ideology and that of the Prisoner of Chillon, but in his anguished imagination he felt they both suffered the similar fate of being cast into a dungeon.

He had also read Oscar Wilde's poem "The Ballad of Reading Gaol" in a Russian translation by Valery Bryusov, and he was struck by its theme, fearing that it paralleled his own situation with Lili.

> The man had killed the thing he loved,
>   And so he had to die.
> Yet each man kills the thing he loves,
>   By each let this be heard,

Some do it with a bitter look,
    Some with a flattering word.
The coward does it with a kiss,
    The brave man with a sword!

On the nineteenth of January, 1923, Mayakovsky wrote Lili another letter, where in his imagination his room has been transformed into Reading Gaol, and he is not only an imprisoned puppy but also Oscar Wilde's hero and Byron's Prisoner of Chillon. Mayakovsky ended the letter with a drawing.

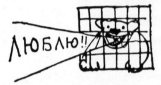

YOUR SJEN
AT THE SAME TIME OSCAR WILDE
AT THE SAME TIME BYRON'S
    PRISONER OF CHILLON

I sit—behind the bars in the dungeon—thin (I am thin, but when it's necessary I'll get fat for you). My beloved, remember me. Kiss the bird Kleist. Tell him not to get out of the cage— I don't get out.

As the weeks of his "imprisonment" wore on, Mayakovsky's letters to Lili became more calm. She gave him "a tiny hope" of being alone together—she agreed to travel by train with him to Petrograd, where they could stay in a hotel for a few days—and he worked intensely in his isolation on a "ten times bigger plaything" which would make her smile, his reference to the poem "About This." Gradually, through his work and his faith that she still loved him, his mood changed until, as time went on, he was encouraging Lili to feel better, instead of begging her for love.

Moscow, end of January 1923

SWEET, SWEET LILYONOK,
    I know, you are still anxious, you are still overcast. Little one, calm your charming little nerves.
    I think of you often.

Remember me a little bit. We really must live happily. But I also prefer this thought, I'll invent some theory or other about how to live together. Love the bird Kleist—he resembles me: a big nose (only mine is red) and constantly clinging to the bars.

I travel with you about the globe.

THE PRISONER OF CHILLON
INNATELY SJEN

Someday I'll kiss you personally. May I?

When Lili came down with the flu, he sent her a note to make her smile, punning on the Russian word for influenza, "Espanka," which has the double meaning of "Spanish woman." Along with the note, he included some essays and short poems recently published in *Izvestia*.

Moscow, the middle of February 1923

KITTEN,

I kiss you and your Spanish woman (to be more exact, Spaniard, because I don't want to kiss any Spanish women).

I send you some of my rubbish. Do smile . . .

I'll even send you some *Izvestia* nonsense.

Maybe then you'll giggle.

I KISS YOU.
YOUR SJEN

Finally, as the two-month separation was nearly over, Mayakovsky sent Lili a flurry of little notes with instructions about the train tickets for their trip. His mood grew increasingly triumphant, until on February 28, the day of his release, he humorously burst into a few lines from an old revolutionary song.

Moscow, Feb. 28, 1923

MY DEAR LITTLE KID,

I send you the ticket.

The train leaves at 8 p.m. sharp.

We'll meet in the compartment.
I kiss you.

YOUR SJEN

Moscow, Feb. 28, 1923

"Gloomy days have passed,
The hour of redemption has struck.
Bravely, comrades, on foot . . ." and so on.

KISS
YOUR SJEN

When the "hour of redemption" struck and Mayakovsky met Lili in their compartment on the train to Petrograd, it was clear to them both that the basis of their love affair was altered. Rita accompanied Lili to the station, where she observed that Lili was very nervous about meeting Mayakovsky again. Despite the bitter cold, Lili took off her beret, and her eyes looked enormous. Suddenly in the crowd on the platform they saw his tall figure standing by the door of a railway compartment; he was smoking a cigarette. Lili shivered, then turned to Rita and said, "There's Volodya. Kiss me and run," and went to meet him alone. When she returned to Moscow a few days later, she phoned Rita exultantly to announce, "Come to the apartment quickly. Volodya has written a wonderful poem and proven he's a genius."

On its most literal level "About This" is a poem about the unhappiness of a lover quarreling with his beloved. But in a larger sense it is the epitome of the Mayakovsky legend, the suffering of a great poet who is martyred when he finds himself completely misunderstood by the world. It is Mayakovsky's most complex dramatization of his role as a romantic poet, the conception that Pasternak characterized as "the poet who imagines himself the measure of life and pays for this with his life."

Mayakovsky's self-dramatization in "About This" is more extreme than in "The Cloud in Trousers" or "Man," which were also tragedies of personal love in a world that must be changed by revolution. In "About This" his situation is hopeless: he blames not the uncaring woman he loves but himself for being jealous, and he can find no plausible resolution for his dilemma. The poem begins with the idea he found in Oscar Wilde's "The Ballad of Reading Gaol," that each man kills the thing he loves. Mayakovsky made this theme personal by suggesting that he was responsible for killing Lili's love for him because of his selfish need to possess her completely.

> The keys to sing ballads in
> > aren't so young.
> But if the words ache
> and the words explain why they ache
> then the keys to sing ballads in get younger.
> Lyubyansky Lane.
> > Vodopyany.
> > > Here is
> the general scene.
> > Here is
> > > the background.
> In bed is she.
> > She's lying down.
> He.
> On the table is a telephone.
> "He" and "she" is my ballad.
> Not terribly new.
> What's terrible is,
> > that "he"—is me.
> and that "she"—
> > is mine.

Despite the simple opening statement of the "ballad's subject," Mayakovsky's sense of betrayal is so intense that he soon must rely on heightened visual images to convey his anguish. His room has no actual "bars to bar the light," but he insists it is a jail. The telephone connecting the lovers is "a straw pulled tight," like the last straw or the inadequate straw offered to the drowning man. When he touches the telephone, hoping it will connect him with Lili, it is hot, hot enough to blister his hand. He imagines that his beloved is sick, perhaps even dying, projecting his own mental state onto her, and he is desperate to talk to her. The urgency of his need to reach Lili is so great that the telephone cable causes an earthquake along the street connecting their rooms. But Annushka, who answers the phone, is too sleepy to comprehend the emergency. As she waddles off to rouse Lili, who is in bed with a cold, the friendly servant is transformed into a second in a duel; what began as a telephone call takes on ominous suggestions of a duel to the death.

The duel image continues as the maid returns with the dreaded answer—no, Lili doesn't want to talk to him. The receiver turns into a gun muzzle pointing between the poet's eyes, but a more terrible fate awaits him. Instead of a quick, merciful death, he is plunged into a living death, assailed by the nightmarish figure of primitive jealousy, first in the form of a cave-dwelling monster, and then in the form of a bear.

At this moment what he has only imagined becomes literally true. Mayakovsky is changed into a bear, the first of his several transformations in "About This." When Lili refuses to speak to him on the phone, tufts of hair sprout under his suit jacket, claws tear through his shoes, and he is a bear driven insane by the pain of rejection. Bleeding, howling, clawing at the walls of his room, he throws himself on his bed, where he weeps such torrents that his tears form a flood to rush him and his bed out of the room. Changed into a white bear from the North Pole, his pillow transformed into an ice floe, he floats feverishly on a river that seems increasingly familiar as he is confronted by a dream city from his past. He is back in Petrograd, where he recognizes a specter of himself from seven years before, the hero of the poem "Man," standing on a bridge over the Neva River. The figure calls to the bear on the ice floe to taunt him with his corruption after the Revolution.

". . . You too are sucking up to their caste?
        Kiss?
                Eat?
                        Grow a paunch?
You yourself
            into their everyday life,
                        into their family happiness,
try to mince like a rooster?!
Don't think!"

Frantically the bear tries to escape, paddling with his clumsy paws down the river on his pillow-ice floe, but the specter's voice pursues him relentlessly.

"You thought to forget the Neva's glittering?!
Can something be substituted for it?!
                        Not by anyone!
Remember to your grave that splattering
that splashed in 'Man'—"

I began to shout.
            Can you cope with this?
The storm is booming—
            you'll never be able to handle it.
Save! Save! Save! Save!
There
        on the bridge
                of the Neva,
                        a man!

In the second section of "About This" the unifying theme is Mayakovsky's attempt to find someone to save the man on the bridge before he commits suicide, to bring proof that "Love/the savior" exists in the world to redeem human selfishness. But his search is unsuccessful. In a series of rapidly shifting scenes he confronts himself as different characters at different stages of his life—as a young revolutionary who commits suicide, as his mother's son, as a famous poet. Neither family nor friends will rise above their petty self-interests to help him save the man on the bridge. Finally, he turns to his beloved. In a remarkable image, as if in a dream, he travels from his friend's apartment miles across Moscow to Lili's building by dissolving and passing through a painting on the wall, Böcklin's Symbolist "Island of the Dead," the same painting Elsa had told him she loved after he'd criticized it for being bourgeois. The four poplar trees in the painting transform themselves into the four columns of the post office near Lili's building, and Mayakovsky finds himself standing before her windows, spread out like cards in a poker game. He is reminded once more that he is gambling for her love.

Again, he loses. Feeling like Dostoevsky's Raskolnikov revisiting the scene of his crime, Mayakovsky climbs the stairs to Lili's apartment, remembering that she has forbidden him to visit her. He describes in the poem what he heard outside the apartment on Vodopyany the one time he had tried to visit her during their two-month separation—the sound of a party, music, dancing, and then laughing voices chattering about him, joking about his emotional breakdown. In reality, in January he had broken his promise to Lili and gone to the apartment without telling her and heard the sounds of the party. Rita met him coming down the stairs in such a hurry that he pushed past her. Since Rita knew about their separation, she thought his presence meant that the quarrel was over, and she was glad to see him, but Mayakovsky was too unhappy to speak. When Lili heard he had been in the corridor, she grew upset and said, "He can't have been here!"

In "About This" Mayakovsky repeats the jokes people made about him at the party, and he protests blindly that this treatment is unfair.

I'll say
    —"Look.

       Even here, my dear,
bombarding with verses the horror of the everyday,
my darling's name I guard,
avoiding
      you
         in my curses."

His beloved is his last hope, and he steels himself to burst into the party and beg her to help him rescue the man on the bridge, but it is impossible. He is the Poet—"soul/nothing else"—whose destiny is to be martyred, massacred in "About This" by a million gunshots fired by jeering, brutal philistines in Red Square.

The third and final section of the poem begins with Mayakovsky speaking after death, mourning his incomplete, unhappy life.

No matter for what I die—
       death is death.
It's terrible—not to love,
       horrible—not to dare.
For all—a bullet,
       for all—a knife.
And when for me?
       And what for me?
From the depths
       of my childhood
I could fish out
       maybe ten bearable days.
But that's for others.
       If only it were for me!
It isn't.
    You see—
       doesn't exist.

If to believe in the hereafter!

                    So easy a trial trip.

It's enough

        to stretch your hand—

and in an instant

          the bullet

             will chart

a thundering path to the life hereafter.

What can I do

    if I

        entirely,

with all the forces of my heart,

I believed in life

      and still

         believe?

Despairingly he looks to science to help him. Perhaps in the future mankind will have advanced to the point of being able to resurrect the dead, and Mayakovsky begs the "Comrade Chemist" for such a resurrection:

Put a heart in me—

      blood—

         to the uttermost vein.

Knock thought into my skull!

My earthly life I didn't live out,

on earth

    I didn't get love to the very end.

It isn't even necessary for him to be resurrected as a poet. He'll be happy doing any job—in fact, instead of raking up the past, he'll be content to be a zookeeper, since he loves animals. And then,

Maybe,
       perhaps,
             someday,
                  along the paths of the zoo
She too—
       she loved animals—
              will come along.
Smiling,
       just like that,
              just like the photograph in my drawer.
She is beautiful—
       she will certainly be resurrected.

Mayakovsky's utopian vision was never more vulnerable than in "About This," since the only way he could imagine being at peace was to be resurrected in the Thirtieth Century's earthly paradise, when the selfish "everyday nonsense" of human reality has been destroyed in a true revolution of the spirit, and the poet's personal love is transformed into a reflection of the complete harmony of mankind.

Your Thirtieth Century
           will leave behind
                all the swarms of petty things
that rend the heart.
The love unfulfilled today
            we shall requite
with the starriness of countless nights.
Resurrect me
      at least
        because
          I as a poet
was waiting for you,
         flinging away the trash of everyday.

Resurrect me,
                  let me live out what is mine.
So that love won't be the servant
of marriages,
            lusts,
                loaves.
Damning the bed,
                getting up from the couches
to let love march through the universe,
so that on the day
                when grief ages you
not to whine and beg in Christ's name,
so that
        at the first cry:
                —"Comrade!"
So that
        when you shout
                —"Comrade!"
the whole earth will turn toward you,
so as not to live
                the victim of households.
So that from now on
                of your kith and kin
                        the father would be
at least the whole world
and the earth the mother.

Of all his love poems, "About This" was Mayakovsky's most extravagant performance. It was also his last love poem to Lili, which he brought to the railroad station to read on the train to Petrograd as their new journey began.

PART TWO

15

Mayakovsky and Osip Brik, Berlin, 1923
(photograph by Rodchenko)

Like melons
　　the years
　　　　came on in maturity . . .
"VLADIMIR ILYICH LENIN"

THE LOVE AFFAIR BETWEEN LILI AND MAYAKOVSKY reached a turning point with their quarrel and separation after her London trip. They went on living together, they became physical lovers again on the trip to Petrograd, but in the years to come they began to drift apart, each of them trying to find with other people the emotional fulfillment that they were unable to find with each other.

Without Brik they might eventually have gone separate ways, but the more Lili expressed her independence, the closer Mayakovsky came to Osip, who had never involved himself in their lovers' quarrels, making light of the upheaval that resulted in their two-month separation. He regarded them as "hyperbolic people"—when love became normal size it wasn't enough for them and they started having what he called their "official affairs." Yet in the next few years Mayakovsky's association with Brik became closer than it had ever been. They worked together on their magazine *LEF* and on advertising projects for the state retail organization Mosselprom, and Brik encouraged him to write the long propaganda poem "Vladimir Ilyich Lenin," which, unlike his other poems up to this point, was dedicated to the Communist Party—and not to Lili.

By this time, the three of them were sharing an apartment on Vodopyany Lane, another communal apartment. Mayakovsky slept in his own room on Lyubyansky, a five-minute walk away, but most evenings he stayed late with the Briks and returned early in the morning for breakfast. Now they had two low-ceilinged rooms, each larger than their old room on Polyektovy, in a building across from the post office on what is now called Kirov Street, a busy, crowded thoroughfare in downtown Moscow. The building had been well constructed, but like most of Moscow it was in poor condition from lack of maintenance. They were one flight up, above a bakery. In

| 223

the foyer a broken cornice hung from one nail, and a dark flight of stairs led to a long, narrow corridor; the entrance to their apartment was directly to the right.

They used their first room as both Lili's bedroom and their living room. Her bed was behind a screen and she had hung a sign above it, "No one is permitted to sit on the bed." An old stove with layers of paint smeared carelessly over the air vents and a table and chairs nearly filled the small room, but they'd squeezed a piano to the left of the door, and on top of the piano was a telephone. An extension was in the corridor, used by the family sharing the apartment who lived in rooms to the rear of the communal kitchen. When someone called the Briks, they could often hear both the voice of the person they were talking to and the breathing of the person listening in, usually "Baba," the son of the other tenants. Lili would call out, "Baba, put the receiver down."

Brik had the second room, furnished with a bed with noisy springs, a studio couch covered with a worn velvet print, a battered desk, and shelves of books. From his window he could see the large clock over the post-office building diagonally across the street. Over the rooftops was the School of Art, where Mayakovsky had studied painting ten years before. Annushka cleaned and prepared their meals, and Lili bought a puppy to replace their beloved Sjen. Aseyev and his wife were living in the neighborhood, and the artist Alexander Rodchenko had his studio and apartment on the top floor of the School of Art. As before, friends came and went, sometimes playing cards until midnight, when Lili expected them to leave. If they tired of cards, they bet on the figures on the electric meter, or on the license numbers of the Moscow cabs on the street below. Lili slept in her bed behind the screen, and Brik read in his room until he fell asleep.

They had formed a new literary alliance, with Lili again the hostess. Just before their quarrel in December, Mayakovsky had gone directly to the Propaganda Department of the Central Committee of the Party with a request to put out a new magazine. The Party gave permission, and discussions about the magazine had already started in the two months he'd been in his room. He threw himself into the new magazine, called *LEF*, which was attempting to unite all the left artists—Futurists, Formalists, Constructivists, as well as disengaged individuals who by this time were called "fellow travelers"—into one cultural front, the Left Front of Art. Mayakovsky was the editor of the magazine, though in reality most of the editorial decisions were made by Mayakovsky and Osip working together with their associates.

It was as much Brik's group who shaped *LEF* as it was Mayakovsky himself. The small circle that had gathered around Brik in Petrograd—the theoreticians, including Shklovsky, who had returned to Russia and was still concerned with the linguistic structure of poetry—were together as before. As OPOYAZ, the Society for the Study of Poetic Language, they'd begun publishing under Brik's own imprint in Petrograd, and during the dislocations of the government's move to Moscow and the hungry months of the civil war they'd managed to meet in the Briks' apartment. After 1917 they'd been recognized by the Party, given an official seal, and registered as a Learned Society.

Despite *LEF*'s stated purpose of bringing together various artists, the language of the magazine was aggressive and rhetorical. The first issue asked, in three lead articles: What Is *LEF* Fighting For? Whom Does *LEF* Bite Into? Whom Does *LEF* Warn?

The position of *LEF*, aesthetically, was that in a proletarian society poetry has no place, since it is of no immediate use in the building of the new society. The passion of the *LEF* group was the making of a new life, and although they argued about how art could be made an important part of this life, in their theoretical discussions they could see no place for poetry in it. This was a confused, confusing, and ultimately self-defeating point for a cultural journal to insist on, but in editorials and articles they went on saying it—at the same time as Mayakovsky went on filling the pages of the magazine with poems. Brik had shifted radically from his position before the Revolu-

tion when, as Lili remembered, "we drank poetry like drunkards."
Shklovsky heard Brik tell a workers' meeting about this time:

"Poetry is not needed, anyway."

And what is needed? "Newspapers."

Someone in the audience said, "Fine. In the morning, a newspaper. But what about the evening?"

Brik answered, "In the evening, an evening newspaper."

There were already dissensions swirling around *LEF* before the
first issue appeared. A Party member, Nikolai Chuzhak, who had
been one of Mayakovsky's most fervent supporters, was included in
the group, and his position was even more doctrinaire than Mayakovsky's and Brik's. After a stormy meeting on January 22, 1923,
Mayakovsky wrote a letter to him trying to keep the group together,
saying that "Communist art . . . is still a vague concept, evading
exact classification and theory, a field in which practice and intuition
are often in advance of the most experienced theoreticians . . ." In a
chaotic period when the writers were assaulting each other in the
most abusive language, Mayakovsky could be conciliatory to someone
who disagreed with his point of view; he could be open to the possibility of new ideas in a way that most of his associates were not.
What was still most important to him was his dogged struggle to
make the Futurist group the center of Soviet cultural life.

The first issue of *LEF* appeared in the last days of March 1923,
published by the State Publishing House (Gosizdat) in an edition of
five thousand copies. It represented a long step from the magazine
Seized, which Brik had published in December 1915, when Lili had
sat painting in the letters on the front cover. Its two hundred fifty
pages included poetry by Kamensky, Aseyev, Kruchenykh, Pasternak,
and Khlebnikov; prose by Brik and Aseyev; theoretical and polemical
articles by Chuzhak, Tretyakov and Brik; and designs by Lavinsky
and Rodchenko. Mayakovsky's own contribution was his love poem
to Lili, "About This."

To critics like Chuzhak, already upset at what they considered Mayakovsky's tendency toward lyricism, "About This" was offensive; even at readings the poet had trouble finding a sympathetic audience for it. To his—and *LEF*'s—credit, Chuzhak was given space in the second issue of April–May 1923 to express his disagreement with the individualistic concepts he felt the poem represented.

During the early years of Lenin's New Economic Policy, Mayakovsky and Brik had turned to advertising to make their living. From 1923 to 1925 they worked for Mosselprom, the state retail organization, where Volodya turned out a stream of rhyming jingles and cartoons urging people not to buy their new galoshes or bottled water on the black market but to purchase goods through government outlets. His best-known slogan was painted in huge letters on the side of the Mosselprom building in downtown Moscow: "You need no more/than the Mosselprom store."

Lili remembers that Mayakovsky was involved in all kinds of propaganda, from urging new weight and length measurements on the wrapping paper for caramel candies, to printing agitation poems on packages of chocolates. She was amused by his apparently inexhaustible power of linguistic invention. When Rita came to visit, Lili enthusiastically took her around Moscow to see Mayakovsky's new advertising posters, saying that many of these poems were among his best.

Mayakovsky wanted to reform the dull, didactic slogans like "Study, Work, Fight," printed on gray paper with black letters, that were common street propaganda in those days. Once when he was bored waiting for Lili and Rita, who were looking at dress materials in a shop, he tore the final letter off the slogan "Study, Work, Fight" to tease Rita. In Russian the word for "Fight" is "Boriss," and without the final "s" it spelled out Pasternak's first name.

Everyone at the Briks' apartment took part in writing the advertising jingles. One afternoon Tretyakov came over just after Mayakovsky had worked out his verse about pacifiers.

You'll never get
                        a better patsy.
I'm ready to suck them
                        into my old age.

Tretyakov and Mayakovsky began laughingly to create a poem about condoms. Mayakovsky recited:

Ding dong,
Ding dong,
Uncle Vanya
Has bought a condom.

Tretyakov went on,

Aunt Annushka,
Come out on the porch,
I've bought you
A diaphragm,

turning all the medical words into a peasant dialect and concluding with the lines

And with a smile on his lips
He gives to his oldest son Misha
Underarm shields
To prevent sweaty shirts.

Of course these jingles were never used.

Mayakovsky's advertising verses were also the logical extension of Brik's aesthetic theories of the social function of art. Mayakovsky wrote jingles about baby pacifiers and cheap sausages because he and Osip felt that poetry should be closer to everyday life, where its power could be a vitalizing force on life itself. Justifying his verses as a search for something new, an experiment in "untested genres," he asserted that "meetings, speeches, front-line limericks, improvised Agitprop playlets, the living radio voice, and the slogan flashing by on the streetcar—all are equal and sometimes valuable examples of poetry."

It was Mayakovsky's work as editor of *LEF* and the propaganda material he turned out during these years that alienated him from many of the writers he'd been associated with before, and it is often writing that he did at this time that is used to attack his work as a poet. But it is too simple to look back at the early years of the Soviet Union and to assess the role of someone like Mayakovsky with the knowledge of what happened later. It seems obvious now that Lenin had already reestablished the bureaucratic apparatus that was to lead to Stalin and the appalling dictatorship of the 1930's, but the faults were not so obvious in the beginning. Lenin and the new government had declared boldly and enthusiastically that they would create a new world, a new society, and for those like Mayakovsky who had supported the Revolution since the beginning, it did seem possible.

Reading the polemic of the *LEF* editorials, one must remember that the total apparatus of control that was to come under Stalin did not yet exist. Disagreements between writers and the artistic factions were violent and acrimonious, but they were conducted on the pages of journals and newspapers. There was still no clearly defined cultural policy beyond the Party's insistence that it would control the cultural life of the state, even if there was no agreement on what the new culture would be. In real terms this meant that even a writer as completely out of step with the times as Osip Mandelstam could find work, even if it was only poorly paid newspaper writing and translating. His widow in her memoirs described the early 1920's as almost a paradise compared to what happened to them after 1928. In 1923 Mandelstam was still able to publish his poetry, there were new editions of his two earlier collections, and among his journalistic pieces is one of the most incongruous interviews conceivable even in those incongruous times—with the young Vietnamese revolutionary who was later to be known as Ho Chi Minh.

Mayakovsky himself was conscious of what he was suppressing in his own work, and there must have been, always, an element of self-doubt in his relationships with poets who were working in different directions. He could write pompously to his Berlin publisher on July 25, 1923: "For us, the masters of words for the Russian Soviets, the petty little problems of making lyric verses yield their place to the broad aims of the way the word helps to build the Commune"; yet about this time, when he saw Mandelstam in a store in Moscow, Mayakovsky leaned across the counter and is said to have shouted in his usual booming voice, "Like an Attic soldier enamored of his enemy!"

Although it is clear from the manuscript revisions of "About This" that Mayakovsky tried to take out some of the personal references so that the context would seem more general, in this atmosphere of endless argument and debate, Mayakovsky's new poem didn't fit in at all. It was a love poem, clearly addressed to Lili, which he defended by insisting that what it described was the ordinary way of life, *byt*, that was betraying the Revolution. When Ilya Ehrenburg returned from Berlin to Moscow in 1923, he observed Mayakovsky's struggle. "We were naïve in those days and didn't know that it is far more difficult to change man than to change the system of a country's government."

With NEP it seemed to the idealistic young writers that "the belly had not only been rehabilitated but exalted." Consumer goods reappeared, and Muscovites grew fatter and more cheerful; restaurants and beer halls opened with phonographs playing records like "Yes, We Have No Bananas." Well-made pre-revolutionary items came back on the market: Singer sewing machines, Swiss watches, porcelain teacups. Through it all Mayakovsky urged that good Soviets buy only through Mosselprom's retail outlets, like the state department store GUM:

Clothe the body,
feed the stomach,
fill the mind—
everything man needs
at the GUM he will find.

Aseyev, his close friend and collaborator on a propaganda poem at the end of 1923, understood Mayakovsky's intent and later tried to explain the mood in Russia at the time.

> The waves of NEP were already rolling overboard the revolutionary ship . . . It was very difficult to remain on board; one had to clench one's teeth and hold on to the balustrades in order not to be swept into the sea of obscurantism and philistinism. Many people with revolutionary pasts found themselves overboard. Many lives were broken by the pressure of growing contradictions. For Mayakovsky, as a revolutionary and as a poet who grasped his world with his senses, who strove to control his sensory reaction through intellectual purposefulness, it was doubly difficult to experience and think all this through . . .

It was a very hard time for idealists. After the NEP began, a good restaurant opened in a private home in Moscow, and Mayakovsky and the Briks—who were paid well for their work at Mosselprom —often went there to eat dinner. Rita Rait tagged along as company for Lili, who loved to show off her new clothes from Berlin, although she laughed that "it was not good form in those days for the *LEF* people to patronize these places."

Lili and Mayakovsky were even more attentive toward each other in public than they'd been before their two-month separation. Lili continued to criticize everything about him except his poetry, but to the people outside the group who already knew them, they seemed surprisingly conventional. The painted scarves and the wall of poems and drawings, the Futurist constructions and ballet tutus that had been part of the decorations of the old Petrograd apartment weren't replaced, even when life became easier again. The people coming to *LEF* meetings for the first time expected to see something startlingly "futuristic" and bohemian, but instead they found ordinary coat hangers, the perpetual samovar, and plates of cold meatballs. Most of the other writers were in shabby tunics and boots, but Mayakovsky dressed like a European businessman. When Lili passed him a glass of tea, he thanked her politely as he took it.

Their relationship was too complicated for most people to understand. Brik's father, a well-dressed, imposing man, used to visit the apartment and he noticed one day that all the birds Mayakovsky had sent Lili were gone—she had released them from their cages after she had returned from Petrograd. "Let's get to the point, where are all the birds?" Brik's father asked pontifically, and he was answered with shouts of laughter. The question "Where are all the birds?" became a sort of joke between the Briks and Mayakovsky, referring to anything that was lost or misplaced.

This difficult period was brilliantly visualized in the photomontage illustrations, the first to be used for book illustration, that their friend Alexander Rodchenko prepared for the separate publication of "About This" in Berlin in September 1923. Rodchenko had begun working with Mayakovsky on advertising materials for Mosselprom, and he conceived the startling juxtapositions of the photomontage technique as a visual counterpart to Mayakovsky's poetic journey. Lili posed for the cover of the little book, a dramatic black-and-white close-up of her face. She remembers that the photographs were taken by David Shterenberg's brother Abram Petrovich, and she was very pleased with the result.

Lili's attitude toward Mayakovsky and the storm he had stirred up by his new poem to her is apparent in a snapshot taken of them at the beach in Norderney, where they'd gone for a short holiday in the late summer of 1923, at the same time as "About This" was being published. He's lying on his side in the sand with three women kneeling behind him, the wife of the critic Boris Kushner, Lili's mother, and Lili—all three of them in dark bathing dresses, smiling at the camera. Lili has her right index finger on Volodya's hip, and despite the glare of the sunlight on the sand, her eyes are looking straight at the camera lens, as if she is asserting, half-humorously, her possession of the man lying before her.

By 1923 the political realities had shifted radically in the Soviet Union. Lenin had been the force behind the struggles within the country since 1917 and the introduction of NEP, but in 1923, just as there was a lessening of the pressures on the government, he suffered a series of strokes and his condition became steadily weaker. On January 21, 1924, Lenin died. As Lili remembered later,

> You have to understand how much we loved Lenin. It was a terrible morning when he died. We wept and stood in lines in Red Square in the freezing cold to get to see him. Mayakovsky had a press card and we could bypass the lines. I think he looked at the body ten times. We were all terribly shattered. The Revolution was mostly a great happiness for us, and we didn't notice the cold and starvation of those years . . .

Mayakovsky had been traveling incessantly to readings and conferences, but back in Moscow he continued to work with Brik and Rodchenko on advertising materials for Mosselprom, as well as on satirical poems for newspapers attacking bureaucracy and petit bourgeois values. After Lenin's death he began writing a long poem that was to be titled "Vladimir Ilyich Lenin." It was his most ambitious propaganda piece.

Before Mayakovsky began the long poem, Brik gave him a crash course in Lenin, and made him read selections from Lenin's speeches and passages from Marx. Brik picked out what he considered particularly important texts and kept the books on his desk for Mayakovsky. Nothing was allowed to interfere with Brik's conversations with Mayakovsky. During the times that Mayakovsky read passages of the new poem aloud to the Briks, the phone was switched off, the doors locked, and Annushka told not to let anyone interrupt.

The result was one of the most easily comprehended poems that Mayakovsky ever wrote, and when he read it for the first time publicly on October 18, 1924, at the Press Club in Moscow, it was an immediate success. As he'd promised Lili at the end of their two-month separation, he had turned away from personal lyricism and his role was

> to infuse
> new glitter
> into the most glorious of words:
> PARTY.

Mayakovsky had refused to join the Party after the Revolution, joking sardonically, "Now I'm the chief Bolshevik, but if I become a Party member they'll send me to some God-forsaken place to edit the local newspaper." But "Vladimir Ilyich Lenin" was as unequivocally a declaration of his political loyalties as Party membership, from the opening lines of the dedication,

> To the Russian
> Communist Party
> I dedicate this poem,

to the paraphrasing of one of Lenin's speeches in the conclusion seventy-five printed pages later.

> Long live
> the Revolution,
> joyful and fast!
> This is
> the only
> great war
> of all,
> that history has known.

As a eulogy to Lenin that glorified every phase of the leader's life and activities, the poem was so patently polemical that Mayakovsky himself broke off to question his approach, anticipating the attacks he'd faced earlier in "150,000,000."

I know,
          the lyricist
                    will turn and twist.
The critic
          will attack
                    and beat with his whip:
—But where's the soul?!
                    This is—
                              rhetoric!
Where's the poetry?
                    This is only journalism!!—
Capitalism
          is not an exquisite word,
much more exquisitely sounds—
                              "nightingale,"
but I
     return to it
                over and over again.
Let the line
          like a fighting slogan fly.

As a Party propagandist he also rejected the kind of freedom he himself had called for in the first public meetings after the February revolution.

Could
     in such a time
                the word "democrat"

ever enter
                some stupid head?!
If one should hit,
                then hit so
                                that the sidewalk gets wet.
    The clue to victory
                    is in iron dictatorship.

Mayakovsky justified everything that had been done in the seven years since 1917 by his vision of the new society that was being created. Despite the continual difficulties he found himself in because of his own truculent individualism, he even asserted that an individual was of no importance to the future.

An individual!
                Who needs him?!
    The voice of an individual
                        is thinner than a chirp.
    Who'll hear it?—
                    the wife, perhaps!
    And only
            if she's around,
                    and not out shopping.

The contemptuous dismissal of the individual and his wife was in startling contrast to his letters and poems to Lili, disparaging his own lyrical voice, but neither he nor the Briks admitted the contradiction. Mayakovsky felt that the brutal tone of his poems was mostly the answer to a similar brutality in his subject. His friend Rita Rait felt that he had to express his social conscience, which was a different matter altogether from his private conscience during the early years of the Soviet state. "The propaganda poets didn't pay close attention to the words they used—they wanted the feeling of *action*. Words like 'annihilate' or 'destroy' were just coins." From Lili's point of view—she loved "Vladimir Ilyich Lenin"—the strident tone in the poem and the justification of the dictatorship were inevitable. Mayakovsky had simply chosen the most effective style for propaganda poetry. "During our entire life together Volodya never raised his voice to me or Osya, not even to our charwoman. The note of shrillness in his polemic poetry is quite another thing. People mustn't confuse the two things."

If Mayakovsky was at odds with his conscience about any of the political aspects of "Vladimir Ilyich Lenin," he never confessed his doubts to anyone. He later said that his only uneasiness about undertaking his eulogy was an aesthetic consideration.

> I felt very nervous about this poem, as it would have been easy to reduce it to a pamphlet in verse. But the workers' attitude to it gladdened me and confirmed my conviction that the poem was needed.

The only flash of the earlier Mayakovsky was his stand against the canonization of any historical figure, which echoed some of his Futurist diatribes against a veneration of the past—but even in this scruple, his sense of duty to the Party prevailed.

> I'm anxious lest
>   processions
>   and mausoleums,
> the established
>   statute of worship,
> should
>   drown
>   in oily unction
> Lenin's
>   simplicity.

I shudder for him,
             as
                   for the apple of my eye
  lest he
       be falsified
            by tinsel beauty.
My heart votes—
             I am
                   compelled to write
by the mandate
            of duty.

Although Mayakovsky sincerely believed what he was writing in "Vladimir Ilyich Lenin," the split had opened again between the private and the public poet. During the summer of 1924 he stopped turning out slogans for advertising posters and planned a lecture tour to cities in the south of Russia. He was deeply involved in the long poem to Lenin, but his lyrical tendencies couldn't be completely submerged, not even when he was intensely at work on his most ambitious political poem. In the late spring of 1924 he found an opportunity to express his private feelings when he was asked to produce a poem for the occasion of Alexander Sergeyevich Pushkin's 125th-birthday jubilee.

Realizing he'd be attacked by critics for his "i-n-d-i-v-i-d-u-a-l" theme if he allowed his personal situation to enter the Pushkin poem, he was nevertheless unable to suppress his melancholy. He had silenced the "bear of jealousy" within him in "About This," but nothing had taken its place, not even the official Soviet bear whom the Briks were encouraging to roar out his slogans for page after page in "Vladimir Ilyich Lenin." He had matured beyond his earlier attacks on Pushkin as a "classic general," and the tone of the poem was softened. Mayakovsky felt so emotionally isolated that he even regretted Pushkin was not alive: "I/would have needed/to come to terms with you/in life." In the poem to Pushkin, "Jubilee Year," he wrote:

I am
                now
                        free
                                from love
                                        and from posters.
Like a skin
                the bear of jealousy
                                        lies with his claws.
One can
                convince oneself
                                that the earth is sloping—
just sit down
                        on your own buttocks
                                        and slide.
No,
        I won't get stuck in black melancholy,
and anyway, there's nobody
                                I'd like to talk to.
Only
        the gills of rhymes
                                pulsate fast
in such as us,
                on the poetic sand.
Dreaming is harmful,
                        and there's no use daydreaming,
one must
                fulfill
                        the official boredom.
But it happens
                        that life
                                rises from another angle,
and one understands
                        the great
                                through the rubbish.

Lyrics

    have by us

        been attacked more than once,

                with bayonets,

we seek a language

        exact

          and naked.

But poetry

      is the most beastly of all things:

it exists—

      no matter what happens . . .

All kinds of things happened:

            standing under the window,

letters,

    the nervous jelly of shaking.

When

    you are not even capable of grieving—

that,

   Alexander Sergeyevich,

          is much harder.

Come on, Mayakovsky:

        loom to the south!

You torment

      your heart with rhymes

and now

    love also has come to an end,

my dear Vladimir Vladimirich.

No,

   the name of this is not old age!

Pushing

    my carcass ahead,

I will

   with pleasure

      cope with two,

and if they tease me—

        even three.

They say

that it's my theme that's i-n-d-i-v-i-d-u-a-l!

Entre nous . . .

        so that the censor won't point his finger,

I'll inform you—

        they say

           one has spotted

even

    two

        members of the Central Committee in love . . .

16

Rose Kushner, Lili's mother, Lili, and Mayakovsky,
Norderney, 1923

Shuffled by millions of feet.
Rustled by thousands of lives,
I furrow Paris—
so terribly alone,
it's terrible—not a soul,
terrible—nobody . . .

"PARIS (CHATS WITH THE EIFFEL TOWER)"

WITHIN DAYS OF THE FIRST READING OF "VLADI-
mir Ilyich Lenin" at the Moscow Press Club in October 1924, Mayakovsky was already on his way out of
the Soviet Union. For the next few years his traveling
was to have an almost compulsive quality, as if he were trying to
run from something. Also, he was intensely curious and wanted to
see some of the world he'd been writing about in his propaganda
pieces. He flew first to Paris, but he'd told the press in Moscow that
he was to travel on to New York, and he'd taken a number of advances on articles and poems to pay for the trip. Once in Paris he
found the situation with American tourist visas even more difficult
than he'd expected, and when he wrote to Lili a week after his arrival, his mood was tired and despondent.

DEAR—DEAR, SWEET—SWEET,
    BELOVED—BELOVED LILYOK,
I've been in Paris for a week, but I haven't written you because I don't know anything about my plans. I'm not going to
Canada, and I'm not even allowed to stay long in Paris. I was
given only two weeks (I'm asking for a longer time), and I don't
know if I should try to go to Mexico—it seems hopeless. I'll
apply again to America for the trip to New York.

How do I live here this time? I don't know myself. My
main feeling is anxiety, anxiety nearly to tears, and a total indifference to everything here (tiredness?).

I want very much to return to Moscow. If I wouldn't be
ashamed to appear before you and the newspaper editors, I
would leave today.

I'm staying at Elsa's hotel (Hotel Istria, 29 rue Campagne
Première). I didn't telegraph my address because Elsa said that

letters get sent on from her old address. They will reach me—
if you write. I'm awfully anxious about you.

What about my new books and contracts? Ask Kolya to
tell the editors that I'm not trying to steal the advance—I'm just
not writing anything because I'm very tired and I'm deliberately
giving myself two or three weeks of rest—then I'll begin to
write about everything.

Nobody met me at the station in Paris because my telegram
arrived only ten minutes before my arrival and I had to look
for Elsa by myself, with my knowledge of French.

I'm staying at Elsa's hotel because it's the cheapest and
cleanest, and I'm trying to save money as much as possible.

I'm very friendly with Elsa and André. We arranged a fur
coat for her from you and me. We always have breakfast and
dinner together. We go strolling with Léger . . .

Little by little I dress myself under André's supervision,
and I even have a corn because of all the fittings. But I don't
feel any enthusiasm in this matter.

We devoted the first day after my arrival to shopping for
you. We ordered a beautiful little suitcase for you, and bought
hats that we'll send as soon as the pigskin suitcase is ready. I've
sent you perfume. If it arrives safe and sound, I'll send more to
you gradually.

I'm sending advertising material and posters for Osya. If
I get permission, I'll go to some little French towns.

It's very difficult without knowing French . . . It's dull,
dull, dull, dull without you. It's not very good without Osya
either. I love you terribly! So many of Elsa's intonations remind
me of you, and I lapse into melancholy sentimental lyricism.

I haven't written such colorless letters in a long time, but
first of all I am literary-exhausted, and secondly I have no happy
optimistic self-assurance.

Do write, sunshine. I stole your letter from Elsa and
locked it in my suitcase. I'll write you, telegraph too (you also!).

I hope to become happier in the future, and then my letters will be more gay.

I kiss you, my little one, and kiss Osya. All your Volodya.

As an afterthought he asked Lili to kiss their friends in Moscow —"They are a hundred times smarter than all the Picassos."

In his loneliness he clung to Elsa. She'd been upset with him after their argument in her apartment in Berlin in 1922, but she was writing herself now and could meet him on a more equal basis. Shklovsky had included some of her letters in his novel *Zoo*, and Gorky, who was living on the outskirts of Berlin during the time, told him they were the best things in the book. Gorky's praise encouraged Elsa to go on with her own writing, and two years later her first novel was published in Berlin.

Elsa's marriage to Triolet was ending, although she continued to see him, and she simply accepted Mayakovsky's presence in Paris when he appeared. Within a few days they'd become friends again. She rented him a room in the hotel where she'd been living since her return from Berlin earlier in the year. It was in Montparnasse, one of the hotels where a number of younger artists struggled to get by, and Mayakovsky felt comfortable enough to stay there whenever he was in Paris. The Hotel Istria was shabby and old-fashioned, from the inside looking like a "tower," as Elsa described it. It had a narrow staircase and hallways like boxes, with five doors leading to five single rooms at each stair landing. The rooms each had a narrow iron bed, a table beside the bed and one near the window, two chairs, a mirror wardrobe, and a sink with running hot water. There was a shabby yellow rug on the floor and the wallpaper was "striped like mattress covers." At the same time that Volodya was staying at the Istria, Marcel Duchamp and Man Ray were living there, as well as Francis Picabia and his wife.

Mayakovsky was still lonely, and the days dragged by as he waited for some word about his visa for America. Sometimes Elsa came to his room and found him sitting on the floor, papers scattered on the bed, writing to Lili. There was simply no one else he felt close to, and he hated to be by himself. Elsa was having her own problems, and when he became too demanding—as moody and sullen as he'd been in Berlin—they often quarreled. There was a sexual tension between them that they left unresolved, though it sometimes led them into ugly scenes. Usually they ended the evening in one of the Montparnasse cafés, Elsa's choice, since Mayakovsky disliked dancing. They sat against the wall, his arm around her shoulders, while he fiddled with a glass of wine with his other hand. Without hearing the orchestra or seeing the dancers, he stared in front of him, chewing on a cigarette while he worked on lines of poetry in his head.

Then he would abruptly ask her, "Do you love Lilitchka?"

"Yes, I do."

"Do you love me?"

She always answered, "Yes, I do."

To this he muttered, "So, watch out!"

Despite their difficulties, Elsa stayed at his side, trying to help with the visa and acting as his interpreter at encounters with officials. He joked that he didn't know any French: "In France I can only speak Triolet." When Paris police told him quite suddenly that he'd have to return to Moscow, Elsa tried, unsuccessfully, to intercede for him through her husband and friends, and finally she accompanied him to the police station.

> We wandered along the scuffed corridors, sent from one office to another. I walked ahead and Mayakovsky followed behind me with the metallic taps on his shoes and the sound of his cane, which he either dragged on the floor behind him or scraped along walls, doors, and chairs. At last we knocked on the door of some important official. He was a very irritated man who stood up from his desk to make a bigger impression and announced in a loud furious voice that Mr. Mayakovsky was to leave Paris within twenty-four hours. I began to tell him something, but Mayakovsky constantly interfered and made it worse, asking, "What did you tell him? What did he tell you?"

"I told him you are not a dangerous man, that you can't speak French." Mayakovsky's face suddenly brightened. Trustingly he looked at the angry official and said in his thick innocent voice, "Jambon." The official stopped shouting, looked at Mayakovsky, smiled, and asked, "For how long do you want the visa?" At last in a big hall Mayakovsky handed in his passport at one of the windows to be stamped. The official checked the passport and said in Russian, "Are you from the village of Bagdadi? I lived there for many years. I made wine!" Both were happy at this meeting. "Think how small the world is. People are always stepping on each other's feet."

One reason for Mayakovsky's increasing anxiety about the travel visa was the money he'd taken as advances for the articles and poems he was supposed to send back from America. If he didn't get there he'd have to find a way to give the money back. His letters to Lili were as filled with his worries over money as they were with his perpetual complaints that she wasn't writing enough. Lili was using telegrams to carry on much of her side of the correspondence, usually to ask him what he was doing when she hadn't heard from him for a few days. She wired him on November 26, 1924, a month after his departure: I WORRY. TELEGRAPH IMMEDIATELY WITH DETAILS.

He answered the next day: "I'm waiting for the American visa. If I don't get it in a month or a month and a half I'll return to Moscow. Do wire and write more often. I kiss, love you. Your Sjen."

In Moscow Lili was as depressed as Mayakovsky was in Paris. She'd begun seeing Alexander Tobinson openly, but he'd been arrested on an accusation that was later proven untrue. He was ill, tubercular, confined in a prison hospital in Moscow, where Lili visited him twice a week with parcels of food. His wife was in the United States and his young daughter Louellen, only thirteen, had no one to care for her. She was at school in Sokolniki, about twenty miles from Moscow, and Lili rented a dacha there so that Louellen could live with her. Over the years the girl became almost a daughter to Lili and Osip, who as always accepted whatever Lili did calmly and without question. Tobinson's illness darkened Lili's mood, since his affection for her had been one of her emotional reassurances.

When Mayakovsky wrote Lili on December 6, 1924, it was still money that worried him the most, but he was also very concerned with his magazine *LEF*, which he'd left in Brik's hands.

What's going on with *LEF*? Did the next issue come out at least? Can I do anything? If it didn't come out, you must have no money. Write me details. What about Lengiz? [The poem "Vladimir Ilyich Lenin" and the collection *Only New* were to be published with Lengiz, the Leningrad state publishing house.] If you don't have any money, then don't send any to Elsa for a while. I'll arrange it myself somehow. Have you managed to place extracts of "Lenin" in newspapers? If it's necessary to help *LEF*, I'll return to Moscow immediately and I won't go to any Americas.

There's almost nothing to write about myself. I have written almost nothing all this time, and now I'm just beginning. Unfortunately, I'm longing to write lyric verses again— a lyric poet! I'm still in Paris because they promised to give an answer about my American visa in two weeks. I hope they won't —then I'd return to Moscow that very second, repay the advances, and not move anywhere for three years. I miss you and all of you quite inexpressibly . . .

Lili's answer did nothing to ease his anxieties. She wrote that without him *LEF* had encountered difficulties with Gosizdat. Even the issue that had been prepared for the press had been stopped, and Brik was to see the head of Gosizdat to try to persuade him to go on with the magazine. The situation for the *LEF* editors was strained, but not in fact as critical as Lili's letters implied. When Mayakovsky was away from her for more than a few days, she often exaggerated the problems she and Osip faced without him. Mayakovsky had two more weeks to wait for some word on the visa; then he finally was told that his application had been refused. He hurriedly left Paris and reached Moscow on December 27, 1924.

His return did little to lift Lili's mood. She was looking for something else, something she didn't find in their relationship. At thirty-four she was beginning to feel old, with a loneliness that neither Mayakovsky nor Osya could alleviate. On January 7, a week and a half after Mayakovsky had returned from Paris, she wrote her friend Rita:

> . . . Volodya has come back. We probably will go to Paris in six weeks. A.T. [Alexander Tobinson] is very sick. He's in the hospital. I hardly ever see him. I'm in a very suicidal mood. I don't want to live. Write me please. Love and kisses.

But before she could go to Paris she became sick herself, seriously ill with an ovarian tumor. On February 23, 1925, she wrote to Rita again.

> RITA,
> I'm really very sick. I've been in my bed for almost three weeks. They found a tremendous tumor and the bitch suddenly got inflamed. Perhaps because I was doing so many exercises trying to get thinner. They thought they'd have to operate, but the doctor doesn't know, because the swelling is diminishing rapidly. The swelling is on the ovary and on the tube. Lying in Sokolniki. Volodya takes care of me like a nanny (it brings tears to your eyes). Everybody visits me, everybody loves me. Nothing hurts, but I'm not allowed to get up. First they used ice, then hot-water bottles and poultices. My temperature was up to 39 degrees C. Now quite normal. In a week they will tell me whether an operation is necessary . . . "O.B. One" is much better. You know he was very sick. I like him very much. That's

all. Of course I want to go to Paris, as usual. I think I've written an awfully long letter for me. Louellen sends you her love. She's quite grown up and very nice. Love and kisses. I love you very much.

LILI

When Lili was ill, Mayakovsky was subdued and patient with her. She wouldn't put up with his moods, and she never found him difficult in the way that Elsa did, because he knew she would ask him to leave if he were too demanding. He was with her as much as possible, trying to nurse her in a gentle way. For greater privacy they were all living in the dacha in Sokolniki now, although Mayakovsky still had his room in the city and the Briks left clothes, books, and furniture in their apartment on Vodopyany.

In the bleak, cold months that remained of the winter, Mayakovsky threw himself into his usual hectic schedule of meetings, readings, disputes, and controversies. On January 5, 1925, he represented *LEF* at a conference of proletarian writers, and from the conference he hurried into a committee that was planning the Soviet Pavilion for the International Exhibition to be held in Paris later that spring. At the same time he was deeply engaged with *LEF*. He and Lili were both involved in the design and layout of each issue.

With "Vladimir Ilyich Lenin," Mayakovsky had become so well known in the Soviet Union that he seemed to have the power to do as he wanted, but the enemies he made were also influential, and the acrimony that had accompanied every stage of his career continued. There were protests against everything he did. Once at a reading somebody in the audience sent him a note asking, "How can you, a proletarian poet, wear a gold ring on your finger? It doesn't suit your appearance." Mayakovsky answered, "That's why I'm not wearing it in my nose." But he took off the ring, the same one Lili had given him years ago, and from then on carried it in his pocket on his key chain as a good-luck charm.

The pressures against *LEF* were also relentless, and there was difficulty continuing with its publication. Some of the pressure was internal, as when Brik speculated that the theoretical dissensions within the group might be diverting the energies of the magazine from the creative process itself. The State Publishing House had never pushed the distribution of the magazine with any enthusiasm, and they began to complain because it was losing money. Mayakovsky was able to get out a seventh issue during the spring, but it was published in an edition of only fifteen hundred copies, and with this issue the magazine ceased publication. His own contribution to the final number was the first part of his poem to Lenin.

In Sokolniki their dacha was small and crowded, but it was more spacious than any place they'd found since they'd left Petrograd six years earlier. It had a large living room, two smaller rooms and one room big enough only for a bed. The living room was used as a bedroom, the warmer of the two smaller rooms was another bedroom, and the colder room was used for storage. Elsa, who stayed at the dacha the next winter, remembered that the storage room was piled with suitcases and boxes. The living room had been filled with so many things that it was difficult to turn around in it. There was a large table, a big sofa, a grand piano, and finally even a billiard table. It was less chaotic out in the country than it had been in Moscow across the street from the post office, but Elsa found the winters difficult and the life sometimes dangerous.

. . . Doors and windows didn't lock very securely, and at night we tied chairs to the doorknobs, in case somebody tried to get in. Then the chairs would scrape on the floor and make a noise to alert us. This was called a "psychological bar." Besides, small revolvers were scattered around everywhere, and sensible people were more afraid of them than thieves. God only knows what could appear to a half-asleep person, and it's easy to shoot a person who gets up from bed in the middle of the night. Those guns were really very dangerous. Somebody who slept over at

our place once shot himself in his own finger. He had a gun
with him because it was dangerous to walk from the train to the
dacha, especially in winter, when there wasn't a soul around
and snow covered all footsteps as if nobody ever walked there . . .

Just as there had been a subtle change in Lili's relationship with
Mayakovsky, so there were changes in her life with Brik, who began
bringing a friend with him to Sokolniki, a woman named Genya who
was married to a film director, Vitaly Zhemchuzhny. She had a job
as a children's librarian and she was later Brik's secretary. Genya was
quiet, but she and Osip seemed to find something in each other that
they both needed. After thirteen years of being married to Osip, Lili
wondered about their involvement. One day when she and Rita sat
in the living room of the dacha and heard a flow of voices from Brik's
room, where he sat with Genya, Lili broke out impatiently, "I don't
know what he finds to talk with her about." Despite Lili's jealousy,
Osip steadfastly insisted that he would continue to see Genya, and
after a while she accepted the relationship, much as Brik, that August
ten years before, had accepted her affair with Mayakovsky. Genya
was welcomed into the household, though she kept her own apartment in Moscow. At the center were still the Briks and Mayakovsky,
and Osip's ideas continued to dominate the household.

With his usual determined energy, Mayakovsky had turned
again to his plans for a trip to America, especially as he hadn't been
able to return the advances he'd received for travel pieces. At the
same time, he was persisting in his efforts to get his other work published. On March 26, 1925, he finally signed a contract with Gosizdat
for a collection of his writings, to come out in a four-volume edition.
The first volume was to appear on June 1, the second on July 1, the
third on August 1, and the fourth on August 15. He and Brik worked
out the plans for the publication, and they agreed that Brik would
follow the work as it progressed. In May Mayakovsky signed a contract for two children's poems with another publisher, and early in

the month—on May 2—he read his poetry over Moscow Radio. Before he began, he pointed to the microphone and asked the engineer how many people were listening. The engineer answered, "The whole world," and Mayakovsky responded, "Well, I don't need any more."

On the twenty-fifth of May he was again on his way to Paris. Halfway to Moscow, he remembered that he had left his keys behind and he had to hurry back to Sokolniki for his gold ring, superstitiously refusing to leave without it. This time, he flew to Königsberg and then traveled by train to Berlin and Paris. The Soviet Pavilion he'd helped plan opened at the Paris International Exhibition on June 4, and he attended the ceremony as an official representative.

Lili again hoped she could go with him, but she was still too weak to travel. Before Mayakovsky left Moscow he gave her a list of things she was to do for him, much of it concerned with the forthcoming volumes of his Collected Works.

Moscow, May 25, 1925

To Kissa:

1.   Keep after Osya about the [Gosizdat] contract, but scold him every day if he spends too much time with this. Don't believe him.

2.   Select the photo for the edition of my complete works. If it's necessary, enlarge the picture . . .

3.   Hurry my sister Olga and everybody associated with *LEF*. [Mayakovsky's younger sister was technical secretary for *LEF*.]

4.   Hurry the printer with the edition of my children's poem.

5.   Collect the money promised by this contract.

6.   About the 15th of July, contact the publisher about a second edition of the children's poem, and if possible when republished, collect royalties of 12% of the listed price.

7.   About the 15–20th of June, contact the *Moscow Worker* and collect royalties from Comrade Kantor for the "Paris" poems . . .

8.   After the printing of the second children's poem, collect royalties . . .

9. Bring all the verses that I mail you to the printers and send me 50% of the royalties. The rest is for you.

10. Take care of my collection of books and add to it with all the new books that will come out . . .

In Paris, some of the posters that Mayakovsky had done with Rodchenko for the state store were included in the Soviet Pavilion of Advertising Posters, and he was awarded a silver medal for his work; it was to be of considerable use to him on his trip. This time he had decided to go to Mexico, where he knew he would have less difficulty with a visa, and then try to arrange for his American visa from there. At least he would be as far as Mexico, and even if the United States still refused to let him in, he could go on to Japan. His tickets and travel papers were arranged for departure on the ship S.S. *Espagne* later in June.

When Mayakovsky wrote Lili on June 2, he had been in Paris only over the weekend (he arrived on May 28), but his mood was already excited, despite his disappointment with the exhibition, which he found dull and unimaginative.

When he wrote again a week later, he had more definite word on his departure, but he was desperately concerned about not hearing from her. Trying as always to please her, his complaining was subdued, especially since he was very excited about the trip.

Paris, June 9, 1925

DEAR, BELOVED, SWEET AND MARVELOUS LILYONOK!

As you know yourself, I haven't had a line from you. I've already sent you two telegrams and a letter, but you didn't even write a line to me in your letters to Elsa! My little one, write soon, because on the 19th I'm leaving. The ship *Espagne* sails from St. Nazaire (eight hours from Paris) and will be creeping toward Mexico for sixteen entire days! It means that your letter answering me will go via Paris (and if it catches a ship) forty days! This is in the back of beyond! Even beyond!

Sunshine, write me before I leave, as much as you can, by any means. All, all, all. Without your letter I shall not go.

What are you doing? What are you going to do?

Kitten, don't take any kind of work until I return. Have a rest and be in the pink of health. My life here is even duller than before. I'm fed up with the exhibition, especially with the talk about it. Everyone tries to present his masterpiece better and exerts all his knowledge of French to say some kind words about himself.

I haven't gone once to the theater. I only saw a Chaplin movie. The heat is unbearable.

I'll exert all my efforts to get around to everything I planned and nevertheless return to you not later than autumn.

Of all the people in the world I envy only Osya and Annushka, because they can see you every day.

What's with money? Did they pay Osya at the publishers? Does anybody write for *LEF*?

Kiss Osya many times.

I kiss you firmly, firmly, love and miss you.

Your always
Sjen

Write! Write! Write!
Immediately.

On the ninth of June—the same day that Mayakovsky had written Lili with the new date for his sailing—he and Elsa went to the bank and drew out the money he'd deposited for his trip, 25,000 francs. The next morning Elsa came to his room, as usual, to sit with him while he ate breakfast, only to discover that all the money had been stolen.

We were probably followed from the bank by a professional thief, who rented a room next to Volodya's in the Hotel Istria, and when Volodya left his room the next morning in his pajamas, not locking the door behind him, the thief came inside, took the wallet from his jacket, and disappeared.

We discovered the loss later. When I came to see Volodya in the morning, he was calmly chewing his *jambon*, sitting without his jacket near the table. Then he got up, put on his jacket (hanging on the back of the chair), patted his pockets to see if everything was in place. I saw how he suddenly turned gray—the wallet! We searched the room, dashed to the owner of the hotel, then the nearest police station.

Volodya walked with his big steps, too upset to keep pace with me, and I hurried to catch up to him. We walked silently, each thinking his own thoughts. The thief didn't leave him a penny, and I wondered what I could pawn. Volodya perhaps was thinking that he'd have to return to Moscow for the second time without success. At last I said to him that we could sell my fur cape and my ring, the only property I had. He laughed and cheered up a little. We don't have to sell anything, he said. We don't have to change our way of life, we'll go to the same restaurants, buy shirts and ties, and entertain ourselves in every way, and he would go around the world too.

Later it turned out to be so. The police search ended with the owner of the hotel, who recognized the thief as someone well known to the police. In the meantime, Volodya telegraphed Moscow and Lili arranged for advance royalties at Gosizdat to be transferred to Paris. I clearly remember Mayakovsky talking to a Russian representative about the robbery, and how he didn't express any compassion for Mayakovsky and didn't offer any help. Instead, vehemently and with apparent joy, he said, "The wisest man can sometimes be a fool." At that time many people were glad Mayakovsky was made a fool of, and they laughed about it.

The royalties from Gosizdat were for the first volume of the Collected Works, and Mayakovsky agreed that the money would be taken from sums owed him in the autumn months. The advance, however, wasn't enough, and he and Elsa began feverishly borrowing money from everyone they could find in Paris. It turned into a kind of desperate game. If friends didn't help him, or lent him less than he thought they could, he stopped having anything to do with them. But if they lent him more than he expected, he was overwhelmed with gratitude. Ilya Ehrenburg, who had known him for years, surprised him with fifty Belgian francs, and even though they'd never been close friends, Mayakovsky suddenly decided he liked him, began calling him by his first name, and told everyone about the fifty Belgian francs. Between the Russians he met at the Soviet Pavilion and Elsa's friends, they managed to borrow enough and disaster was avoided. He had wired Lili the same day he'd discovered the loss, but he didn't wire again until June 17, when the Briks worriedly inquired, TELEGRAPH HEALTH, AFFAIRS. He answered the same day, I'M WELL. EVERYTHING IS FINE. GOING TO MEXICO. THANKS. LOVE, KISS BELOVED KISSA AND DEAR OSYA. ALL YOURS, SJEN.

Two days later, as he was finally preparing to leave, he wrote a last letter to them with a somewhat sheepish account of the theft. He finished the letter just before catching the train to St. Nazaire and his waiting ship. His voyage to the New World had begun and his last thought, as always, was of Lili.

> Little one, I'm finishing writing in the morning, and I leave for the terminal in ten minutes. I kiss you, Solnik. I kiss Osya. I love you awfully and I miss you.
>
> ALL YOUR MEXICAN SJEN

17

Mayakovsky, Mexico, 1925

I, VLADIMIR MAYAKOVSKY, *citizen of* RUSSIA, *holder of passport no. 36258, issued* JANUARY 12, 1925, *in* MOSCOW, RUSSIA, *intend to visit the United States of America* . . .

I was born on JULY 7, 1893, *in* BAGDADI, RUSSIA. *Occupation practiced in the last two years*—ARTIST-PAINTER. *At present*—LIKEWISE.

I want to go to the United States in order to EXHIBIT MY WORK THERE *and I intend to stay for the period of* UP TO 5 MONTHS. *My address in the U.S.A. will be:* WILLY POGANY, 152 WEST 46 STREET, NEW YORK.

. . . *I solemnly swear and declare that all my answers given above are absolutely true in the sense I understand them.*

VLADIMIR MAYAKOVSKY
(MAYAKOVSKY'S APPLICATION
IN MEXICO CITY FOR A VISA
TO ENTER THE UNITED STATES)

J UST LIKE ANY OTHER TOURIST CROSSING THE ATLAN-
tic on a slow vessel, Mayakovsky found his ship, the *Espagne*,
exciting at the beginning of the voyage, and then hopelessly
boring. He took advantage of the stops along the way to
send letters home. He was writing to Lili almost as soon as the ship
was out of the harbor.

The ship *Espagne* 22 VI 1925

DEAR LILINOCHEK,

. . . My *Espagne* is not a bad ship. I haven't yet discovered any Russians. There are men in suspenders and belts
(they are Spaniards) and some women in enormous earrings (they
are Spanish women). Two short dogs are running around.
They are Japanese, but red-haired, both quite the same.

I kiss you, my dear, and run to be able to send this letter off
to you.

ALL YOUR SJEN

By the time he reached Cuba, after twelve days at sea, he was
so restless that he mailed her a letter the day he arrived, July 3, 1925,
and then hurried back to the ship and immediately began writing
her again.

The ship *Espagne* 3 VII 1925

DEAR, DEAR, SWEET, SWEET, SWEET AND MOST BELOVED MY
LILYONOK!

Are you receiving my traveling letters? Now we're approaching the island of Cuba—the port Havana (cigars); we'll stay here
a day or two. I use the opportunity once more to helplessly put
the letter in a mailbox.

The heat is unbearable! We have just crossed the Tropic of Capricorn itself.

To my right the first real land (not counting small things like islands), Florida, begins to appear. I have to write verses about Christopher Columbus, which is very difficult because it's hard to find out what is the diminutive for Christopher, and to rhyme "Columbus" on the word "Tropic" is an ordeal.

I can't say that I'm happy aboard a ship. Twelve days of water are good for fish and for professional explorers, but for land people it's too much. I haven't learned to speak French or Spanish, but instead I work on the expressiveness of faces, because I converse in pantomime.

My dear, telegraph me about your health and work. Unfortunately, I don't know the address of our Embassy.

I work very hard.

I miss you inexplicably.

I kiss you 1,000 times and Osya 800.

ALL YOUR COLUMBUS SJEN

The ship *Espagne* 3 VII 1925

MY DEAR, MY OWN, MY BELOVED KISSANKA,

I've just put a letter in the mailbox today, and now it's evening and I'm feeling awful again and already missing you.

I walked on the upper deck where there were only machines and no people, and suddenly I saw approaching me a very young, gray cat that I'd never noticed before.

I wanted to caress her instead of you, but she ran away from me behind the lifeboats. Kissik, won't you come out from behind the boats? My beloved, don't do it!

I love you terribly, terribly!

The two red Japanese dogs and one Spanish greyhound greet you. They understand everything and talk to me in Russian.

I'm being called for dinner.

Every day when I get up, I think why is everything so bad and why don't you get up from the empty berth next to me?

I want to see you terribly.

I kiss you, my dear, and love.

ALL YOUR SJEN

Whatever Mayakovsky later wrote about Mexico in his published pieces, he seemed to spend most of his time there in determined efforts to get out of the country.

Regarding Mexico City, it's very dull, unpleasant, filthy, and immeasurably dull.

I didn't come here in the proper season (winter). It rains regularly for half the day, at night it's very cold, a rotten climate. Since it's 2,400 meters above sea level it's awfully difficult to breathe (only for the first two weeks, I'm told) and the heart beats at a very high rate, which is very bad.

Mayakovsky had some plans to travel in the countryside if he wasn't successful with his American visa, and he already had booked passage back to France (to save 20 percent on the ticket); he was only waiting to see what his chances were for the trip to the United States. To save money he stayed with the Russian consul instead of at a hotel. His first days were spent with Diego Rivera, who met him at the railroad station after he'd taken the train up from the port at Veracruz, and his descriptions of Rivera and the museum they visited together were earnestly innocuous in the sketches for what he later titled *My Discovery of America*. He was writing poetry at a relentless pace, trying to pay back the advances he'd taken for the trip, and much of his letter to Lili in mid-July was concerned with money for the poems he was sending her.

. . . When you get this letter I'll not be in Mexico evidently, because after my trip to the countryside I'll go straight to the ship. That's why by any means write me everything, everything to Paris by the first of September, so I should receive your letter as soon as I arrive. And please don't write that you don't love me any more. I miss you terribly, not knowing anything about you. How is Osya? How is *LEF*? What about the Collected Works? Little one, I'm sending you verses and bothering you with frightful requests:

1. "The Discovery of America"—send to *LEF*.
2. "Spain"—send to *Ogonyok*.
3. "Nuns"—try to send to *Izvestia*.
4. "The Atlantic Ocean"—send to *Projector*.
5. Offer everything to Radio-Rosta.

Certainly don't take money from *LEF*. From the rest, get one ruble per line, and from Radio-Rosta, two or three chervontsa per verse. I beg you to send this money to Elsa's André from whom I borrowed money before leaving. I have to repay him by the first of September.

If you don't get this money or anything at all, then please don't send your own money. Only telegraph me and I'll arrange some loan.

Thank you, little one, for the telegrams. They are awfully, awfully nice and lie on my chest in a beautiful pigskin-leather case.

I won't send it now, because first they'll lose it, and second, I haven't taken a look around, and third I want to bring it to you myself.

In the photographs taken of Mayakovsky in Mexico City he looks worried and cold. Standing in front of a thick cactus with the sun blazing in his face, he's wearing a starched collar and tie, and a heavy woolen suit and vest, his expression as grim as ever.

His efforts to get his American visa became heroically strenuous. He visited the United States embassy almost daily, telephoned and bombarded the office with telegrams. It was finally the prize from the

Paris International Exhibition that cut through the red tape. He somehow convinced the embassy people that he was only a graphic artist interested in commercial display, and his silver medal overcame any lingering doubts. The American artist Willy Pogany wrote from New York to help, his letter mentioning only advertising art and posters. The United States didn't officially recognize the U.S.S.R. until October 1933, and if the embassy had realized that Mayakovsky was a propagandist writer, he never would have gotten into the country. His persistence and his apparent naïveté at last got him through. He packed a pair of Mexican castanets in his suitcase to bring back to Lili, and on the thirtieth of July he reached New York.

Whatever else he was to say about New York, he could never say that he was bored. On one of his first days there, he had one of his usual exchanges of telegrams with Lili, who was now well enough to travel and wanted to join him in the United States. On the thirty-first of July he wired her: KISS FROM NEW YORK. BEGINNING AUGUST VOLYUSKY BRINGING *LEF* VERSES. TELEGRAPH HEALTH. ADDRESS 3 FIFTH AVENUE. KISS LOVE. YOUR SJEN. She answered him, WIRE DETAILS, and on August 2 he protested, DEAR KISS. NO DETAILS YET. JUST ARRIVED. KISS LOVE. YOURS SJEN.

On August 6, he wired again, this time about his efforts to get her a visa so that she could join him. STRIVING FOR VISA. IF NOT I'LL COME HOME. MISS YOU AWFULLY. KISS LOVE. YOUR SJEN. After that Lili didn't hear from him for a month.

Mayakovsky's work was unknown to the United States embassy in Mexico City, but to American socialists, especially to recent émigrés from Russia, he was a hero of the Revolution. It wasn't only the leftist community in New York that was excited about having him there. His old friend and fellow Futurist David Burliuk was in New York too, where he had finally ended up after his long journey from Russia and Japan. They hadn't seen each other since April 1918, but Mayakovsky telephoned him as soon as he got to the city and said simply: "Mayakovsky speaking."

Burliuk managed to say, "Hello, Volodya, how are you?"

Volodya, in his loud voice, answered impassively, "Thank you, I'm all right. I had a cold only once in the last ten years."

Burliuk, in an article in a Russian-language paper on August 2, described their meeting with his usual hyperbole.

> From the distance I already noticed his big "Russian" foot on the doorstep and a couple of heavy suitcases in the doorway. I recognized that foot at once: it could only belong to Mayakovsky. We looked at each other for a long time, first in the dark hall. Then I watched Mayakovsky take a bath; he washed the dust of tropical Mexico and hot Texas from his lion's mane and powerful body. And Vladimir Vladimirovich is just as young, tells his jokes just as before. There is nothing strange in this. After all, he is only thirty. And who will be weighed down by fame, even if world fame, at the happy age of thirty?

Burliuk had found life in New York difficult after his arrival, but he'd managed to settle with his wife and two sons and continue his work as an artist, even though they were desperately poor. He went along as Mayakovsky was interviewed by the papers, read his poetry, and attended meetings, concerts, and picnics. Mayakovsky was interviewed by Mike Gold for the New York *World* and Shakno Epstein for the Yiddish paper *Freiheit*. These interviews were printed in the form of essays on the theme of the decline of capitalism and the bright future of socialism, and they contain more of the standard propaganda line than they do Mayakovsky's own responses.

In America Mayakovsky felt hopelessly limited by his inability to speak English. He stayed close to Burliuk whenever possible, using him as an interpreter, but there were many awkward moments, for example, the New York party Mayakovsky later described with great humor.

> But just consider my situation in America. A poet's been invited. They've been told he's a genius. A genius—that's even

better than being well known. I arrive and right off I say, "Gif
me pliz sam tee."

They serve me. I wait a bit and then, "Gif me pliz . . ."

They serve me again.

And I keep it up, varying the intonation and the phrasing.
"Gif me de sam tee; sam tee de gif me." I say my say.

The evening proceeds.

Respectful old fellows listen reverentially. "There's a Russian for you. Doesn't waste words. He's a thinker . . . Tolstoy
. . . The North."

But the ladies move away when they hear for the hun-
dredth time that same request for tea, even though it's enunci-
ated in a pleasant bass voice. And the gentlemen distribute
themselves in the corners of the room laughing at my expense.

So I shout to Burliuk: "You translate this for them. Tell
them that if they knew Russian I could, without even dirtying
my shirtfront, nail them with my tongue to the cross of their
own suspenders, that I could roast this whole collection of in-
sects on the sharp turnspit of my tongue."

And the honest Burliuk translates. "My eminent friend
Vladimir Vladimirovich wants another cup of tea."

But people in America wanted to hear him and they wanted to
hear what he could tell them about the Soviet Union, even if they
couldn't always understand what he had to say. Mayakovsky's first
reading at the Central Opera House in New York City on August
14, 1925, was packed, and he was an immediate success. During the
month of September he went to weekend camps in upstate New
York organized by *Freiheit*, reciting ceaselessly to attentive listeners,
once reading the entire "Lenin" poem in a Catskill clearing in the
woods. He read a total of seven times in New York City, and even
once in Coney Island. On the twelfth of September, a Jewish group
named Icor, which was working to help Jews colonize in the Soviet
Union, got him out to Coney Island for a benefit reading with
Burliuk. A photograph of them taken at the beach shows them with

their coats off in the sun, but still in long, hot trousers, neckties, and suspenders, with straw hats for shade. Usually the picture is printed as a close-up of the two of them talking, but in the original negative they're surrounded by girls in bathing suits who look like bathing beauties from the background of a Mack Sennett movie.

He did meet girls in the United States, although this part of his life, like the girls in the Coney Island photo, was in the background. His poetry—usually the most truthful expression of the realities of his emotional life—doesn't suggest that he became seriously involved with anyone. But Lili thought that a woman bore him a child in America and later brought the child, a daughter named Ellie, to visit him in France. The details became confused as the years passed, with various versions of the story, and if a serious relationship ever existed, he never referred to it later.

Mayakovsky's efforts through these weeks to get a visa for Lili were unsuccessful. He'd become closely attached to a Russian in New York named I. Y. Khurgin, head of the Soviet agency Amtorg, who promised to help with the visa, but on August 27 Khurgin was drowned, and ten days later Mayakovsky wired Lili, VISA HELD UP AFTER ACCIDENT. SEPT. 10 BEGIN LECTURES HERE. IF VISA IMPOSSIBLE THEN COMING HOME. ANSWER TENDERLY.

Lili's telegram in answer was anything but tender. She told him that the State Publishing House, in violation of their contract with Mayakovsky, had refused to go on with the publication of his Collected Works, and she was upset with him for not writing more frequently. The news from Moscow made it impossible for Mayakovsky to consider staying on in America, though he had offers to lecture as far west as San Francisco. He wired her again on September 25, this time upset about her lack of money to pay for a trip to Italy to help her recuperate from her illness of the months before.

Lili certainly could have kept Gosizdat's bad news about the Collected Works from him, since there was nothing he could do about it from America, but as always she was impatient with him when he was away from her on a long trip. She went off to Italy while he hurried through the rest of his reading engagements so he could get a ship back to her as soon as possible. He read in several cities, among them Philadelphia, Pittsburgh, Cleveland, Detroit, and Chicago. On October 3 he wired her: KISSES FROM CHICAGO. I MISS, LOVE YOU. TRYING FOR ITALY. ALL YOUR SJEN. The next day he went back to New York, and almost distracted at the thought that he would miss her, he wired again when he arrived. For the next three weeks he tried to get an Italian visa while he waited for a ship to get him back. But his visits to the Italian consul were unsuccessful, and on October 28 he sailed for Le Havre on the S.S. *Rochambeau*. Lili had left for Italy on October 16, and when Volodya got to Paris on November 6, he immediately contacted her. She answered him at the Hotel Istria on November 9, saying that an Italian visa for him would take three weeks. ". . . What should I do?" she asked. He wired back,

DEAR KITTEN,
Let's meet as soon as possible. Come to Berlin Saturday 18. Telegraph immediately day, time, terminal of arrival. Short of money. Wiring $250 to bank Credito Italiano. I kiss you, love, miss.

YOUR SJEN.

On the fourteenth of November he reached Berlin and Lili joined him there. They left for Moscow by way of Riga, and they were back on the twenty-second of November. Elsa, who had been sleeping in Mayakovsky's room at Lyubyansky, was at the station to meet them and she remembered that Lili was wearing a new squirrel coat when she came off the train. Mayakovsky followed her out of the compartment, happy to have his long trip over.

Mayakovsky's *Discovery of America*, published later, was a mixture of journalistic impressions and poetry. The journalistic pieces were uneven, often banal, but even at their best they lacked his raw energy, and his New York descriptions were too often of the "As I leave the gleaming skyscrapers of Manhattan my deepest memory is of the unhappy faces of the poor people thronging its streets . . ." variety that Soviet writers have been turning out for the last fifty years. As limited as his view of America was, he sometimes liked what he saw, especially the vitality of New York City in its best moods (despite his confusion over its geography).

I LOVE NEW YORK in the fall, on working days, on weekdays.

One dresses by electric light, streets in electricity, houses in electricity, evenly cut by windows like the pattern of a commercial poster. Buildings spread endlessly, traffic lights blink with colored signals, traffic is doubled, tripled, multiplied ten times on the asphalt, on the rain-licked mirror. In the narrow precipice of buildings the wind hoots, tears, rattles the signboards, tries to sweep people off their feet and runs away unpunished, unarrested by anyone, through the miles of dozens of avenues cutting through Manhattan Island—from the ocean to the Hudson. On both sides the countless weak voices of very narrow streets assist the howling of the thunder, also cut evenly by a ruler across Manhattan from water to water. Under an awning—or on dry days just on the pavement—big piles of newspapers are scattered, brought earlier by trucks and thrown down here by newsboys . . .

The most awkward aspect of his American writing, however, isn't its insistent propagandist bias. He disliked capitalism intensely, and since many aspects of New York life reflected capitalism at its worst, there's no reason why he should have hidden his views about it. The difficulty with his descriptions is their inconsistency. Since he wasn't able to talk to anyone except a handful of Russians, and since he had no real plan of what he wanted to see and do, he was at the mercy of anyone who dropped by to tell him about life in the United States. Some of what they said was penetrating, some of it wildly imaginative, but he never got close enough to the society around him to know which was which.

His most successful writing about the United States was his poem to the Brooklyn Bridge, an exuberant response to American technology, his feelings as fresh and open as his poem on the meeting with the sun five years before. This time the subject overwhelmed him, as it had many artists and writers before, despite his standard approach of disparaging Western culture for his Soviet audience. As he wrote in the opening lines of "Brooklyn Bridge,"

Give out, Coolidge,
with a cry of joy!
I'm not stingy with words
                   about good things.
Blush,
       with my praise,
                  red as our flag's dear material
though you are
              the Unitedest States
of America.
As the fanatical believer
                       going
                           to a church,
to a cell
        retreating
                  sternly and simply,
so I,
     in the evening's
                    graying mist,
set foot humbly
              on Brooklyn Bridge . . .

He uses many of his familiar devices in the poem—the future historian looking back at the ruins of the past, even a momentary

brush with religion in the early image about "the fanatical believer."
The old egoism is there, as it had been in his earlier Futurist
days, but even it is muted into the poem's larger tribute, as in the
lines

> could anyone with bare hands
> planting
> one steel foot
> on Manhattan
> pull Brooklyn
> up
> by the lip . . .

Or Whitmanesque phrases like

> this mile-long iron arch
> welded
> oceans and prairies together.

The mood of "Brooklyn Bridge" is molded with maturity and
restraint. While it is clear that he had seen, and genuinely admired,
the bridge, most of his American poetry was as uneven as his prose
accounts, and he was also publishing didactic propagandist poems
that show how little he understood of New York.

Mayakovsky had, however, made a serious discovery in the
United States, something that was to help shape his vision in his
final plays. Ever since his childhood he had gloried in machines,
writing in his autobiography of a rivet factory which, as a boy, he'd
seen lit up at night in the Caucasus: "After seeing electricity I lost
interest in nature. Not up-to-date enough." America challenged his
earlier beliefs and in a startling passage in *My Discovery of America*
he revealed a prophetic glimpse of the problems of the technology
he usually extolled.

The futurism of naked technology, of superficial impressionism of smoke and cables, whose great task was to revolutionize the moribund, village-ridden mentality, that primeval futurism has finally been confirmed by America . . .

Before the people of art there arises the task of *LEF*, not extolling technology but curbing it in the name of humanity's interests; not looking for aesthetic admiration in iron fire escapes of skyscrapers but in simple organization of living quarters.

What is there in automobiles? . . . There are many cars; it is time to think how not to let them stink up the streets.

And skyscrapers? A place where it is impossible to live, and yet one lives.

Dust is spitting from the wheels of the rushing subway and it seems the trains are running through our ears.

Not to extol noise but to put up sound absorbers—we poets must talk in the cars . . .

It was a thought that he put aside for a time when he returned to Moscow and found himself again in the middle of the struggles that dogged his life in the Soviet Union.

Elsa stayed on in Mayakovsky's room in Moscow, where she found it hard to keep the sheet from slipping off the oilcloth covering on his couch. Volodya was with the Briks in the dacha in Sokolniki, and often he met Elsa when he went to Moscow. For the first time she realized how famous he had become.

> Later when I was walking with Mayakovsky on the Moscow streets, I understood the fame he had. Even a cabman looked back—people turned their heads—to look at him, and passers-by said, "Here is Mayakovsky coming!"

18

Lili and Osip Brik, 1933

You,
      who could do things
                  with words
   that no one else
          on earth
              could do . . .
      "TO SERGEI ESENIN"

MAYAKOVSKY'S LIFE WITH LILI CHANGED AFTER HIS return from his American trip in November 1925. They never were physical lovers again, a decision that Lili found more difficult to accept than she later admitted. Years afterward she said,

> When he came back he didn't ask for my physical nearness. He said to himself—he was very clever, he understood everything very well, he knew—"If I push myself on her she will leave me." And that would have been so, because I had decided I didn't want to be his physical partner.

But at the time she felt his decision not to "push" himself on her as a lover was a form of rejection, just as she was hurt when Brik lost interest in making love to her a year after their marriage. When she and Mayakovsky were reunited in Berlin after his American trip, they took separate bedrooms as usual in a hotel, and after dinner Lili waited for him to join her. She was not looking forward to making love with him, but to her surprise, when he came to her room, he leaned against the door instead of approaching her bed and said softly, "Good night, darling. I won't torture you any more." At first she felt relieved, but then as she lay in bed after Mayakovsky had left her, she found herself weeping.

She had many more casual affairs after this, but none of her lovers satisfied her and she would drop them as abruptly as she'd started, bewildering them by her lack of interest. One time when she was infatuated with the film director Pudovkin, who refused her, Lili was so depressed that she took an overdose of sleeping tablets in an unsuccessful suicide attempt. She felt herself getting older, and

Brik didn't offer much emotional support. He was spending his time with Genya, who considered herself his "shadow."

Lili had never had a completely successful physical relationship with anyone, not even Mayakovsky, and the lack of fulfillment intensified her restlessness. During this time Rita felt it was very sad that Lili, courted by so many men for her charm and beauty, was most concerned with finding a satisfactory sexual partner. Her involvements flared up, burned intensely, then died away, leaving her dissatisfied until she moved on to someone else. Rita remembered:

> Once, when her life with Mayakovsky was in its last stage and they all moved to the Gendrikov apartment, Lili told me about some new man. She was very excited, her eyes were shining. "Do you think it will last long?" I asked her. "Right now, it's for eternity," Lili said with great seriousness.

She was in better health, but she was dieting compulsively and visitors to their apartment, including the American writer Theodore Dreiser, commented on her pallor. Dreiser saw Lili as "a fair woman no longer so very young, and with that tired look about the skin and eyes which is rather common among Russian intellectuals. She had the broad, white brow which is the charm of so many Russian women; clear, sensitive, comprehending eyes, and a dazzling smile. At the tea table she shone . . ."

Dreiser met the Briks and Mayakovsky in 1927, when they'd finally managed to get an apartment to themselves on Gendrikov Alley after years of communal living in Moscow. It was in a dilapidated two-story stucco house with a garden in a run-down working-class neighborhood that had a quiet, country feeling to it. They kept the dacha at Sokolniki, but it was the new apartment that they finally felt was home.

Although Lili and Mayakovsky were no longer lovers, he still felt his home was with the Briks and moved his clothes and personal articles into his own room at Gendrikov when it was ready. He kept his small room on Lyubyansky Passage as a convenient office—it was in the center of Moscow—and as a place to bring his girl friends (he kept a box of their letters and photographs there). His neighbors on Lyubyansky weren't always friendly. Shklovsky told a story that humorously described the poet's relationship with the people who lived in the next apartment. When he occasionally stayed overnight, he used to borrow a Gillette razor from the brothers who lived next door. He'd ring their bell, take the razor, shave, and bring it right back. But after a while the boys' mother decided the borrowing had to stop. She was a very proper lady, with her hair combed back tightly over a roller, and she told her sons that Mayakovsky returned the razor without drying it properly, so he couldn't use it any more. The next time Mayakovsky came for the razor she said, "The razor is being used, Vladimir Vladimirovich, and will be for a long, long time to come." "I understand," replied Mayakovsky, "you are shaving an elephant."

On Gendrikov their apartment was on the second floor; it was spacious and comfortable after being repaired under the supervision of "Big Jim," Louellen's uncle, who was a building contractor in Moscow. Mayakovsky had a front room with windows opening to the garden, and Osip and Lili's small rooms were off the hall, which had been ingeniously partitioned to include a triangular bathroom with a tub, a luxury in those days. The toilet was in a separate compartment. The dining room, the center of the apartment with its fine white tile stove and long inlaid table, was off Mayakovsky's room. There were no soft chairs, because Lili didn't want guests to sprawl, but they found a long leather sofa which they placed along the wall of the dining room, and it became their favorite place to sit. No paintings hung in the apartment, since Mayakovsky hated anything superfluous; he called most paintings "lies." In his room he had a low couch covered with a striped wool Mexican blanket in soft colors, an American rolltop desk with almost nothing in it (a twin to the one in his room on Lyubyansky, which was filled with papers), and a large bureau for his clothes, with a mirror on the door placed high enough for him to shave easily.

Lili remembered that Mayakovsky was usually the first one to get up, and he waited impatiently for the Briks to join him.

Restlessly he passed the door of Osip Maximovich's room every few minutes, and if he heard that Osip Maximovich was not sleeping any longer—when Mayakovsky heard him reading or solving chess problems in a journal—he asked Brik immediately to come and eat breakfast. The samovar was boiling and Mayakovsky made a big heap of open sandwiches—butter and white cheese, sausage—and then we sat at the table and ate and drank and read the day's newspapers and journals. When Osip Maximovich researched the literature of the 1840's, Vladimir Vladimirovich demanded that he should discuss the latest discoveries in his work, or anything else that kept Brik busy at that time.

Breakfast was Mayakovsky's favorite time of the day. Nobody disturbed us, and our heads were clear after the night's rest. He was always in good temper in the morning, and we spent all our mornings together in such a way. Osip Maximovich always talked to Vladimir Vladimirovich about what he had read and thought about. Mayakovsky almost never had time to read. He wrote. But he was interested in everything, and Brik told him about everything in an interesting way. Often after these morning conversations Mayakovsky would come to Brik and kiss him on the head and say, "I kiss your little baldness."

The Briks also shared his public life through the numerous friends, literary associates, and visitors who came to the apartment daily for meetings, talks, and conferences. Mayakovsky was a celebrity, and the Briks served in a more or less formal capacity as his reception committee. Visitors would phone the apartment, ask the housekeeper if they could meet Mayakovsky, and when they arrived,

Brik would talk to them. He was always ready to talk, and usually the room was filled with people sitting on the couch and around the table, sometimes even perched on the single chair or on the top of the bureau in Brik's room—poets, theatrical producers, artists, photographers, critics, architects, musicians, philologists, journalists.

Vasily (Vasya) Katanyan, a younger colleague who was publishing some of Mayakovsky's poems, felt that Brik was "useful to many creative people as a friend, a catalyst, an advisor to check plans, listen to doubts, clear up tangled problems. He could reveal an unexpected side to a subject, and his suggestions were often fine and witty . . . Most likely at the end of his life he could have written memoirs under the title 'Notes of a Secret Advisor.' I don't remember who made this joke—wasn't it Brik himself?"

Brik's friend Roman Yakobson noted that he seemed entirely without ambition. He was content with being Mayakovsky's associate and editor. In 1927 he published a chapter of what he envisioned as his second book of Formalist literary criticism, "Rhythm and Syntax," but his own work never came first, perhaps because he lacked a certain sense of organization. He published over a hundred articles between 1915 and 1930, but they were mostly short editorials in journals that he and Mayakovsky were involved with together. The majority of his scholarly articles were never finished, and as an editor of *LEF* he was often behind schedule. Katanyan remembered that at the beginning of July 1927 they were sending the May issue of the magazine to the printers.

After ten years together the Briks and Mayakovsky had begun to go in different directions, but the hours they shared remained the center of their lives. For Lili, certainly for Osip, and to some extent for Mayakovsky also, the justification for their way of life was a book that had influenced all three of them, just as it had influenced generations of Marxist intellectuals, including Lenin. It was the novel *What Is to Be Done?* by Nikolai Chernyshevsky, one of the most popular nineteenth-century reform novels in Russia. Lili remembered:

Chernyshevsky was our spokesman in his novel *What Is to Be Done?* If we had a problem, we had a choice: either we advised each other or we looked to Chernyshevsky. His philosophy was very near to us. The last book Mayakovsky read was probably *What Is to Be Done?*, because the book lay near his sofa. There Chernyshevsky says that woman is the crown of creation and everything is allowed to her. Perhaps he says this because women had no rights at that time.

The other day I met a woman I've known for many years and she asked me, "Lili, can you explain how three people can live together?" Her question can be compared with a situation where a teacher explains how the effect of steam makes a steam engine work. Then he asks his pupils if there are any questions. One of the pupils asks the question "Can the engine work without steam?" It means that the pupil understood nothing. People now don't understand anything of my life with Mayakovsky and Brik. They think it was a terrible sin.

But we had a dream of some other kind of perfect life. It was the life Chernyshevsky recommended, life as he thought it should be—Chernyshevsky guided our thoughts. You must read *What Is to Be Done?* to understand our relationship, our life of three people together. Our great eternal friendship has not ceased to exist today, even when Brik and Mayakovsky are no longer here.

Today Chernyshevsky's novel is considered old-fashioned even in the Soviet Union, but Lili insisted that her love for Mayakovsky could only be understood on its terms. When he entered her life, their situation seemed to her to have already been described in Chernyshevsky's novel. Osip had given it to her to read shortly after their marriage, and Lili passed her copy on to Mayakovsky. He wasn't nearly so enchanted with the novel, but for Lili the book was almost a bible.

Lili saw herself as a counterpart of Chernyshevsky's heroine,

Vera Pavlovna, who had been taught by her first husband, Lopukhov, a way to live that revolutionized their marriage, freeing her of the bondage of the conventional wife's role. Brik had encouraged Lili to set up their life together in the same spirit as the characters in *What Is to Be Done?* In the novel the husband and wife each had a separate bedroom, and each used the same small parlor as a common meeting room to receive guests and eat meals and talk together, because for Chernyshevsky the important thing was that neither individual was to sacrifice any freedom in the marriage. As a couple they saw each other only when they wished to meet, and they were as considerate of each other as they were of strangers. A husband and wife were two equally free individuals, neither possessing the other, each free to develop in the highest degree the characteristics that Chernyshevsky enumerated as the superior personality of what he called "the new man"—"tact, coolness, activity, all well balanced, the realization of common sense in action."

In the novel, when the heroine fell in love with Lopukhov's best friend, the husband as a man of honor faked a suicide so they could marry. First Lopukhov wrestled with the problem of jealousy, which Chernyshevsky defined in the novel as a "distorted feeling, a false feeling, an abominable feeling." Furthermore, "a man with a developed mind should not have it." Chernyshevsky's rationality seemed to Brik to justify his decision early in his marriage not to have children or even involve himself in the sexual challenge of a full physical relationship with Lili.

There seems to have been only one moment in all the years when Osip felt jealous of Lili and Mayakovsky. In 1916 Lili came back radiant after a short trip to Moscow with Mayakovsky a few months after they'd become lovers, and Brik later told a close friend, "I was very upset. But Mayakovsky understood that Lili and I would never separate because of our great human relationship. Our long friendship and intimacy didn't depend on anything and couldn't end because of anything." It was Brik, the rationalist, who had first read Chernyshevsky.

For Mayakovsky, until the quarrel that led to the poem "About This," jealousy tormented him nearly every moment of his years with Lili. Although love was defined clearly and logically in *What Is to Be Done?* and Lili was certain that if he only would read it carefully, he would be able to accept her point of view, she was overlooking the fact that since his early Futurist days Mayakovsky never had much use for the knowledge that came from old books and he certainly wasn't a rationalist. It was Mayakovsky, the romantic, who had the deepest misgivings about Chernyshevsky's book. He tried several times to read it, and loyally he told Lili that he considered Brik to be a "blueprint of the 'new man.'" The role was temperamentally impossible for Mayakovsky. Publicly he could be a spokesman for the Communist utopia, but privately he understood the novel's limitations clearly enough. He once asked a friend,

> Have you read Chernyshevsky's *What Is to Be Done?* I'm reading it now. The book interests me from a special angle. The problem then consisted of how to get out of the family. Now it's how to get into it, how to create a family. This is very difficult, and in the aspect of time, it is easier to build socialist cities.

Mayakovsky was now so well known in the Soviet Union that he was traveling almost continuously, lecturing on his trip to America and reading his propaganda poems. After his return from America at the end of 1925, he stopped writing advertising jingles and began to earn a living for himself and the Briks from journalism. He wrote for *Izvestia, Trud, Komsomolskaya Pravda, Rabochaya Moskva*, and many other journals and newspapers. His income was large but unpredictable, and it was always a brutal, grueling schedule. On his travels, his letters to Lili were filled with money worries, as for example when he wrote her from Simferopol on July 8, 1926:

> All the money from Odessa has been spent, and I have to go on with my lectures to earn anything.

Unfortunately, even this gives almost nothing. For example, in Sevastopol the organizers . . . not only refused to pay according to the agreement but also canceled the lecture and insulted me in public with what in my opinion was bad language. I had to waste the whole day on this nonsense, assembling a meeting of the district committee, and the secretary of the committee gave a good talking to to the insolent little tyrant who had gone too far. I had full moral satisfaction, but my pocket remained empty. Moreover, instead of poems I write only letters to editors . . . The most unpleasant thing for me is that you must be sitting without a ruble, everybody is bothering you, and Osya has no money to go to the Volga . . .

There were so many problems on his trips that he even wondered if his poetry was suffering. He joked about the situation to Lili while he rested between readings in a resort town on the Black Sea. "According to my observations I've become an awfully proletarian poet. There's no money and I don't write poems." Despite his reputation he had no help during his tours, making all the arrangements himself. Traveling was difficult with the irregular train schedules in the Soviet Union, and Mayakovsky was disturbed about the often primitive sanitation facilities in the hotels along his lecture route. In his fear of contracting infections, he insisted on boiling his water and washing his own dishes, even carrying along a folding rubber tub for his baths. Once when he was at a place where he was warned that the water system was polluted, he wrote Lili that he bathed in mineral water and was beginning to bubble over himself.

Finally in Odessa an unemployed Jewish actor named Pavel Lavut saw him at a poorly attended reading at the Sailors' Home. Lavut went up to him afterward and offered to arrange some readings in the Crimea, where he had contacts. They agreed on a financial arrangement, and Lavut became Mayakovsky's agent, traveling with him, taking care of details, and freeing him of some of his anxieties over money. It was the final anomaly, the Soviet's leading propagandist forced to hire a Jewish business agent so he could make a living as a traveling lecturer, but Mayakovsky wasn't troubled by the ironies of it. Between 1926 and 1930 Lavut booked him for more than two hundred appearances in over fifty cities in every part of the Soviet Union. Mayakovsky regarded the tours as more "compulsory loneliness," and at the end of them his voice was so hoarse and painful that he could barely talk.

Emotionally, his life was far from happy. His relationship with Lili and his poetry seemed at a standstill. The most eloquent expression of his many conflicts was in an elegaic poem he wrote about Sergei Esenin, one of the most popular poems on his reading tours. They had been rivals; in fact, Mayakovsky had been annoyed when Gosizdat decided in June 1925 to issue a large collection of Esenin's poetry, about 10,000 lines, and pay him at the rate of one ruble a line, the highest advance ever paid to any poet. But less than a month after Mayakovsky's return from America, on December 27, 1925, Esenin hung himself in a hotel room in Leningrad. The day before his suicide he cut himself to write in his own blood:

> Goodbye, my dear, goodbye.
> Don't be sad, don't cloud your brow,
> In this life to die is nothing new,
> But of course life isn't any newer.

The suicide shocked people on every level of Soviet life. Mayakovsky, as publicist for the Party doctrine, interpreted the event as showing that Esenin had stood aside from the poets who had accepted the Revolution and who "saw before them a wide and optimistic path." But in his long poem about Esenin's death, "To Sergei Esenin," Mayakovsky was unable to suppress signs of his own difficulties in writing poems to order for the Party. His respect for Esenin as a poet was evident in the first lines.

> You have passed,
>> as they say,
>>> into the other world.

Emptiness . . .
>Fly,
>>cutting your way into the stars.
No advances,
>no saloons for you there.
Sobriety.
No, Esenin,
>this
>>is not in derision.
In my throat
>not laughter
>>but sorrow strangles me . . .
You,
>who could do things
>>with words
that no one else
>on earth
>>could do.
Why,
>what for?

He also described with some irony what would have happened to Esenin if he had been closer to Soviet political ideology: he would have been watched, as in a way Mayakovsky was watched by Brik, and forced to emphasize the political aspect of his poetry.

They say,
>someone should have been attached to you,
>>one of the On Guardists
and
>your content
>>would have shown
>>>much more talent.

You would have
>
> written
>
> some hundred lines
>
> a day . . .

And the individualist in Mayakovsky broke free when he said suddenly that he couldn't have done it himself.

But, in my opinion,
>
> should such nonsense
>
> be realized,
>
> I would have
>
> laid hand on myself earlier.
>
> It's better
>
> to die from vodka
>
> than from boredom!

The lines seem to contradict what he had written earlier about the duty of the artist to serve the Revolution, and at the end of the poem, when he asserted that the most important argument for life was that it was difficult and that it was a weakness in Esenin to commit suicide, it was almost as if Mayakovsky were forcibly taking himself in hand. He had so often fought off suicidal impulses himself that his poem seems like a polemic against himself. In his conclusion, Mayakovsky echoed Esenin's suicide note:

In this life,
>
> it's not hard to die.
>
> To make life
>
> is much harder.

On January 24, 1926, just before the Briks moved into the new apartment, Mayakovsky left for a long tour on which he was continually questioned about Esenin. At a reading in Kharkov he startled the audience by answering a question about the suicide with: "After death I spit on all memorials and wreaths . . . Take care of poets!" There was a moment of complete silence as the audience stared at him in confusion. He was writing to Lili as he traveled, apologizing that she was left with supervising the repairs of the apartment while he was gone. "I feel very sorry that you have to take care of the apartment yourself, and yet I envy you because it's so interesting." At the same time, as if he were thinking of Esenin's lonely death, he added, "I'm missing you very much, my dear. Everybody needs someone, and in my case I need you. It's the truth."

19

Lili Brik and Mayakovsky, Crimea, 1926

Mayakovsky, V. Stepanova, O. Beskin, Lili Brik,
in Gendrikov apartment, 1927 (photograph by Rodchenko)

Love
    for us
        is no arbored paradise—
to us
    love
        says, humming,
that the heart's
        stalled motor
has begun working
        again.

"LETTER FROM PARIS TO COMRADE
KOSTROV ON THE NATURE OF LOVE"

THEIR LIFE IN MOSCOW BEGAN TO REFLECT THE darkening political situation. In addition to Mayakovsky's propaganda writing, he and the Briks were associating more frequently with government officials, including members of the secret police. Although Brik was no longer a Party member, he was still close to people he had worked with at the Cheka. He and Mayakovsky thought of the secret police as "the conscience of the Revolution," repressing all "enemies of the state" who tried to subvert or weaken the government.

> And he who doesn't sing with us today
>   is against
>   us!

The Briks' relationship with their friends in the government was so strong that they could intercede for people who had been arrested. However, they could be coldly indifferent if they chose, even when confronted with the persecution of those close to them. When Brik was told of the arrest of his cousin Isadore Roumer, who had spent so much time with him during the early years of his marriage to Lili, he did nothing to help. Roumer's two brothers came to the Gendrikov apartment, but Osya refused to telephone his contacts in the Cheka, saying, "He must have done something." Heartlessly, Lili asked the brothers, "Why are you so sad? I've heard that conditions in the camps are good. He can work there and the time will pass quickly for him."

Lili never joined the Party, but she was sympathetic to the activities of the police. When Rita visited her after an unhappy period of her life in Leningrad, Lili suggested that she might consider working as a contact in Berlin, where "friends" would help her set up a comfortable apartment to meet writers and intellectuals in the émigré group. Rita had always felt awkward with the members of the police she'd met at the Briks' apartment, but she consented to meet Lili's "friend" at Gendrikov to see if he wanted to use her. She was so nervous and talked so uncontrollably that afterward the agent told Lili he didn't feel Rita would be satisfactory for the kind of work she'd be expected to do.

Brik was bringing in very little income at this time. After leaving Mosselprom, he and Mayakovsky collaborated on a radio play, and in 1927 Osip began experimenting with a short story, but he didn't have much talent as a creative writer and often his projects didn't get beyond the speculative stage. His most serious interest was scholarly research in the theory of poetic language, subjects like the relationship between rhythm and syntax in poetry or studies on Pushkin's epithets or Russian trochaic tetrameter with dactylic endings, chapters of the book of literary criticism he never completed.

Brik's scholarly interest was not confined to subjecting poetry to rigorous scientific analysis; he also leaned to sociology. His theories of the "social demand" of art had grown out of his involvement with Futurism, but as he steadily lost his power to influence the Soviet government in cultural areas, he grew increasingly cynical. Ten years after the Revolution, while asserting that "art is nothing but vanity," it was from Mayakovsky's art that he derived most of his income.

Mayakovsky signed contracts and drew large advances for a variety of projects with Gosizdat, including a three-act play, *Comedy with Murder*, and a novel about his life in Leningrad and Moscow which never progressed beyond the first twenty pages. However Soviet socialism was defined, he earned his living with endless hack writing and grueling lecture tours like any writer in the capitalist countries. Lili was often away herself during this period: one of the men she was involved with was the film director Lev Kuleshov, and she was working as a director's assistant for some documentary films.

The summers were especially difficult, since Lavut booked Mayakovsky on reading tours to the crowded resort areas along the Black Sea coast. In the summer of 1926 Lili and Volodya saw each other only for a few days when their schedules coincided. Lili came to the Crimea in July with Alexander Tobinson for a two-week vacation, before beginning work as an assistant to the director Abraham Rohm on a film about Jews in an agricultural collective. Mayakovsky was traveling in the Crimea at the same time, on one of his lecture tours, alternating *My Discovery of America* with a talk on "How to Make Verses" and his poem to Esenin. She telegraphed him in the middle of July that she could meet him, and he answered her on July 19:

> I am extremely glad. On Friday, Saturday I lecture in Yalta. Come right to Yalta. It's better by ship from Sevastopol. You'll get a bad shaking in the car. Bring Osya with you. Telegraph. See you soon.

The script for the film, titled *Jews on the Land,* had been written by their friend Shklovsky. Mayakovsky wrote the titles and probably had a hand in some of the final script changes as the filming went on. Lili did the routine work of locating props and film and scheduling the shooting. In the photographs of the two of them taken during the summer they look very settled, almost like a vacationing couple. Volodya, in his undershirt, long trousers, and cane, still leaned his head toward Lili when they sat together to be photographed.

With Lavut taking over some of the details of his schedule, Mayakovsky was able to turn again to his other concerns, the most important of them being the magazine *LEF*. He continued stubbornly to believe in the *LEF* ideals, and on September 1, 1926, he signed an agreement with Gosizdat for a magazine to be called *New LEF*, the first issue to come out in December. He even solicited funds himself for the magazine during his readings, taking in 96 rubles for advance subscriptions to prove to Gosizdat that people were still interested. Because of the usual delays, it was January before the magazine appeared. It was smaller than the first issues of the old *LEF* had been, but many of the names were the same—Pasternak, Aseyev, Brik, Shklovsky, Kushner, Tretyakov—and there was the same strident ring to the editorials. The journal provoked the same relentless critical response to what the other groups regarded as the magazine's elitism and unintelligibility.

There was a lack of energy in much of Mayakovsky's new work, including the long propaganda poem "Good!" which he wrote for the tenth anniversary of the events of October 1917. Eisenstein, one of the early contributors to *LEF*, created a patriotic masterpiece for the Soviet anniversary in his film *Ten Days That Shook the World*, but in Mayakovsky's poem the political enthusiasm seemed predictable and forced even to Soviet readers; in one of the Moscow papers it was dismissed as a "lackey's poem." The only personal note was his description of his life with the Briks during the hard winter of 1919–20 in Moscow, when Lili became ill and he searched desperately for fresh carrots to help cure her eyes.

After Stalin emerged as leader in the struggle for power that followed Lenin's death, the pressures on Mayakovsky and other "individualists" became even more intense. The proletarian writers' groups, the enemies of the Futurists, had now become more dominant in the formation of cultural policies. Mayakovsky still considered himself a spokesman for the government, even if critics attacked him for not exhibiting the correct proletarian class consciousness. Determinedly he appeared on public platforms reciting "Good!" before assemblies of Party activists at the Moscow Polytechnic Museum and the Leningrad Press House. The Little Opera Theater in Moscow staged a "collective verse-reading" of the poem. Although the Jubilee Year of 1927 was supposed to be a triumphant celebration of the first decade of Communism, the mood of the country was no longer heroic. Philistinism had triumphed, as in a malicious review of Mayakovsky's poem printed in a Rostov provincial newspaper after he read "Good!" in that city.

> For the tenth anniversary, working people of the Soviet Union have offered the republic valuable gifts: power stations, factories, railways.
> Mayakovsky's poem is not one of those gifts.

It is rather like gaudily painted jubilee triumphal gates and pavilions made of plywood and cardboard for the feast day.

Such a gate, as one knows, is not durable. A month or two will pass, the gate will get wet, the paint will peel off, the passers-by will look at it with indifference . . .

In the face of the savage newspaper attacks and bitter attempts to denigrate his work as a writer, Mayakovsky continued to insist that he would not be silenced. When he was accused of glorifying the poet —not the worker—in the new society, he answered angrily:

I don't give a damn whether I'm a poet. I am not a poet, but first and foremost a man who has placed his pen at the service—note, at the service—of the present hour, of the present reality and its guide—the Soviet government and the Party.

His situation was growing increasingly intolerable. It was, as Pasternak described it later, a time "when all poetry had ceased to exist, either his or anybody else's." Among the poets in the *LEF* group in these years, Aseyev was the only follower of Mayakovsky whose poetry was well received because of its patriotism and simplicity. In 1924 Aseyev achieved fame from his collection of anti-NEP poems, *Lyrical Digression*. The next year his "Twenty-six," a ballad about the twenty-six Red Commissars executed by the British in Baku, was published with great success.

At first Pasternak had stayed with *LEF*, even though he was personally disillusioned by Mayakovsky's propaganda poetry. But he became increasingly angry at the wranglings and disagreements within the group and, in an obvious effort to disassociate himself from the others, he wrote a letter to the critic V. Polonsky to say that he was ending his association with *LEF*. In his letter of June 1, 1927, Pasternak explained to Polonsky his reasons for breaking away.

I am leaving *LEF* definitely this time. I probably will formulate this in a letter to Vladimir Vladimirovich. You know

how much I like and still value him. Here is part of the letter
concerning yourself . . . "The way you turned out to appear in
Polonsky's eyes is the only way a poet can appear when he takes
as the basis LEFist aesthetics, LEFists' role in disputes concerning Esenin, LEF's polemical tricks, and above all LEFist artistic
perspectives and ideals. Glory to you as a poet, since the foolish-
ness of LEF's premises has been shown up by your example . . .
I consider LEF's existence, now as before, to be a logical puzzle.
The key to it has ceased to interest me." This break is not easy
for me. They do not want to understand me, and many others
do not want to understand either. I shall remain more lonely
than before.

Mayakovsky even quarreled with Shklovsky over New LEF at a
meeting at the Gendrikov apartment. In the middle of their argument,
when Lili tried to give her opinion, Shklovsky rudely tried to silence
her by saying, "Let the hostess pour tea." Lili was so hurt that
Mayakovsky told him, "You'd better leave."

In an attempt to escape the pressures on him in the Soviet Union,
Mayakovsky arranged another trip to France, and during the next
eighteen months Paris became almost a second home to him. Elsa
was there again, working on a novel published as Wild Strawberry,
about two girls very much like herself and Lili. After a number of
affairs during her months in Moscow, none of them very happy, she'd
returned to Paris to get a divorce from Triolet and decide what she
would do next. She was ready to pick up the old relationship with
Volodya, interpreting for him and going out to restaurants and cafés.
    Elsa remembered him leading processions of friends down the
streets of Montmartre, shouting jokes and trying to imitate popular
singers. He was spending many nights gambling and he was drinking
more. There were also lots of girls, often much younger than he was.
    Elsa began to be disturbed by his continual involvements, but
he wouldn't listen to her criticism. Once when she said something to

him about a poem he'd written—"We don't divide love into days/ Don't change the names of the lovers"—she asked him how he could write it with so many women around him, and he answered sharply, "I have never been unfaithful to Lilichka." Elsa shrugged.

Very well, it was so, but he himself demanded from women that absolute feeling that he wouldn't give them himself, since he would never be unfaithful to Lili. No woman could hope that he would ever separate from Lili. Meanwhile, when he happened to fall in love and the woman, out of her need for security, didn't want to risk an involvement knowing Mayakovsky would destroy her little life and knowing Mayakovsky would never take her into his big one, then he became desperate and furious.

In June 1928, the Central Committee of the Young Communist League contacted a number of organizations to try to set up a world tour for Mayakovsky, and he planned to go to Paris as the first stage of his journey when he was through with the usual Crimean reading tour that Lavut had arranged. He spent the rest of the summer in the country, and as the trip was delayed into the fall, he had some time in Moscow in September. He had begun thinking about the theater again, since his attempts to realize a number of film scenarios had been unsuccessful. He began to sketch out a play based on one of the scenarios, "Forget about the Hearth." It was to become his brilliant satirical play, *The Bedbug*.

He and Lili saw each other irregularly over the months, though their relationship went on as it had since his return from America. Their feelings toward each other at this time were captured in a photograph Rodchenko took of them in the apartment. It is the end of a summer luncheon and they're sitting opposite each other over a littered table in the dining room at Gendrikov. Two other people are sitting at the table behind them, but they are outside the current of tension between Volodya and Lili. He is in shirt-sleeves, staring across to her with a tight half-smile, as if he were waiting for her to respond to something he's said. Lili, in a stylish sundress and pearls, is staring down at her plate, her thin body tense, as if she were warding him off. Their love had become a series of uncomfortable evasions.

Lili began working on another film as co-director with Vitaly Zhemchuzhny, a half-documentary, half-parody called *The Glass Eye*. They chose at random a pretty young actress named Veronica (Nora) Polonskaya to play the heroine of the parody on commercial romantic films that was the second part of their scenario. When Mayakovsky left for Berlin and Paris on October 8, 1928, both he and Lili were preoccupied with their own work. It was Lili's most ambitious project in years, a complex scenario juxtaposing a narrative film with a "visual poem." Brik was also beginning his most successful commercial projects as a writer, creating opera libretti and film scenarios, like the one for Pudovkin's *Heir of Genghis Khan*.

Mayakovsky's letters to Lili at this time were concerned mostly with his attempts to buy a car. He was trying to sell a film script to René Clair to get the money for it, but he went ahead anyway when Clair turned down his scenario. On November 10 he wired Lili that he'd bought a gray Renault, "a fine specimen," and two days later he wrote a long letter about the car, going on to say that he was working on the play, and asking her to tell Taras Kostrov, editor of *The Young Guard*, who had commissioned him to write some propaganda poems for his magazine, that he was finishing an assignment for him. The letter ended with a subdued and enigmatic paragraph saying that he'd tell her what was happening to him when he got back to Moscow. "My life is somewhat strange, without events, but with numerous details. It's not material for a letter, but only to tell you."

What was happening to Mayakovsky found its voice in his poetry, and what he wrote for Kostrov, along with the propaganda pieces, was one of the freshest poems he'd written in years, a lyric, excited poem called "Letter from Paris to Comrade Kostrov on the Nature of Love."

To love
      means this:
            to run
deep into a yard
          and, until the rook-black night,
chop wood
      shining with an ax,
playing
    with my
        strength.
Love
   for us
      is no arbored paradise—
to us
   love
      says, humming,
that the heart's
        stalled motor
has begun working
          again.
You
   have broken the thread
            to Moscow.
Years—
   distance.
How can I
     possibly explain
         to you
this state of mind? . . .
The square begins its noise;
the carriages move;
I walk
   jotting some verses
in my notebook.

Cars
> dash
>> along the street
but they can't knock me down.
They understand,
>> the smart ones:
the man is
> in ecstasy.

The poem was inspired by a girl named Tatiana Yakovleva, whom Elsa had met just before Volodya's arrival in Paris. Looking at Tatiana, Elsa said, "You're as tall as Mayakovsky," and decided to introduce them as a kind of joke. But, at his first glance, Mayakovsky had fallen in love.

Tatiana, who was only eighteen, seemed to Elsa to be little more than a fashionable beauty. "Tatiana was in full swing . . . She had a youthful exuberance, an affirmation of life that brimmed over; she talked chokingly fast, swam and played tennis, counted her suitors . . ." Elsa was obviously jealous of Tatiana and Volodya, and she envied what she thought was Tatiana's easy life. To Elsa, in her thirties, her marriage to Triolet over, her career as a writer uncertain, unsure if she would even stay in Paris, Tatiana must have represented many things that Elsa herself had been forced to do without in the interminable years she'd lived in shabby hotel rooms teaching herself to write. Tatiana herself says simply, "I wasn't a beauty as he described, but I was very pretty."

Tatiana's family, like so many others, had been broken apart by the struggles in Russia during the civil war. Her father, an architect who designed theaters, left in 1918 for the United States, where he had a difficult life as a factory engineer. She was only eight when her parents separated. In 1921 her mother married again, but her stepfather died of malnutrition. Her mother married again in 1924, but the family was still near starvation, and when Tatiana contracted tuberculosis, she left to join an uncle, Alexander Yakovlev, who had a successful career as a painter in Paris. Tatiana's grandmother was already there, and Tatiana found a poorly paid job making hats. Elsa had met her at the apartment of a friend a few days before Mayakovsky's arrival, and then introduced her to Mayakovsky at the office of a doctor, another friend, who was treating Tatiana for bronchitis. As Mayakovsky wrote in the poem,

> Imagine:
>   a beauty
>   enters the hall,
> framed in furs
>   and necklaces.
> I
>   took this beauty
>   and said:
> —did I speak right
>   or wrong?—
> Comrade, I'm
>   from Russia,
> famous in my own country,
> I've seen
>   more beautiful girls,
> I've seen
>   more slender girls.
> Girls
>   like poets.
> I'm smart
>   and loud-voiced;
> I can talk your head off—
> you only agree
>   to listen.

Mayakovsky took her home in a cab and proposed to her on his knees while they were still riding in the taxi. He was wild and impetuous, insisting in a frenzy that he'd fallen in love with her. When he took her to dinner he found out something else about her, that she knew the poems of Akhmatova and Blok by heart and that she loved poetry as much as he did. Tatiana remembered: "Mayakovsky couldn't believe a White Russian girl living in Paris knew Russian poetry as he did. I think this was really the beginning of everything between us."

As they sat at the table in the restaurant, he recited his poetry to her, political pieces like "Left March," and she answered by reciting other poems back to him. He flattered her by saying that she had a better memory than he did, and he told friends afterward that she had an absolute ear for poetry, just as a musician has absolute pitch. They went out together the following day, and she helped him buy a knit suit for Lili. They were together every day, meeting in cafés and restaurants, once at the opera. Tatiana had to lie to her family, because she knew they would be upset if they found out she was seeing him.

It was almost as disturbing for Elsa as it was for Tatiana's family, but at this moment her own life suddenly changed when she met Louis Aragon, the French Communist and writer who was to become her second husband. She saw Tatiana with Mayakovsky, but she still couldn't accept the seriousness of his new love.

> As Tatiana was Volodya's friend, I had to take her into account, even if I was strongly irritated that she both over-estimated and underestimated his love. But one must remember how young she was, and how short a time she knew him. Besides, he was soon to leave for Moscow. They knew each other only three or four months. Naturally she assumed that she could be the only love in Mayakovsky's life. His frenzy, his possessive-ness, his wild desire to take her alone, or together with Paris, how could she know that it wasn't the first or the last time he'd felt that way in his life?

It was in his lyric poetry that Mayakovsky was completely open, and as it was only to Lili that he'd written love poems before, so it was only to Tatiana that he wrote love poems now. He was writing propaganda verses in Paris, reading them to Tatiana as he was composing them, and then one night in November he filled nine pages in his notebook with two poems to her, one the "letter" to Kostrov on the nature of love, and the other "A Letter to Tatiana Yakovleva," a love poem to her that was one of the most tender and gentle poems he had ever written. The next day as they were having lunch at the restaurant La Petite Chaumière he read the poem to her. He was trying to persuade her to come back to Moscow with him, and the "letter" was part of his persuasion.

> You alone
> > equal me in height.
> Stand beside me now,
> > > forehead to forehead,
> and about that
> > (oh so) important night
> let's talk
> > like human beings . . .
> You and I
> > are needed in Moscow,
> there's a lack
> > of the long-legged.
> It isn't for you,
> > who's walked
> through snow and typhus with those legs,
> to give them here
> > for caresses
> at banquets
> > with oil magnates.
> You furrow your forehead—
> > > don't be afraid—
> eyebrow half circles straighten to lines.

Come here,
>   or to the crossroad
of my big
>   and
>   clumsy hands.
You don't want to?
>   Then stay behind and spend the winter,
and that
>   insult
>   we'll put to the general account.
Just the same,
>   sometime or other,
>   I'll take you,
alone
>   or together with Paris!

After he read the poems he'd written to Tatiana for groups of friends in Paris, she asked him not to publish them, but he was careless of any consequences that might come of his new feelings. Tatiana was overwhelmed by the strength of his passion.

> He had a talent for violent love. I have never known a man with a greater capacity for love—his love was an explosion. What he said in the poem about love, "If you can control this, then try . . ." It was true.

Elsa, who heard him read the poems about Tatiana, was frightened. She understood how catastrophic the affair would be. His only word to Lili was an answer to a telegram she'd sent after he bought the car; at the last minute she'd wired him to buy a Ford instead of a Renault. He replied on November 19, 1928: CHANGE IMPOSSIBLE. CAR READY. SOON GOING TO MOSCOW. KISS. YOUR SJEN.

Mayakovsky was so overwrought that Tatiana was confused by him. She had no idea of the pressures on him in the Soviet Union, but she knew she didn't want to return there. She didn't understand how he could be so deeply involved with Lili, and she wasn't sure of herself or of him. Before Mayakovsky entered her life she'd had many suitors, some of whom she continued to see between her meetings with Mayakovsky. His visa was expiring, he had to leave, they were together constantly, she couldn't decide what to do. There was no question of his staying with her in Paris; she would have to live with him in Moscow as his wife. He finally had to go back without her, but before departing he left money and a series of little cards with a florist so that every Sunday Tatiana would have a flowering plant from him in the months they'd be separated. (She had told him she didn't like cut flowers—they reminded her of death.) Then, despairingly, he left on the train for Moscow.

20

Drawing of Tatiana Yakovleva, 1929

Citizens! My people! My own people! Dear ones! How did you get here? So many of you! . . . Why am I alone in the cage? Dear ones, my people! Come in with me! Why am I suffering?

THE BEDBUG

WHEN HE WAS IN PARIS, MAYAKOVSKY HAD SENT "Letter from Paris to Comrade Kostrov on the Nature of Love" to Lili and asked her to pass it on to the magazine. She thought it was an excellent poem and was unconcerned with the emotional involvement it suggested, shrugging it off as merely another flirtation. But when he returned to Moscow and read "A Letter to Tatiana Yakovleva" to Lili, she cried as she listened, knowing that he had been unfaithful to her.

> When he came back to Moscow and read his poem about Tatiana Yakovleva, I wept a little. It wasn't pleasant for me to hear. Because once he'd written, "Where in my songs/was I false to my love?" In some way he had been unfaithful and it was hard for me, of course. But my mood passed very quickly. My character is light . . .

Lili's sadness didn't pass quickly. She was extremely upset. She had tried to set up boundaries to their relationship, but they were boundaries that neither of them could accept. Mayakovsky had broken through them in his unhappy search for someone he could love, and she had broken through them as she moved from man to man, pretending for a moment that she loved each of them. Love as he defined it, with its possessiveness, hadn't worked for her. Love as she defined it, as an association of two free individuals, didn't work for either of them.

Kostrov went ahead and printed the "Letter from Paris" poem in the January issue of *The Young Guard*, the Communist youth magazine. There was an immediate angry response from Mayakovsky's enemies. During this period the entire resources of the Soviet Union were being organized behind the first Five Year Plan, and the romantic individualism of the poem was in opposition to the whole direction of the new cultural policy. Mayakovsky had already been through so many storms of criticism that he shrugged this one off as well and immersed himself in the final work on his play.

At the end of December 1928, he read the play to Meyerhold, and the response was direct and enthusiastic. *The Bedbug* was accepted for immediate production. This time Mayakovsky and Meyerhold seemed to have been able to work without unintentionally getting in each other's way. With the same persistence with which he had driven himself to finish the play, Volodya persuaded people to work with the production, whether they wanted to or not. Part of the decor was to be done by Rodchenko, but they needed designers for the opening scenes. Mayakovsky rushed off to the Herzen House, went to the table of three young painters who were sitting in the canteen, and told them he'd written a play that Meyerhold was about to produce. "Will you help with the designs?" They tried to protest, saying that they'd never done anything for the stage, but he refused to listen. The next day they went to the theater, read the play, and agreed to work, "terrified."

He turned to Dmitri Shostakovich for the music. Shostakovich at this time was a twenty-two-year-old whose compositions as a student, among them his first symphony, had already attracted much attention. It was Meyerhold who contacted Shostakovich and arranged for him to meet Mayakovsky. Later the composer remembered that Mayakovsky asked him, "Do you like firemen's bands?" Shostakovich replied that sometimes he liked them and sometimes not. Mayakovsky said, "I like firemen's music best of all, and such music is needed for *The Bedbug*." When Shostakovich played his "firemen's music" for Mayakovsky, he said only, "Well, in general it will do," which the composer decided was a compliment.

Lavut had booked a short lecture tour through the Ukraine, but after the first two performances Mayakovsky complained of a bad throat and hurried back to Moscow, canceling the rest of the appearances. He wrote Tatiana that he didn't want to delay "as much as an hour" reading her letters, and at the theater he was closely involved in the production of *The Bedbug*. He told Tatiana,

> I work until my eyes go hazy and my back breaks. Besides writing I now have daily readings and rehearsals of the play. I hope to complete my work here in a month. I will rest then. When I am altogether tired, I say to myself, "Tatiana," and again, animal-like, bite into the paper.

For Meyerhold, Mayakovsky had written a play that was bitterly tragic, yet one that could be played as a wildly comic farce at the same time. It was a biting, relentless satire on the grasping vulgarity of the new Soviet society and a pained, despairing glance at the future he was helping to create. In his propaganda poetry he had begun to lie, he had turned out poems without thought or meaning, dully tramping off after each new order of the Party. In *The Bedbug* he expressed himself in a voice that was completely honest.

What was clear in the play was that he had misgivings about what was happening in the Soviet Union. He was dedicated to the ideals of Communism, but something had gone wrong, and he created a play that expressed criticism of the realities of the "new life" while staying within the context of Soviet art in the early years of the Revolution. The complexity and imagination of his "farce" made *The Bedbug* a masterpiece, one of the century's most important theatrical experiments.

The plot was strong and effective. A young, vulgar, socially ambitious member of the working class during NEP is going to be married to a girl who is a cashier and manicurist in a beauty parlor. For her sake he changes his name from Ivan Prisypkin to the more elegant-sounding Pierre Skripkin, shops for new clothes, leaves his comrades in their workers' hostel where they've been living together, and deserts his old love, a poor girl who shoots herself (not fatally) in despair. The wedding is hopelessly drunken and disorderly, and in the middle of it the bride's veil catches fire, the building where they're celebrating burns to the ground, and everyone perishes.

Fifty years later, when Communism has been established everywhere on earth, a group of workers finds Prisypkin frozen in a block of ice in the ruins of the cellar, where he'd fallen in a drunken stupor as the house collapsed. The Institute of Human Resurrection desires to bring him to life, but the experiment is so dangerous—who knows what diseases he might be carrying?—that the newspapers of the world, all Communist now, are asked if the experiment should go ahead. They approve and the hero is brought back to life, and brought to life with him is a bedbug which was on him when he died. The Institute, having revived him, has no further use for him.

After a period of freedom which is nearly disastrous for the authorities, Prisypkin is turned over to the zoo, where he's put in a cage labeled PHILISTINUS VULGARIS. His use, so far as they can determine, is to be a home for the bedbug, which is the pride of the zoo. As the director says eloquently, holding the bedbug in a special glass case,

> We have captured a very rare specimen of an extinct insect which was extremely popular in the early days of the century. Our city may be proud of itself—scientists and tourists will come here in throngs . . . Right here in my hands I hold the only extant specimen of the *Bedbugus normalis* . . .

Because Prisypkin has found the new society a total disappointment, he must be isolated. In the brief time that he was allowed to live among other people, he began to infect them with his degenerate habits, like drinking beer, crooning love songs, and dancing the foxtrot and the Charleston. He has been put in a cage where he just wants to eat and drink, dance and sing, play his guitar and read romantic novels filled with dreams and roses. When he asks for the novels the elderly attendant, who is the working-class girl friend he deserted, though he doesn't recognize her, comes back with a bundle of books.

I don't know if these will suit you. They didn't have what you asked for, and nobody knows anything about it. Only the manuals on horticulture say anything about roses, and fantasies are mentioned only in the medical books, in the section on dreaming. But now here are two very interesting books from about the same period. A translation from the English. Herbert Hoover—*An Ex-President Speaks* . . .

A large part of the effect of the play is the unending rattle of jokes that makes it possible for the audience to avoid facing any confusion they might feel at his bitter satirical jibes. Hoover was, of course, President of the United States at that time, and Mayakovsky lightened some of the tension by joking at Hoover's possible inability to stay in office. The other book that was brought to him is "by somebody named Mussolini. The title is *Letters from Exile*."

But the satire cut the other way as well. Prisypkin complains that he can't dance any more and he's told that he can witness one of the dance exhibitions of the new Communist state. He complains, "What *is* all that? What did we fight for? Why did we spill our blood if I, a leader in our new society, can't enjoy myself doing the new dance steps, and so on?" He's answered: "Tomorrow I'll take you to see a dance performed. Ten thousand male and female workers will move across the public square. It will be a joyous rehearsal of a new system for field work on the farms."

A worldwide social revolution has been achieved, but the revolution of the spirit is still missing. Unlike *Mystery-Bouffe* and "About This," which were also concerned with the future Communist utopia, *The Bedbug* didn't idealize the future. Now Mayakovsky had placed himself on the streets of the commune, and for the first time, when both the private and the public poet were fully engaged, he established his most profound link with his audience.

In the last scene Prisypkin is being exhibited to a group of visitors as he lies back on his bed in his cage, drinking vodka, scratching, and singing his songs. He is taken out of the cage to entertain the crowd, and he stands with his back to the theater audience, beginning to play his guitar. Then he turns suddenly, sees the people in the theater behind him, smiles joyously, pushes the zoo director aside, and rushes to the footlights of the stage to implore the audience:

> Citizens! My people! My own people! Dear ones! How did you get here? So many of you! . . . Why am I alone in the cage? Dear ones, my people! Come in with me! Why am I suffering? Comrades!

He is dragged off by the zoo attendants, the director apologizing to the audience as the play ends, with the orchestra banging out the firemen's march.

On a symbolic level, the conclusion of *The Bedbug* is a brilliant dramatization of Mayakovsky's emotional state at this time. He has matured beyond the narcissism and posturing of his first play, *Vladimir Mayakovsky: A Tragedy*. The easy political slogans and anarchy of *Mystery-Bouffe* have been replaced with a portrayal of a society seen in human terms. From the idealistic vision in "About This" six years before, where his hope that resurrection into the future commune as a humble worker would reunite him with his beloved on the paths of the zoo, Mayakovsky has moved his worker, *Philistinus vulgaris*, into one of the zoo cages where he is captive, unloved, and alone, a victim of the technological society the poet had once welcomed so eagerly as a Futurist, but which now appears totally depersonalized and inhumane. Communism was still a religion for Mayakovsky, but even as a "True Believer" he let himself reveal his doubts about the government in his last plays. The repressions of the Soviet regime were coming closer to him all the time.

Whatever his inner misgivings about the society, he was now one of the leading figures in Soviet literature, the most gifted Soviet theater ensemble was using all its resources to bring his play to life, and he was sure of a large audience. The production was ready on February 13, 1929, only a few weeks after they'd begun rehearsals, and the audience's response was loud and enthusiastic. At whatever level they chose to take it—as a burlesque of NEP times or a bitter, half-veiled protest against the government—the play was an immediate success. Mayakovsky lurked backstage during the performance and had to be pulled out to the footlights by the actors when the audience insisted that he take a bow. The people around him were surprised to see that he was nervous. The next day, without waiting for reviews, he was already hurrying back to Paris and Tatiana.

Mayakovsky stayed in Paris until the end of April. He was with Tatiana almost continually, trying to convince her to return with him. Her family had reluctantly accepted the situation, and she and Mayakovsky were able to travel together to Le Touquet-Paris-Plage, near Deauville, where he spent his days gambling. For the first time there were no letters to Lili, although she was trying to get some money for him from Gosizdat and she wired him from week to week with details. He began one of his usual letters to her, complaining about Paris, but he never sent it. Tatiana still was hesitating; she was not sure of Mayakovsky or of what she'd find in Moscow. He wanted her to return there and marry him; she wanted him to marry her in Paris, and then they would return together. Elsa was dismayed and frightened by their affair.

Tatiana had continued to see other men when Mayakovsky was working on *The Bedbug* in Moscow, and she wasn't able to keep them all at a distance when he returned. Once, after seeing her home, Mayakovsky told Elsa he had glimpsed a man waiting for her in a dark entranceway, and spying on her a few minutes later, he saw them kissing. In despair he told Elsa, and she tried to console him, but he said, "No, it's finished. A broken cup can be glued, but nevertheless it's broken."

In confusion Mayakovsky left Paris for a few days in March and went alone to Nice on a gambling trip. While there, he met a friend from Russia, the painter Yury Annenkov.

> I'd been walking on a very old street leading to the sea, and I noticed a familiar profile. I opened my mouth to say hello as Mayakovsky said to me, "Have you a thousand francs?" He ex-

plained he was coming back from Monte Carlo and he'd lost everything gambling. "This France, it's a disgusting country," he concluded. I gave him a thousand francs. "I'm hungry," he added. "If you give me two hundred francs more, I'll invite you for a bouillabaisse." I gave him the money, and we went to a cozy, fashionable restaurant near the beach. The bouillabaisse was remarkable. We talked about the Soviet Union. Mayakovsky asked when I thought I'd return to Moscow. I replied that I'd stopped thinking about it because I'd decided to remain a painter. He shook my shoulder and then said in a shrill voice, "But I'm going back, because I've stopped being a poet."

Then there was a dramatic scene. Mayakovsky began sobbing and whispered, "Now I've become a clerk." The people in the restaurant, frightened by his sobbing, ran over to us. "What's wrong? What's happening?" Mayakovsky replied, "Nothing happened. A little fishbone has stuck in my throat."

We left the restaurant and shook hands. I said, "I hope to see you in Paris." Mayakovsky, "Of course, in Paris."

Back in Paris again, he and Tatiana were as inseparable as they'd been before his short trip. He had already introduced her to all his friends, among them Ilya Ehrenburg, and she had introduced him to some of the people she knew. Through her uncle, who was extremely successful during this period, she met people like Chaliapin and Diaghilev. On March 20, Lili had wired him that Gosizdat had said it was impossible to send money out of the country, but Mayakovsky stayed on in Paris, not realizing that the first steps had already been taken to force him back to the Soviet Union. Tatiana's family had finally turned to him for help, asking him to arrange an exit visa for her sister so she could join them in Paris, and he hastened to do what he could. It was a serious mistake. Trying to get someone out of the Soviet Union, particularly someone from a family with known White sympathies, was inexcusable for a man in his position. He was, after all, officially in Paris as a correspondent for the Communist youth newspaper.

At the end of April 1929, when his visa expired, he was forced to go back to Moscow. Tatiana promised that she would marry him in October. Mayakovsky was to come to Paris for her and they'd be married there, and then they'd return to Moscow. Almost as an engagement party they had a farewell luncheon for friends the day he was to leave.

When he returned to Moscow Lili was disturbed and anxious. She hadn't realized how serious the affair was. There had been so many girls before that she hadn't taken Tatiana seriously, but now he was planning to marry her. There had never been the thought before that he might marry someone else or become seriously involved, as Osip was with Genya. Lili argued with Mayakovsky, saying that Tatiana would never come to Moscow, that she could never be sympathetic to the Soviet government. But Mayakovsky insisted that she would return to the Soviet Union with him in October. Lili lost her temper and began breaking china.

She was also feeling other pressures. One of her lovers was a high-level official in the secret police, Yakov Savlovich Agranov. Lili learned that agents were following Mayakovsky and Tatiana in Paris. Mayakovsky regarded the secret police as his friends—he and Osip had always welcomed them at the apartment—and he couldn't believe that they would take action against him. The Briks must have been approached and asked what they knew of Mayakovsky's plans, if not on an official level, certainly on a personal level through their close contacts with the members of the police.

Through all the confusion Mayakovsky went on writing, as he'd done when he returned from Paris the previous winter. Encouraged by the success of *The Bedbug*, he rushed to finish another play, driving himself with the same furious determination, trying to earn money for his marriage to Tatiana. He continued to write and wire her, his letters often tired and desperate, but still clinging to the promise of their meeting in October.

> I am only now beginning to work: I shall be writing *The Bathhouse* . . . Please do not grumble and do not reproach me—

I've experienced so much unpleasantness—both great and small
—that you must not be angry with me.

Again he wrote: "I can't imagine life without you after October (the
date we fixed). In September I'll begin constructing wings so that I
can fly to you."

Despite the success of *The Bedbug*, Mayakovsky found himself
more vehemently criticized than ever before when he appeared in
front of audiences. At readings hecklers jeered when he said his reason
for not joining the Party was that he had "acquired a lot of habits that
cannot be reconciled with organized activity." He was forced to
account for having the large apartment on Gendrikov when he was
so often away from Moscow on his trips abroad. There was criticism
of the Waterman fountain pen he always carried in his pocket (a gift
from Tatiana), and there were pointed remarks about his tailored
English suits and new French car, which he had to bend himself
almost double to climb into.

The little gray Renault was especially difficult for many people
to accept. It was a period when there were almost no private cars in
the Soviet Union, and Mayakovsky not only had a car, he also had
a chauffeur to drive it, since he couldn't drive himself. Demyan Bedny,
a powerful figure in the Proletarian Writers' Group, said to him, "It
looks like you've turned bourgeois, driving your own car." When
Mayakovsky answered, "As far as I know, you've been using a car
for years," Bedny said sharply, "Yes, but it's a state car, not a private
car."

The car also caused difficulties for Lili. She used it to go to the
film studios when she was looking for work, and they told her that
since she had a car she obviously didn't need a job; there were others
who needed work more than she did. It seemed to Mayakovsky's
vociferous critics that he was becoming bourgeois, and—as always with
him—he'd chosen the wrong moment to do it. It was futile for them
to criticize him for bourgeois tendencies, since he was incapable of
becoming something he wasn't, but he was as stubbornly individualist

as ever, and his enemies never let up their incessant drumming on his insistence on standing alone.

He'd become more isolated with the collapse of his *LEF* group and the magazine *New LEF*, even though he was no longer acting as editor when the magazine ceased publication. But he was still loyal to Brik. In the last issue of *New LEF* in 1928, Mayakovsky wrote an article describing how he'd revised the poem "Homewards," which he'd first written on the ship bringing him back from the United States, a poem expressing his dedication to Communism.

> Proletarians
>   arrive at communism
>   from below—
> by the low way of mines,
>   sickles,
>   and pitchforks—
> but I,
>   from poetry's skies,
>   plunge into communism,
> because
>   without it
>   I feel no love.

When "Homewards" was published in *The Young Guard* in 1926, its concluding lines were

> I want to be understood by my country,
> and if I am not—
>   never mind,
> I will pass
>   over my native land
> sideways,
>   as a slanted rain passes.

Brik had criticized this as being too individualistic and inconsistent with the ideology of the poem as a whole, and when
"Homewards" was next published, the concluding lines were dropped.
Mayakovsky wouldn't listen to the din of his many critics, but in 1928
he admitted that he'd accepted censorship from his friend Brik, and
he even joked that

> I will pass
> over my native land
> sideways,
> as a slanted rain passes,

was one of his more sentimental images; "people reached for their
handkerchiefs."

Yet even Brik's aesthetic theories no longer had their tight hold
on Mayakovsky. If the discussion turned to the insignificance of
poetry, Mayakovsky would say that such talk was really nonsense, "but
useful for the purpose of revolutionizing art." Brik adjusted to the new
situation with his usual agility. When Mayakovsky showed signs of
breaking free of his theories, Osip proceeded to modify them. Shklovsky
is said to have joked that if they ever cut off Brik's legs, he would
simply decide that he found it more convenient that way.

Through the spring and early summer Mayakovsky and Tatiana
continued to write each other. He was driving himself to finish the
play, he was desperate to get back to her, he was waiting for October.
Life is not always what it pretends to be. Tatiana, who was traveling, wrote her mother at this time, perhaps to reassure her, that she
hadn't committed herself to Mayakovsky yet. "There are an awful lot
of dramas in my life. Even if I wanted to be with M., then what
would happen to Ilya, and besides him there's still another. It's a
charmed circle." Meanwhile, Volodya was wiring Tatiana, "Am very
depressed . . . impossibly depressed . . . absolutely depressed . . .
yearning for you unprecedentedly . . . yearning for you regularly and
recently not even regularly but even more often." He was begging

her humorously to come back to Russia as an "engineer" so they could migrate to one of the distant regions of the Soviet Union together. His letters couldn't have been more ardent, completely hiding the fact that he had thrown himself into a new love affair. After he came back from his second trip to Paris, he met the young actress Nora Polonskaya, who had been in the film, *The Glass Eye*, that Lili had worked on the previous summer. They had met when he was gambling at the race track. She was married to one of the actors in the Moscow Art Theater and was struggling with her own career, but Mayakovsky threw himself at her with some of the same impetuousness he'd shown toward Tatiana only a few months before. By the end of the spring they had become lovers.

To Lili his new affair meant that he had never really been in love with Tatiana. She wasn't jealous of Nora, who seemed to be only one of a succession of pretty young girls he'd been involved with over the years. But why did he act that way? Had he meant what he said to Elsa, that it was over for him when he saw the other man waiting for Tatiana in the doorway, that "a broken cup can be glued, but nevertheless it's broken"? Or was he so unstable and his need for love so desperate that he had to turn to someone in the months that he was separated from Tatiana, since Tatiana herself still seemed to hesitate, despite their "October promise" to each other? Now, even though the Briks were in the apartment with him, he still felt desperately alone.

Lavut, his agent, had scheduled a series of readings in the summer, first in the Caucasus and then as usual in the Crimea. He noticed the difference in Mayakovsky the first day they met on the tour, July 15, 1929. Mayakovsky was to have met Nora near Sochi, but she never showed up; he learned later that she was sick with malaria. He was in such low spirits that Lavut was unable to distract or entertain him, and in his public readings he was more easily irritated than usual by the hecklers in the crowd. In the Crimea he read fragments of *The Bedbug* and tried to follow it with audience discussion. One critic was so outspoken that Mayakovsky invited him to come onstage, where he stood up beside the poet and made a particularly venomous speech attacking the play, insisting it misrepresented socialism. Mayakovsky kept his temper with great difficulty, and when he began his reply and someone tried to interrupt him, he protested angrily, "I kept quiet! Now you have to sit quietly and listen to me!" A group in the audience began to clamor, and Mayakovsky turned on them, so furious that he broke out in sweat, and insisted in a tremendous voice, "There isn't a person born yet who could shout me down!"

In Moscow on August 25, 1929, he met his friend Vasya Katanyan, who went with him to the Dynamo Stadium for a reading at the Pioneer Rally. Mayakovsky was sullen in the car, but the sight of the amphitheater full of marching children and thousands of people waving red handkerchiefs raised his spirits briefly. He said to Katanyan, "What's happening here! This is socialism already! To think that fifty thousand people have come to look at some children . . ." He disappeared into a small radio booth to read his poems, his voice booming over dozens of loudspeakers, and when he came out again, he said with elation to Katanyan, "To write an excellent poem and read it here—then one can die!"

Mayakovsky finished writing *The Bathhouse* on September 15, 1929, and as soon as he was through with it, he hurried to make arrangements for the trip to Paris. October was only weeks away, but he was nervous and anxious, almost as if sensing that something was going to go wrong. Then Tatiana got a hopeless letter from him, the saddest he had ever written her. His application for a visa had been refused. He was not permitted to leave the Soviet Union.

21

Osip Brik, Lili Brik, and Mayakovsky, 1929

Listen,
            comrades of posterity,
to the agitator,
                    the rabble-rouser.
Stifling
        the torrents of poetry,
I'll step over
            my volumes of lyrics;
as a living being,
                addressing the living.

"AT THE TOP OF MY VOICE"

A s USUAL, MAYAKOVSKY RESPONDED TO HIS UN-
happiness by throwing himself more intensely into his
work. Perhaps he thought the refusal of a visa was only
temporary and he would be permitted to leave after a
short delay. However confused his emotional situation had become,
he was clinging to the idea of marrying Tatiana.

On September 22, Mayakovsky read *The Bathhouse* aloud to
about thirty people in the Brik apartment. On the next day, he
read the play to Meyerhold's theatrical company. It was a tremendous
success. As Mayakovsky read, there was laughter, shouting, excitement, and applause. Then everyone turned to Meyerhold, since he
would decide about accepting it for production. Meyerhold sighed
and said only one word, "Molière," and the excitement broke out all
over again. The writer Mikhail Zoshchenko, who was also there, was
swept along in the general enthusiasm, but he was worried about the
play at the same time. His first impression was that it was theatrically
clumsy, but not wanting to hurt Mayakovsky—there was always the
possibility, Zoshchenko thought, that he didn't understand something
in it—he agreed with the others.

There was even talk that the Moscow Art Theater would produce *The Bathhouse*, though Mayakovsky had already given it to
Meyerhold's company. Nora Polonskaya's actor husband, who knew
nothing of his wife's involvement with Mayakovsky, had come with
her to listen to the reading. He liked the play and suggested to his
associates at the Art Theater that it should be staged there, and on
October 2, 1929, several representatives from the theater came to the
Gendrikov apartment to talk with Mayakovsky.

Whatever Lili had said about the "new marriage" Chernyshevsky
described in his novel *What Is to Be Done?*, in which neither person
was to stand in the way of the other's happiness, she felt jealous and

possessive of Mayakovsky and hoped that his marriage to Tatiana would not take place. Despite Lili's arguments with him, only the authorities' decision had stopped it. She must have felt that the work with the new play would make him forget the worst of the pain, as "About This" had taken him through the crisis when they'd quarreled six years before. Then on October 11, just as he was about to leave for a series of readings, there was a final blow. It was less than a month since he had written to Tatiana telling her that he wouldn't be able to come to her in Paris. Lili remembered:

On the evening of October 11, 1929, we sat quietly in the dining room of the apartment waiting with Volodya for the car that would take him to the station to catch the train for Leningrad. There were several readings planned. On the floor stood his suitcase, packed and locked.

Just then a letter from Elsa was delivered to me. I opened the letter, and as usual, I began reading it aloud. Among other things, Elsa wrote that Tatiana, whom he'd met in Paris and whom he still loved, was marrying a viscount. She was to be married in church in a white gown, carrying orange blossoms. Elsa was terribly worried that Volodya might get to know about it and kick up a fuss that could damage or even break up the marriage. At the end of the letter Elsa asked me not to say anything to Volodya. But the letter had already been read. Mayakovsky grew gloomy. He stood up and said, "Well, I'm going now." "Where shall you go?" we asked him; the car hadn't yet arrived. But he took his suitcase, kissed me, and left. When the chauffeur returned, he told us that he'd met Vladimir Vladimirovich on the street, that he threw his suitcase into the car, climbed inside, and swore violently at the driver, which he'd never done before. Then he was silent, but when they came to the station he said, "I'm sorry, Comrade Gamazin, don't be angry at me. My heart is breaking."

I worried all that night about Volodya. In the morning I telephoned him at the Hotel Europe in Leningrad. I told him that I was very anxious about him. He answered with a phrase from an old Russian saying, "This horse has died. I'll begin riding another." Don't worry, he told me.

"But perhaps you'd like me to join you?" He wanted that very much. I left that evening. He was so terribly glad to see me that he didn't let me move away from him a single step. We went together to all his performances, always in large halls crowded with students.

At the beginning of October one of Tatiana's suitors, a young Frenchman, Vicomte DuPlessix, had come back to Paris from his diplomatic post in Warsaw and asked her to marry him. She'd been badly shaken by Mayakovsky's difficulties with the visa, she was no longer sure that he'd be able to come to her, and her mother was as opposed to Mayakovsky as she had been when the affair started. Tatiana hesitated, and then told DuPlessix she would be his wife. They planned the ceremony for December.

Lili wrote later:

> After a time it was evident that the pain ceased for Volodya, but his pride continued to bother him. He felt himself foolish in his own eyes and before me. He'd told me so many times, "She's ours. She'll never stay abroad."
>
> Mayakovsky often felt lonely, but it wasn't because people didn't love him, or because he had no friends or needed more recognition. His poems were published, people read his work and listened to him in crowded halls. There were countless numbers of people who were devoted to him and loved him. But it was all only a drop in the ocean for him. He was, as Brik said, a man who had "an insatiable thief in his soul." He felt it was necessary that he should be read by the people who didn't read him, that he should be heard by the audiences who stayed away from his readings, and that he should be loved by the woman who, it seemed to him, didn't love him. There was nothing to be done.

He had been deeply wounded, but as he'd done before, he tried to throw off his unhappiness. The night after their return from Leningrad on October 14, he met with writers and artists from his old *LEF* group in the apartment on Gendrikov. He proposed that they organize into a new group called REF, making one of his strong speeches and holding his own in the discussions, but to the relentless critics who opposed him, it represented a continuation of the old "literary salon," with Mayakovsky and Brik again working outside of the Party. The new group came into being only a short time.

Lili stayed at the apartment as he went on with his tour, helping him come out of the worst of his depression. On November 25, 1929, *The Bedbug* was premièred in Leningrad, and despite some criticism, it repeated its Moscow success. Then, in what would seem to be an emotional reaction to Tatiana's rejection, Mayakovsky decided to organize a display of his work, an exhibition that would include all of his books, posters, advertising slogans, Rosta cartoons, announcements for his films—everything he had done, from early editions of "The Cloud in Trousers" to Mosselprom matchboxes. Hoping to force his critics to see what he had accomplished, he called the exhibition "Twenty Years of Work," though the period covered was some years less. He rushed into his latest project with his usual impetuousness. The exhibition wasn't an official event, but he'd been given space for it in the Writers' Union building the next month. Living with Mayakovsky at the apartment, Lili realized how important the exhibition was to him, and she helped him gather materials. By the end of the month, he was working day and night preparing the exhibition, pasting up albums, working out displays, filling a large book with the questions he'd been asked at his readings.

Despite the fact that his work was going well, his friends were concerned about him, and on the evening of December 30 they crowded into the apartment to give him a party, telling him to stay in his room on Lyubyansky Passage and not come back until they'd got everything ready. Meyerhold and his theater company had brought props, make-up, and costumes, and everyone dressed up in shawls and capes. The table was moved out of the dining room so there'd be more room, old posters were put up on the walls everywhere in the apartment, and on the ceiling they'd pasted a long banner running from one wall to the other, reading M-A-Y-A-K-O-V-S-K-Y. Aseyev impersonated one of the critics who had worn down Volodya at many meetings and conferences by delivering a wandering, pompously garbled speech which ended up praising someone else whom he'd mistaken for Mayakovsky. David Shterenberg, who'd been with them after 1917, since the days in Petrograd when IZO was organized, came in with a schoolgirl hairdo and read his "Greetings from the Schoolchildren," ending with the lines

> We are all your children now,
> Since we are your—pupils!

Through all of it Mayakovsky, wearing a billy-goat mask, straddled a chair and answered all congratulations by bleating loudly. The small apartment was jammed with actors and actresses from Meyerhold's company, along with people from GPU, the secret police, friends of the Briks. When the tributes were over, the guests acted out charades, making Volodya guess which line from his poems they were thinking of. One sat behind a desk; another took out his fountain pen, put it angrily down on the desk, and walked away. Mayakovsky shouted, "I've got it! I've got it: 'Conversation with a Tax Collector about Poetry'!"

> . . . if
>> you think
>>> that all I have to do
>> is to profit
>>> by other people's words,
>> then,
>>> comrades,
>>>> here's my pen,
>> and you can
>>> write
>>>> yourselves!

There was supper and champagne, the noise and excitement grew, people laughed until they cried. It was only when they demanded that Mayakovsky read for them that the mood changed. He refused at first, saying that his voice was gone, that his old poems weren't interesting. When they insisted, begging him in unison, he finally gave in and began to read his poem about the exhausted horse he'd seen lying on a Moscow street in 1918, when he was making *Fettered by Film* with Lili. One of his friends at the party, Lev Kassil, described the scene.

> He got up, his hand gripping a corner of the cupboard, and, looking around at us slowly with a never-to-be-forgotten look on his face, read quietly and with unexpected moroseness:
>
> > Horse, don't cry.
> > Listen to me, Horse.
> > Why d'you think you're any worse than they?
> > Horsey dear,
> > we're each a bit of a horse,
> > everyone's a horse in his way.
>
> . . . and everyone around suddenly became very serious. This was no longer a joke, not a merry jubilee for a poet, not a party of friends. Suddenly, everyone felt—like a cold draft passing through the convolutions of the brain—that this moment was to be remembered . . . and he turned his yard-wide shoulders, as if harnessed . . . climbing up a great hill . . . and softly turning round, as if afraid to hurt anyone, he went into the other room and for a long time stood there, bending over the bureau, clutching in his hand a glass of undrunk tea. Something of helplessness, loneliness, heartache, something then not understood had come over him.

In January the rehearsals began for the Moscow production of *The Bathhouse*. Mayakovsky was at the theater for most of the first readings, and the actresses noticed that he wore a clean shirt and a new tie every day and they teased him about his revived interest in clothes. He was more often with Nora, trying to convince her that their affair should become open, even that she should marry him. He was also looking forward to the première of the play on January 30 in Leningrad and the opening of his exhibit in Moscow two days later. On January 21, 1930, there was an evening at the Bolshoi Theater, honoring the sixth anniversary of the death of Lenin, where Mayakovsky read the third part of his poem "Vladimir Ilyich Lenin." Present for the ceremonies were Stalin, Molotov, Kalinin, and most of the important members of the ruling group.

There was a desperateness to Mayakovsky's public appearances now. The criticism of his work had grown to a deafening chorus around him, and he felt more and more isolated. At readings it was more of an effort for him to face the audiences, and there were frequent emotional outbursts in public. At a reading in October he had blurted out, "Only after my death will you understand that a wonderful poet has died."

One of his most difficult appearances was in the middle of January 1930, when he went to Kharkov to give a lecture, "To the Left of *LEF*," and read poetry and sections from *The Bathhouse*. A friend, A. Poltoratsky, noticed that he was unusually nervous, and then in the midst of the confusion and noise that were always part of his readings, someone in the audience shouted, "Louder!" Mayakovsky stopped as if he were suddenly afraid. Lamely he joked, "Well, if you ask *me* to speak louder, comrades, you must be out of your minds." But the next morning Poltoratsky was in Mayakovsky's room as he called his doctor. After a long discussion over the phone Mayakovsky became deeply disturbed about his throat, which was red and swollen. Volodya feared cancer but the doctor told him that he had strained his vocal cords with all the readings. He should have trained his voice years ago, like an actor, but now it was too late. He said despairingly to Poltoratsky, "What shall I do?"

On January 30, 1930, the first production of *The Bathhouse* opened in Leningrad, directed by Meyerhold's pupil V. Lutse, and it was abruptly clear how disturbed Mayakovsky had become. He released his anger in the play, but his reckless confidence and Meyerhold's enthusiasm for his work had blinded them to the realities of what he'd written. *The Bathhouse* was a violent, undisguised attack on Soviet bureaucracy, on the ambitious Party hacks like the petty officials responsible for turning down his visa application only a few months before. Important figures in the government were described and mercilessly lampooned, and the workings of the official Soviet apparatus were held up for bitter ridicule.

In the play an inventor named Chudakov has built a time machine in his apartment, but he's unable to get money to test it even though he lives downstairs from the Chief of the Bureau of Coordination, a vain, corrupt bureaucrat who is having difficulties with his wife. The machine brings them a woman of the future who begins to organize a group to take with her to the Communist paradise of the year 2030. The Chief of the Bureau attempts to make the people working for him prepare vouchers for travel pay and his per diem expenses, shows up for the departure with all of his office paraphernalia so he can set up the bureaucracy again in the future, and insists that he must be given a position as important as the one he has now before he'll agree to go. When the machine takes off with the inventor, the woman of the future, and a group of enthusiastic workers, the bureaucrat is left behind. The last line of the play is his suspicious question, "All of you—she and you and the writer—what were you trying to say? That people like me are of no use to Communism?"

No audience in the Soviet Union in 1930 could risk approving a direct attack on the authorities. In *The Bedbug* Mayakovsky had begun the play as a satire on a NEP wedding, so everyone was free to laugh at the grasping selfishness and vulgarity of members of the working class, the "eternal philistines," but in *The Bathhouse* Mayakovsky was clearly satirizing the repressive bureaucratic tendencies in his own government. Zoshchenko, who was present at the performance, described it as the worst failure he had ever seen in the theater.

There wasn't one laugh from the audience, and at the end of the
first two acts there wasn't even applause. The audience sat in stony
silence, and the next day there was fierce criticism in the newspapers.

Two days later, on February 1, Mayakovsky opened his exhibition
"Twenty Years of Work" at the Writers' Union in Moscow. Hundreds
of young people came to see it, but it was boycotted by the official
writers' groups. Lili described his mood in the diary she had begun
to keep:

> Volodya was most unhappy. The tickets printed for ad-
> mission to the exhibition were so poorly designed that it was
> disgusting to present them at the entrance. I really wished that
> everything at the exhibition should be a model of its kind. The
> next day some friends wanted to add an explanation above one
> of the showcases—"The masses do not understand Mayakovsky."
>
> At last, on February 1, the exhibition was opened. At 6 p.m.
> he went to the official opening. Crowds of people, but only
> students. The exhibition wasn't complete, but all the same it
> was interesting. Volodya was overstrained. He spoke in a tired
> voice. Several people delivered speeches, then he read the pro-
> logue of his new poem. It left a tremendous impression, although
> he read it from the paper as if forcing himself to read it.
>
> I remember that Volodya was tired and gloomy that day.
> He took offense easily, he didn't want to speak with his friends.
> When people telephoned, he didn't bother to answer. About
> a young REF member he grumbled, "He ought to have brought
> cigarettes for me from the shop around the corner, but he hasn't
> even driven a nail in the wall of the exhibition."

Brik tried to explain Mayakovsky's depression in one of the few
notes he wrote about him later.

> We didn't grasp it at that time; we couldn't understand
> why Volodya was so nervous and angry with us. He reproached

us by hints and indirect comments for not organizing his ex-hibition for him. He became querulous, capricious, rude. Finally he quarreled with all the members of REF. He told me, "It's only REF that keeps us together. I would have fought even with you, but there is something else that binds us."

I saw that he was in a very bad temper, that his nerves were shattered, but I didn't guess the real cause of his condition. It wasn't characteristic of Volodya to seek official recognition. I was accustomed to him fighting recklessly, to being aggressively controversial.

Lunacharsky was one of the old friends who'd come to the open-ing of the exhibition, and he left deeply disturbed at Mayakovsky's condition. He looked very tired; his hair was beginning to be touched with gray at the temples. It wasn't only the exhaustion, the bad temper, the hoarseness—Mayakovsky seemed almost indifferent. He was under so much strain he no longer seemed to care what was hap-pening. To Lunacharsky, who'd seen him through so many violent struggles, this was more upsetting than if he'd raged at the lack of official recognition.

The poem that he'd read at the opening of the exhibition was a new one, still unfinished. It was titled "At the Top of My Voice," and it was an impassioned defense of himself as a poet, saying that it would be the future that would judge what he'd done. In an out-burst he even lashed out at some of the poetry he'd been forced to write by the circumstances of the times, suggesting the pain he'd felt at stifling his lyric voice in one of his most unforgettable images.

Agitprop
    has stuck
        in my teeth too,
and I'd rather
    compose
        romances for you—

more profit in it
                    and more charm.
But I
        subdued
                myself,
                        setting my heel
on the throat
            of my own song.

He went on defiantly,

My verse will come to you
                            over the peaks of the ages,
and over the heads
                of poets and governments.
My verse will arrive,
                    but it won't arrive like that—
not like an arrow
                in a cupid-lyred chase,
not like a worn penny
                    reaches a numismatist,
not like the light of the dead stars reaches you.
My verse
        by labor
                will break the mountain of years,
and will present itself
                    ponderous,
                            crude,
                                tangible,
as an aqueduct,
            by Roman slaves
constructed,
            enters into our days.

When in mounds of books,

                  where verse lies buried,

you by chance discover the iron filings of lines,

touch them

        with respect,

            as you would

some antique

        yet awesome weapon.

And he ended with the boasting assertion,

When I appear

        before the Communist Central Committee

                of the coming bright years

as a Bolshevik Party card

        I'll raise

above the gang

        of self-seeking

            poets and rogues,

all hundred volumes

        of my

          Party books.

The previous fall Mayakovsky had helped with the formation of the Committee of Proletarian Writers, which had grown out of the old RAPP group that had been so obdurately opposed to his own *LEF* group. At the time he'd said, "We of the Left Front accept RAPP because it is the precise channel of the Soviet and Party line and because it must be such." RAPP was still unalterably opposed to him and the individualism of his writing, and when they had more power, their criticism of his work grew even more shrill. It was not only Mayakovsky; they attacked every writer in the Soviet Union who wasn't part of their group. Their aims were rigidly defined. They declared that "the depiction of the Five Year Plan and of the class war within its framework is the one and only problem of Soviet literature." The quarrel between Mayakovsky as the leader of *LEF* and his old antagonist Chuzhak of RAPP had been going on for years, and the positions of both groups had moved still further apart as RAPP began to push for a complete standardization of literary expression.

Then early in February, after the fiasco of *The Bathhouse* and the official boycott of his exhibition, Mayakovsky abruptly joined RAPP. It was a complete turn away from the principles he'd been defending since the first meetings of revolutionary writers in February 1917. Clearly he did it to end the isolation he felt as intolerable, but his membership had the opposite effect. Lili remembered, "Volodya considered it his duty to join RAPP. He considered them his comrades in the common battle, but it wasn't like that at all. They simply couldn't stand him. They met him with drawn bayonets. They talked to him about morals and how to live. It was dreadful." Brik had suggested that Mayakovsky join RAPP, but his other associates were bitterly disappointed at what they felt was the poet's betrayal, and RAPP was almost as confused by his change of position as they were.

One of the RAPP group who knew Mayakovsky, K. Zelinsky, presided at the meeting when he joined. It was the evening of February 6, 1930. Mayakovsky recited "At the Top of My Voice" with "inspiration and bitterness," his fingers drumming on the green baize table as he read the poem from his manuscript.

With RAPP the repressive tendencies that had been implicit in most of the Soviet cultural policies finally became unmistakable. Mayakovsky joined them, expecting to be involved in the full spectrum of RAPP's activities, but on their side, they were dismayed by his presence. They might admonish him in their articles as if he were a neophyte, but no one in the RAPP group had his prominent position as a writer. The reading before Stalin two weeks earlier made it clear that he was no longer in official disfavor.

This was the final, defeated action of the public Mayakovsky, who felt that if he wanted to participate in Soviet cultural life he had to join RAPP. He hadn't realized that, once he joined the organization, it would change to accommodate him. It was like the incongruous scene in his early poem describing the extraordinary occurrence at Pushkino when he'd asked the sun to have tea with him. The sun had come into his room, almost crowding him out and burning him up as the afternoon went on. For most of the group heading RAPP, Mayakovsky was the same kind of apparition.

Their answer to Mayakovsky was to quickly reorganize the group. They divided RAPP into two sections, one an "October Caucus" consisting of RAPP's leadership plus the other writers considered important enough to bring in with them, and the other group—Mayakovsky and various minor writers. He had joined RAPP to break out of his isolation, only to find himself more isolated than ever.

But he already knew it was difficult to work with RAPP. In Rostov, as Shklovsky remembered, Mayakovsky had been told about a local writer who'd been encouraged by RAPP to dress in a peasant kerchief and pose for a photograph that was later captioned "Kolkhoz poetess." Then they no longer published her work, and in despair the woman shot herself in the chest, attempting suicide. Volodya read her verses and went to see her in the hospital. He told her he'd try to help with her medical treatment and convalescence.

Then he asked her, "Is it bad?"

She answered, "You know, a gunshot wound doesn't hurt. You feel as though someone suddenly called out to you. The pain comes later."

"What you say isn't nice," said Mayakovsky.

22

Mayakovsky's funeral procession, Moscow, 1930

Lili and Osip Brik at Mayakovsky's coffin, 1930

Why does death occur so frequently in the spring and also at dawn? You would think that winter and night would be more appropriate. But dawn and spring are the beginning of a cycle, and when he enters it, a man whose hour actually came in the winter and at night is at once revealed as a supernumerary, a cipher. He does not survive at the beginning of the new cycle because his life has been completed earlier, at the end of the preceding one, and his time has now run out. The new day dawns and, no longer needed, he departs.

ANDREI SINYAVSKY,
A VOICE FROM THE CHORUS

ON FEBRUARY 18, 1930, THE BRIKS LEFT MOSCOW to travel to London, a trip they'd been preparing for months. With cruel irony they weren't able to obtain an exit visa until Mayakovsky gave them his financial assistance, although he had been held in the Soviet Union himself. They were to go first to Berlin, and then on to London to visit Lili's mother. They weren't planning to be back until the middle of April. In Berlin they handled literary matters for him, and his letters to them were filled with details of things he wanted them to do. He missed them, and he and the bulldog Bulka, who'd also been left behind at Gendrikov, had only themselves to console each other. Their housekeeper came in during the day, but she was gone by the time Mayakovsky returned to the empty apartment. On February 24 he wrote, with his usual affection:

DEAR, DARLING, SWEET AND BELOVED KISSITY,

Thank you for the two telegrams and the postcard. And where are the rest? I wish so much to receive different letters and telegrams from you—it's so dull because you both left together . . . My exhibition will go to Leningrad from the 5th to the 12th of March, and I'll go as an exhibit.

Kissya, don't forget to write down in the notebook all your writing and the reviews.

Bulka really misses you. When I come home at night she not only jumps, but in my opinion she's even learned to stay in the air until she licks my face.

I miss you, love you, and wait.

He also passed on the news that he'd signed a contract with the State Circus for a political-satirical revue entitled *Hold Out*, about the 1905 revolution. Three weeks later, on March 17, he sent a petulant telegram complaining that he wasn't hearing from them, but two days later, when a letter and a picture arrived of Lili holding a lion cub in the London zoo, he wrote them a long letter, stubbornly cheerful, and as always filled with details of his activities.

Mayakovsky went to Leningrad for the opening of the exhibition of his work. As in Moscow, there was a crowd of young people, and a devastating silence on the part of the official writers' groups, including RAPP, despite his gesture in joining them the month before. He turned even more desperately to Nora Polonskaya, but she was beginning to tire of their affair. She remembered that Mayakovsky "seemed a little old for me. He was thirty-six, I was only twenty-two." She had become interested in one of the actors at the theater, a handsome young man named Lininov. Her husband knew nothing of her tangled involvements. Mayakovsky was jealous of her young friends and tried to persuade her to marry him, but she refused, though she went on seeing him.

Two months was a long time for Mayakovsky to be in Moscow without the Briks. He'd been separated from them before, but it was the first time that they had both been away from the apartment at the same time. He still needed Lili for her love and emotional support, and Osip to talk to about his work. Suddenly he was without them, at a moment when he was too depressed to struggle with all the things that were overwhelming him. In his room at 2 Lyubyansky Passage he kept a small camel on the mantelpiece, and he quoted a melancholy jingle to Shklovsky:

> Every cow has a nest,
> every camel has children,
> but I have no one,
> no one in the whole world.

He was still appearing at meetings and lectures, but his voice was strained and the exchanges with the audience were becoming more difficult for him. In early March he was admitted to a Moscow hospital with what was described as a nervous breakdown but seems to have been more like exhaustion. He left the hospital after a short rest and again flung himself into his work. Friends were dismayed at his appearance, at his haggard face, at his distracted moods, at his deepening depression, but no one realized quite how desperate he had become. He sent another telegram to Lili—like the one he'd sent in March—which had read WE MISS, WRITE—BUT I CAN'T UNDERSTAND WHOM YOU WRITE—NOT ME, AT LEAST. Lili answered with an impatient postcard from London. "Please invent a new text for telegrams."

His agent Pavel Lavut was close to him, and he was disturbed at Mayakovsky's emotional condition, but didn't know how to deal with the situation. On April 11, a week before the Briks were to return to Moscow, Mayakovsky missed a lecture for the first time. Lavut had called in the morning, as he usually did, but to his surprise Mayakovsky wasn't at the apartment. He spoke to the housekeeper, who assured him that Mayakovsky had remembered the lecture. He asked her to remind him again and told her the address of the auditorium where the reading was to be held. But Mayakovsky didn't appear. After an hour Lavut sent someone in a car to find him. The person he'd sent went to all possible addresses, then saw a car like Mayakovsky's Renault in front of him. He pulled even with the car, saw that it was the poet's, and asked his chauffeur to drive in front of it. They stopped in Tagansky Square, and had an argument. Mayakovsky said that he knew nothing about the reading, slammed the car door, and drove off. Nora was in the car with him. Lavut had to announce to the audience that Mayakovsky was sick and that the reading would be postponed.

The next morning Lavut went to the apartment and found him still in bed. Lavut started to come toward the bed, but Mayakovsky stopped him.

He was writing something. I stood in the doorway, and when I wanted to approach him, he stopped me sullenly. "Don't come near me, or you can get infected." I was surprised. He had been taken ill so many times in my company on our travels and he had never said anything like that. Later I realized he had something on his mind . . .

In the early evening Mayakovsky called Aseyev and asked him to invite Nora and her husband to his apartment. Aseyev protested, saying he had nothing to offer them to eat and it was too late to go shopping for food, but when Volodya insisted, asserting that a pretzel and tea would be enough, Aseyev agreed to call them. But when he telephoned, they had just left. He called Mayakovsky back immediately. He was silent for a while, as if thinking about something, and then said, "Well, we must put it off to some other day."

Mayakovsky managed to reach Nora later in the evening. When she came to his room after the theater, he told her that he had mentioned in a letter to the government that he considered her a member of his family. Did she object? Confused, she said, "I don't understand what you mean. But please mention me whenever you think necessary."

Everyone remembers final moments, as if these cruel memories of pain and grief are among the clearest glimpses we have of a man and the people around him. The next day Mayakovsky clattered into the empty building of the State Circus, rattling his cane against the wooden seat backs and demanding to know when the rehearsals for another of his theater pieces, *Moscow in Flames*, would begin. The only one there was the stage designer, Valentia Khodosyevich, who had known him for years. He insisted that she leave with him for a drive in his car. She tried to refuse, saying she had a rehearsal. Suddenly he flew into a rage, his face white and twisted, his eyes furious. He banged his cane against the chair next to him, roaring "No!" and then suddenly whining, nearly sobbing, "No? Everyone answers me 'no.' Only 'no.' Everywhere 'no.' " He turned and ran up the theater aisle, banging his cane even more wildly against the backs of the chairs, such a frightening sight that she rushed out after him. She caught up with him at his car and joined him for a drive. After a long silence he said to her quietly, half apologetically, that he would sleep in his room on Lyubyansky to be close to the theater and would she call him there about ten? Then he asked the chauffeur to stop, suddenly leaped onto the sidewalk, and scattered pedestrians with a wave of his cane. He told his driver to take her wherever she wanted to go. Now he wanted to walk.

Sometime during his walk, about four in the afternoon, he tried to reach Aseyev by telephone, but the only person in the apartment was Vera, the sister of Aseyev's wife. She was a friend, but he only asked if Aseyev was there. When Vera said no, he was silent for a moment. "Well, it means that nothing can be done," he said and hung up. Next he tried to phone Louellen, to invite her to have dinner with him, but she and her husband were both studying for exams and couldn't meet him. He sighed and put down the receiver.

In the evening after the theater he and Nora went to supper at the apartment of Valentin Katayev, who remembered Mayakovsky's hands, his nervousness, when he later described the evening.

My memory has retained nothing of the most important details of that evening except for Mayakovsky's large hands, his nervously twitching fingers—they were before my eyes all the time, right at my side—they mechanically plunged into a bearskin cover and tore it, plucked at it, pulling out tufts of dry brown fur, while his eyes stared across the table at Nora Polonskaya, his latest infatuation, a very young, delightful, fairhaired girl with dimples on her pink cheeks, in a tight knitted sweater with short sleeves . . .

With a slightly frightened smile she would write on bits of cardboard torn out of a chocolate box answers to Mayakovsky's messages, which he tossed to her across the table from time to time with the gesture of a roulette player . . .

The little cardboard squares flew across the table over a bowl of dumplings, and other bits of paper flew back. At last the chocolate box was destroyed. Then Mayakovsky and Nora moved to my room. Tearing scraps of paper from anything that came to hand, they continued their rapid correspondence, which was like a silent duel to the death.

It was a disastrous party. Katayev aggravated the situation by making tactless jokes about Mayakovsky, saying that his plays shouldn't be called *The Bedbug* or *The Bathhouse*, but *Othello*—a cruel reminder that Mayakovsky was jealous of Nora and her young friends. At three in the morning Mayakovsky and Nora finally left. Katayev tried to persuade her to spend the night at his apartment, but they left together and went to Mayakovsky's room in Lyubyansky Passage.

Later that same morning their quarreling began again. He shouted that she had to stay with him, that she couldn't leave him alone, but she insisted she had to leave for a rehearsal at the theater. It was her first important role. She told him that if he continued being jealous, they would have to stop seeing each other. Just after 10 a.m. she broke away from him and went out the door.

I went out and walked a few steps toward the front door. I heard a shot. My legs gave way under me. I began to shout and rave in the corridor. I could not make myself open the door to his room . . .

From his desk Mayakovsky had taken the pistol he'd used in the film *Not Born for Money* twelve years before and, holding the pistol in his left hand, shot himself through the heart with the single bullet he'd left in the chamber. The room was splattered with blood, and on the desk was the letter he'd been writing when Lavut had surprised him two days before.

To All of You:
Don't blame anyone for my death, and please don't gossip about it. The deceased hate gossip.

Mama, sisters, comrades, forgive me. This is not a good method (I don't advise others to do it), but for me there's no other way out.

Lili, love me.

Comrade Government, my family consists of Lili Brik, Mama, my sisters, and Veronica Vitoldovna Polonskaya.

If you can provide a decent life for them, thank you.

The verses I have begun give to the Briks. They'll figure them out.

As they say, "The incident is closed."

Love's boat
    smashed on the everyday.
Life and I are quits,
    and there's no point
in counting over
    mutual hurts,
      harms,
        and slights.

Best of luck to all of you!

Vladimir Mayakovsky
4/12/30

Comrades of the Proletarian Literary Organization, don't think me a coward.

Really, it couldn't be helped.

Greetings!

Tell Yermilov it's too bad I've removed the signboard—we should have fought it out.

V.M.

In the desk drawer I have 2,000 rubles. Use them to pay my taxes. The rest can be obtained from the State Publishing House.

Among his papers were fragments of an unfinished introduction to the second part of "At the Top of My Voice," variants of the lines quoted in his suicide letter:

It's past one o'clock,
                        you must have gone to bed.
    In the night,
                the Milky Way shines
                                like a silvery Oka.
    I'm in no hurry,
                and there is no point in
    waking
            and disturbing you
                            with the lightning of cables.
    As they say,
                the incident is closed.
    The love boat
                has crashed against the everyday.
    You and I,
            we are quits,
                        and there is no point in listing
    mutual pains,
                sorrows,
                        and hurts . . .

Look! what stillness in the world.
Night has covered the sky with a starlit tribute.
At such hours, you rise and you speak
to the ages, history, and the universe.

Pasternak was in Moscow, and he was one of the first to rush to the room in Lyubyansky Passage. He later wrote:

The beginning of April surprised Moscow in the white stupor of returning winter. On the seventh it began to thaw for the second time, and on the fourteenth when Mayakovsky shot himself, not everyone had yet become accustomed to the novelty of spring.

He reached the staircase of the building an hour after the suicide, between eleven and noon, when "the waves were still flowing in circles around the shot. The news made the telephones tremble, covered faces with pallor, and urged one toward the Lyubyansky Passage, across the courtyard into the house, where the staircase was already choked with people." The body, completely covered, was brought down on a stretcher and placed in an ambulance to be driven to the Gendrikov apartment. Pasternak followed in a streetcar, and as he stood inside holding on to the strap, he imagined he heard Mayakovsky's "A Cloud in Trousers" "as if it were being spoken loudly by someone at my side . . . 'I feel that my "I" is much too small for me' . . . made my lips cling together like fingers in mittens."

At Gendrikov there were many people crowded into the hall and dining room. Mayakovsky had been placed on his own bed in his room, and he lay in a clean blue shirt, his face uncovered as if in sleep. The door from the hall into Lili's room was open, and on the threshold Aseyev was weeping. Suddenly the house porter came into the room carrying a chisel in his boot top, and with it he carefully removed the storm window and opened the windows slowly and noiselessly. It was still cold outside, but Pasternak could hear sparrows in the trees in the garden and the faint voices of children.

Someone asked if a telegram had been sent to Lili. It had been done, and Pasternak imagined "that scarcely conceivable London, far, far beyond the trees, where the telegram had gone. Soon, over there, someone would cry out, stretch her hands toward us, fall down unconscious. My throat was constricted. I decided to enter his room once more and weep my fill."

What Pasternak saw was marked on his memory forever:

He lay on his side, his face turned toward the wall, somber, tall, a sheet covering him to his chin, his mouth half open as in sleep. Turning proudly away from us all, even when he was lying down, even in his sleep, he was going away from us in a stubborn endeavor to reach something. His face recalled the time when he had spoken of himself as "handsome, twentytwo-years old . . ."

Pasternak was most shocked by Mayakovsky's face, wearing "the expression with which one begins life, but does not end it. He was sulking and indignant."

That day the Briks were in Holland. They spent the afternoon shopping and bought presents for Mayakovsky—cigars, a walking stick, ties. Lili sent a postcard with a view of a field of multicolored hyacinths to Rita Rait and then took the night train to Berlin. The Briks remembered:

On the morning of April 15 we arrived in Berlin and registered at the Kurfürsten Hotel as usual. We were greeted by the manager and her dog Schneidt. The porter gave us letters and a telegram from Moscow. "It's from Volodya . . ." We took the elevator to our room, unpacked, and then opened the telegram.

At our embassy everything was already known. They immediately gave us the necessary visas and we left for Moscow that same evening.

The morning of April 17 we arrived in Moscow. The coffin was at the Writers' Union. Tremendous crowds of people came to say goodbye to Volodya. Everyone was excited. Nobody had expected that Mayakovsky would commit suicide. According to the Old Style calendar, April 14 is April 1, and many people laughed when they were told that Mayakovsky had shot himself, thinking that it was a joke . . .

For Rita, who was teaching languages at the Leningrad Military Academy, the news came late in the afternoon.

The 14th of April, 1930
Leningrad

Coming home from my work I went into my aunt's room. She whispered to me, "Mayakovsky has shot himself." It wasn't a shock, not even a heartache. Quite automatically I loosened the collar of my jacket and could only whisper, "It's a lie." Down from the third floor to the newsstand. My hand is trembling. I'm throwing down copper coins, grabbing the paper. "Wait for your change!" But I'm off. Before going upstairs I open the paper and I hear his voice:

> I don't advise others to do it.
> Best of luck to all of you!

But how recently he phoned me from the Hotel Europe. "Rita, I'm very sick. Do you know a doctor who isn't a quack? Hurry up and send him to me." I rang up Doctor K., our old family doctor, and he said with some misgiving, "Mayakovsky? Is it that one, the Futurist?" The doctor later showed me Volume 5 of Mayakovsky's collected works with the inscription, "To dear Doctor K., for internal use only." And the old man added, "You know, he was very nice. Quite human, after all."

I go upstairs, rereading five, ten times: "Lili, love me." Oh, God. Lili isn't there. Osya isn't there. Has anything happened to them?

It seemed to me that only the most horrible catastrophe with his dearest, nearest friends could have killed him. Late in the night, lots of phone calls. Some friends, some writers, don't remember who.

"I don't know. Don't understand a thing. Leaving for Moscow tomorrow."

Morning of April 15. Lessons at the Academy. Nobody to replace me. The two hours a torture, asking, correcting, explaining. At the end of the class, a slick-haired nonentity making a vulgar joke: "Did you read about the suicide? In Esenin's footsteps. Poetry—nothing good will come of it. But of course, what sort of poetry is his?"

I couldn't stand it. How many times during those ten years of friendship with the poems and the man have I risen to defend Mayakovsky before those fools—aesthetes, petit bourgeois, even camouflaged counter-revolutionaries? How many times have I shouted down all those voices? How could I now keep from shouting in a voice strangled by discipline and rage, "A man is judged by his life and not by his death. You are Communists. You ought to know. Revolution and Mayakovsky are inseparable. All his life . . ."

The bell. Not being able to finish, not even dismissing them, I run out of the classroom straight to the lavatory to cry my heart out. For the first time in the last twenty-four hours.

The 15th of April
Moscow

I leave late at night. The trip to Moscow used to be the greatest joy. My friend Leonty would meet me at the station the next morning, and then when Lili was awake, to Vodopyany, Sokolniki, Gendrikov.

Going in the morning to see Lili, breakfasting together, watching her bathe, looking through a new book of Volodya's or Osya's photographs in Sokolniki. Catching up on the news of the one or two months I'd been in Leningrad.

Or coming to dinner, "Five sharp, don't be late." Volodya returning from the publishers. Often bringing packages—books, bread, wine, fruit. Saying hello to me, always kindly. Always, even if tired and irritable. Trying to be pleasant. First kiss for Lili. First question always, "Is Osya home?" And immediately, meticulously washing hands.

Now I'm coming to Moscow and what will be there?

Morning of April 16.

There was a car waiting for me at the station. Straight to the Writers' Union. A long line of silent people stretched from the Koudrinsky Place all around the courtyard of the Writers' Union. A small side door. I am in with my friend. The large hall is unrecognizable. Red flowers. Music, official funeral music. I am afraid to look at what lies in the middle of the hall.

Somebody takes me by the hand and leads me to a row of chairs beside the red coffin. There among unknown crying women, Volodya's tiny mama. She hugs me silently. With trembling hands she takes a small handbag and a handkerchief from a chair and makes me sit down beside her. When I raise my eyes, I see his head, his brow, his profile, and his large hands, folded. She says very quietly, "If Lili had been here, it would never have happened."

Morning of April 17.

We meet Lili and Osya. Vasya Katanyan came with them from the German border. Louellen, Liova [Grinkrug] and I and other friends wait at the station.

The platform is empty, quiet, clean. There is the train, there is the car. Osya is at the door, and behind him—her eyes. Frightening. So full of tears, tortured, frightened—frightened to death. We are afraid to recognize her, afraid to move. And only when she's down on the platform can we approach her, one by one, trying not to cry, not to say anything. I press my cheek to the familiar fragrance of her fur collar, and listen to her helpless words, "Just think what has happened!" I can only repeat, "Kissia, Kissia," before somebody takes her away from me.

The funeral on April 17 was hasty and disorganized. Instead of flowers beside the coffin, a huge wreath was quickly constructed out of an enormous iron flywheel with hammers, screws, and bolts attached to it. On a red ribbon was an inscription in golden letters, *To the iron poet—an iron wreath.* The body was on display for three days at the Writers' Union in a casket that was too small—Mayakovsky's shoes with their heavy metal tips scarcely fit inside. The coffin was mounted on a platform and driven through the streets of Moscow with tens of thousands of people following it, but the driver was inexperienced and drove too fast, leaving the crowd behind. Those who had been close to Mayakovsky were scattered in the confusion. At 7:30 that evening his body was given over to the flames of the crematorium to the accompaniment of the Communist anthem, "The Internationale."

23

Lili Brik, Moscow, 1976 (photograph by Marianna Volkov)

Why did Volodya shoot himself? The question is complicated and the answer must also be complicated . . .

Mayakovsky loved life ecstatically. He loved all its manifestations —revolution, art, work, myself, women, excitement, the air he breathed. His amazing energy helped him conquer all obstacles. But he knew that he would not be able to defeat old age, and with a morbid fear he waited from early youth for it to come.

LILI BRIK

I N THE FIRST DAYS OF DISBELIEF THAT FOLLOWED
Mayakovsky's suicide the questioning had already begun. Why did
he do it? The event seemed to represent the end of a literary
epoch. How could Mayakovsky commit suicide? The Soviet Union's
most prominent literary figure—how could he follow in Esenin's footsteps? A year after Esenin's death Mayakovsky had publicly de-
nounced suicide; he said in a lecture that his purpose in writing the
poem "To Sergei Esenin" had been

> to deliberately paralyze the action of Esenin's last lines; to make
> Esenin's end uninteresting; to set forth, in place of the easy
> beauty of death, another kind of beauty. For the working class
> needs strength in order to continue the revolution which de-
> mands . . . that we glorify life and the joy that is to be found
> along that most difficult of roads—the road towards Communism.

Mayakovsky's treatment at the hands of the Proletarian Writers'
Group, political disappointment, the failure of his love affair with
Tatiana, Nora's refusal to marry him, Lili's absence, the physical
troubles with his voice—each of these was present in those last moments
in Lyubyansky Passage, but Lili insisted that the idea of suicide had
always been there for him.

> How often I heard Mayakovsky say the word "suicide"! At
> every trifle he would threaten, "A bullet in the head"—that was
> his favorite expression. He told me he wanted to live until he
> was thirty years old, and no longer.
> Of course his constant references to suicide didn't frighten
> me, but there were occasions when I thought he was close to a
> disaster. I remember when he came home from Gosizdat after

someone had kept him waiting for a long time, or he'd had to stand in a long line to collect his money, or he'd been forced to argue and justify some petty detail. Then when he got home he threw himself full-length on the leather sofa and literally howled, "I cannot stand it any longer." I would begin to cry out of sympathy and fear for him, and he would forget about himself and try to console me.

When Volodya shot himself I was not in Moscow. Perhaps if I'd been at home death would have been postponed for a while, but one never knows. Had circumstances been more favorable, perhaps the suicide might have been postponed. But at the time everything was going wrong: Nora hadn't verified that he was still young and irresistible, *The Bathhouse* was a failure, RAPP. People whom he'd expected to attend his "Twenty Years" exhibition hadn't come. He didn't have enough sleep the night before.

He was completely wrong about all this, but he was the POET. He had to exaggerate everything. Without exaggeration he could not be the man he was.

Mayakovsky's friend Shklovsky felt that he had not really meant to kill himself. There had been only one bullet in the cylinder of his revolver, and "there had been no friend attentive enough to remove that bullet." Mayakovsky's old associate Lunacharsky recognized that at the end the poet had been overwhelmed by his personal suffering. He was a double personality, an unstable mixture of a tough exterior and a soft interior, and the circumstances of his life had defeated him.

Not all of us are like Marx, who said that poets experience a great need for kindness. Not all of us understand this, and not all of us understood that Mayakovsky was in need of great kindness, that often he needed nothing as much as a kind word, perhaps even the simplest of words; it would have reached the heart of this double, it would have balanced the deep sadness inside him.

Despite the fact that he liked his double, despite the fact that Mayakovsky at times wondered: Am I not the double?—despite all this, he stepped on his double's throat. And his double killed him for this. He succeeded in killing Mayakovsky because, though he had only managed to mix in a certain amount of slag in Mayakovsky's works, in his private life he had been much more powerful.

The Briks explained the suicide as the inevitable result of Mayakovsky's hyperbolic attitude toward life, that he hungered for complete acceptance in everything he did—if one person in the audience didn't like a poem he read, then the reading was spoiled for him, even if all the others applauded tumultuously. As *The Bedbug* and "At the Top of My Voice" showed, the political pressures against Mayakovsky had never been more overwhelming, while at the same time his private life had never been more unhappy.

But the outer world was less important to Mayakovsky than the dynamo of his inner creative self. There was an inner self that couldn't be silenced, that spoke out insistently through the accumulation of painful rejections in his career and love affairs, when he sat alone writing his suicide letter and his entire being reached out to cry, "Lili, love me."

Perhaps it was another poet, Marina Tsvetayeva, who most clearly saw the conflicts within him. She wrote that he "committed suicide because of his unfortunate love in spite of all his reproaches to Esenin . . . Mayakovsky did away with himself the way he would an enemy." His truest life was in his poems, his love for Lili, and his belief in the socialist revolution, and it was clearly impossible for him to go on living in the terrifying abyss of "loveless times" that stretched before him in April 1930.

For Lili the year after Mayakovsky's death was one of emptiness and loneliness. As deeply affected as she was by the suicide, she felt that Osip, in some way, was even more grief-stricken. "When Mayakovsky died I think Brik suffered even more than I did. Osip said, 'We were like circus trapeze artists, and I feel as if my partner had died.'" The suicide letter had stated that all of Mayakovsky's papers should be turned over to the Briks, and Lili started sifting through them almost immediately. In May 1930 she wrote Rita: "I can't come to Leningrad yet. I'm rummaging in Volodya's little papers, and sometimes it seems to me I do what I have to do. I'll send you a good photo of him. Nothing to write about. I kiss you very much. Love to everyone, Lili."

"I do what I have to do" included Lili's destroying the letters and photographs she found in Mayakovsky's room from the other women in his life, including all the photographs he'd begged Tatiana to give him. She also began to bring order to his manuscripts with the help of Brik and Vasya Katanyan, sorting through the scraps of verses she had saved over the years, clarifying the different versions of long poems like "About This," preparing the manuscripts for an archive library the Briks wanted the government to establish at the Gendrikov apartment.

The official attitude toward Mayakovsky's poetry became even more ambiguous after his suicide. The Proletarian Writers' Group, RAPP, continued their attacks on him during the next two years, when they dominated Soviet culture, but their excesses finally turned the Party against them. In 1932 the Party stripped them of all authority and ordered the organization of a new Writers' Union under its direct control to supervise all literary activities in the country. Since there was no official attempt to assess Mayakovsky's work, it was much more prudent to stay silent until Stalin's policy was known. Later the arrests and persecution of the intellectuals began—Meyerhold, Babel, and Eisenstein, to name only a few of Mayakovsky's associates —and Stalin's second Five Year Plan proceeded with waves of prisoners flooding the work camps.

By the middle of the 1930's, the cultural current had shifted, and under the influence of the Writers' Union it appeared that Pasternak was to be considered the greatest poet of the Revolution. Mayakovsky's books had become almost unavailable, and the plans for a literary museum and archive for his materials at Gendrikov had been unofficially stopped. Lili was so disturbed that on November 24, 1935, she performed what she considers her most important act of love for Mayakovsky.

When he wrote in his final letter, "Lili, love me," he meant that I should defend him. But I didn't in the usual way. I didn't write letters until 1935, when I wrote Stalin.

The Briks composed a letter to Stalin protesting that Mayakovsky's poetry was being ignored. Two days later there was a telephone call from the Kremlin. The Fourth Secretary of the Central Committee spoke with Osip, who was in Leningrad working on an opera libretto, and it was decided that Lili should go to the Kremlin. She was met there by Stalin's assistant Yezhov, one of the Party secretaries, who showed her Stalin's answer. They spoke for one and a half hours about Mayakovsky, Lili urging him to open a museum honoring the poet and an archive in the Gendrikov apartment. The letter that she sent read:

November 24, 1935

DEAR COMRADE STALIN:

After Mayakovsky's death, everything was left with me. I have all his archives and rough drafts, his notebooks, manuscripts, all his things. I edit his works. Everybody asks me for materials, data, and photographs.

I do everything I am able to do to have his poems printed, to keep his belongings intact, to satisfy the growing interest in him.

His poems haven't aged. Today they are still contemporary and are the strongest revolutionary weapon.

Almost six years have passed since Mayakovsky's death, and nobody has taken his place. As he was, he remains the greatest poet of our Revolution.

But not everybody understands this, not by a long shot.

Almost six years have passed since his death, and only half

his complete works have been published, and only in an edition of 10,000 copies.

For more than a year, there has been talk of a one-volume edition of his work. It has been given to the publishers, but it hasn't been sent to the printers.

His children's books are not reprinted.

After Mayakovsky's death, a government edict established a special room dedicated to Mayakovsky at the Communist Academy with all his manuscripts and materials. Nothing has been done yet.

Some materials belonging to him are scattered everywhere. Part is in the literary museum, which is not interested at all. This is shown in the bulletin of the museum, where Mayakovsky's name isn't even mentioned.

About three years ago, the Regional Soviet of the Proletarian District asked me to reconstruct Mayakovsky's apartment and organize a library in the name of Mayakovsky. This hasn't been done.

Instead, after some time I was told that the Moscow Soviet refused to give any money for the project, although the sum was very small.

It's located at 15 Taganka Gendrikov, a small wooden house with four apartments in it. One apartment belonged to Mayakovsky. The others were to be remodeled into a library. The District Soviet promised to relocate the inhabitants of the three other apartments.

This apartment reflects the character of Mayakovsky's everyday life—simple, modest, clean.

Any day now this house could be pulled down. Isn't it better, while we are still alive, to reconstruct everything now, instead of regretting it after fifty years, and to collect bit by bit the materials of the everyday life and the working conditions of this great revolutionary poet?

Aren't we thankful for that ink pot and that little desk and chair which we are shown now in the Lermontov house in Pyatigorsk?

There has been talk of renaming the Triumphal Place in Moscow and Nadezhdinsky Street in Leningrad, Mayakovsky Place and Mayakovsky Street, but that hasn't been done either.

These are the main things. I don't mention the petty facts; for example, according to the Ministry of Education, the poems "Lenin" and "Good" have been eliminated from the textbook of contemporary literature. They are not even mentioned there.

Our government does not understand the colossal role of Mayakovsky as an agitator, his revolutionary actuality. They underestimate the tremendous interest in Mayakovsky taken by the Soviet youth.

That's why he is so reluctantly published. There should be hundreds of thousands of copies of his poems being printed now.

That's why nobody cares to collect all the Mayakovsky materials before they get lost.

Nobody cares to preserve his memory for future generations.

I cannot overcome this bureaucratic apathy and resistance by myself. After almost six years of work, I address myself to you because I do not see any other means to realize the tremendous revolutionary heritage of Mayakovsky.

LILI YURYEVNA BRIK

Stalin replied with a scrawled note on the margin of her letter, which Lili copied: "Comrade Brik is right: Mayakovsky was and remains the most talented poet of our Soviet epoch. Indifference to his memory and words is a crime. The best thing to do would be to call her to Moscow. Contact the head of the State Publishing House and the head of *Pravda*. If my help is necessary, I am ready. Greetings. Joseph Stalin."

The next day Stalin's comment "Mayakovsky was and remains the most talented poet of our Soviet epoch" appeared as a headline in *Pravda*, and overnight Mayakovsky became the poet-hero of the

Revolution. The Central Committee resolved to do everything Lili's letter had asked for. She remembered that Mayakovsky "had had many enemies, but there was no trouble after Stalin's recommendation." No one in the Soviet Union wanted to risk the crime of indifference toward his work. Moscow's Victory Square was hastily renamed Mayakovsky Square, one of hundreds of squares in his honor everywhere in the Soviet Union. Speeches, articles, poetry readings proliferated, and more statues of him were commissioned than there were monuments to Garibaldi in Italy.

Lili and Pasternak were to quarrel later over Pasternak's interpretation of what happened after her letter to Stalin. Pasternak had written an eloquent tribute to Mayakovsky in his first autobiography, *Safe Conduct*, in 1931. In that memoir Pasternak wrote as if Mayakovsky were for him a symbol of the violent disruptions and catastrophes that Russia had endured since the Revolution. But many years after Lili's letter to Stalin, Pasternak published *I Remember: Sketch for an Autobiography*, and it was this later memoir that Lili found offensive. Here his tone was completely different, and his judgment of Mayakovsky's role in Soviet society had changed.

> Mayakovsky was beginning to be propagated compulsorily, like potatoes in the reign of Catherine the Great. That was his second death. For that he is not to blame.

Lili saw the truth in what Pasternak had said, but she was still angry with him.

> He was right, of course, but he shouldn't have written it. It was wrong to say it of a man whom he had once adored. But it was true, because Mayakovsky was being spread like potatoes in the time of Catherine the Great. Of course it did great harm to Mayakovsky's poetry among young people, because when students are forced to read a writer, then they don't want to read him. Such was the case with Mayakovsky.

In writing to Stalin, the Briks had done what they felt had to be done, and for Lili the recognition of Mayakovsky's role in the shaping of the revolutionary society justified the excesses of the petty Soviet bureaucrats who scrambled to show their enthusiasm for the poetry they had done everything to obstruct in the years when Mayakovsky was alive.

As Mayakovsky's "widow," Lili mourned him for a year, and then she became the "wife" of a man she'd met before the poet's death, a hero of the civil war, General Vitalij Markovitch Primakov. He was six years younger than Lili, and he was the first man in her life with whom she had a satisfying physical relationship. Primakov, like Mayakovsky, was devoted to her. His nickname for Lili was *Deti* ("children") because he took such good care of her.

She lived contentedly with Primakov in Leningrad for several years. He had a large apartment, and there was a room set aside for Osip and Genya, who came frequently to stay. In 1935 Primakov carried the Briks' letter about Mayakovsky to Stalin. At a staff meeting Stalin glanced at the letter, put it in the pocket of his tunic, and said, "I'll take care of it." Two years later Primakov was a victim of one of Stalin's massive purges; he was seized and shot along with many other generals in the Red Army. Unlike the other military wives, Lili was not arrested in 1937. Stalin crossed her name off the list with the note "Mayakovsky's wife."

Lili was so despondent after Primakov's death that she began to drink heavily "in order not to think." Vasya Katanyan, the Briks' friend and Mayakovsky's associate since the mid-1920's, saved her. His own marriage was ending, and he moved into Lili's apartment. Although at first he had no thought that they would stay together permanently, they lived together for nearly forty years. He worked as a scriptwriter while devoting himself to scholarly research on Mayakovsky's life. Talking to Katanyan, a gentle, quiet man who was very solicitous about her, Lili always used the formal Russian "you," not "thou."

Of the people who were part of Mayakovsky's life, only a handful live on now. During World War II Lili, Katanyan, Osip, and Genya were evacuated to the Urals. Lili's mother, who'd returned to Moscow in 1933 and stayed with her brother in the South, died in 1942. Brik died of a heart attack in 1945, just before the war's end. He was back in Moscow, coming home from his office for dinner—he was editing Mayakovsky's poetry for a new edition—when he fell dead on the steps to his apartment. Rita saw him two days before his death and they had a pleasant conversation as they walked together to the Metro. He told her, "I was always Volodya's editor. He hated to put in periods and commas. When he wrote he always gave me the manuscript and said, 'You put in all the damn commas.' Now probably the academic scholars will break their heads over the problem of why he put those commas there." Over the years Brik often spoke of writing his memoirs, but he never did. Jokingly he said to Lili, "To me Mayakovsky is an event, not a human being. My book will be called *Vladimir Mayakovsky: An Eyewitness Relates*."

Lili's love for Mayakovsky continued until her death. Visitors frequently came to her apartment in Moscow to pay tribute to the poet's memory, and Lili shone as a hostess with her intense interest in new poetry and art and her spontaneous encouragement of new projects. Mayakovsky's gold ring was always on a chain around her neck, together with the ring she had given him. In the spring of 1978, at the age of eighty-six, she broke her hip; during her convalescence she was moved to her summer dacha next door to the Pasternak family's dacha in Peredelkino. Confined to her bed, she told her visitors that she would kill herself if she thought she would never be able to walk again. She wasn't in pain, but she grew increasingly weaker. She died of an overdose of sleeping pills on August 4, 1978. Later, going through her papers, Katanyan found a note from 1968, when she was close to suicide after two insulting articles in a Soviet literary journal denigrated her place in Mayakovsky's life. In her note she requested that her body be cremated and that her ashes be scattered in the wind so they wouldn't be found by her enemies.

When Mayakovsky wrote "Lili, love me" in his last letter, she understood that he was saying to her, "Forgive me, don't forget me, defend me, don't give me up after my death. I want to be first in your thoughts even after my death, as I wanted it when I was alive." As she said later, in an effort to explain their shared life, "Many years have passed since Volodya's death. 'Lili, love me.' I love him. Every day he speaks to me through his poems."

The voice of the poems is the voice of his love.

> Everything will perish.
> It will all come down to nothing.
> And the one
> who moves life
> will burn out of the last suns
> the last ray
> over the darkness of the planets.
> And only
> my pain
> is sharper—
> I stand,
> entwined in fire,
> on the inextinguishable bonfire
> of inconceivable love.

A NOTE ON THE TRANSLATIONS

THE SELECTIONS FROM MAYAKOVSKY'S POETRY IN THIS BOOK are, in the careful meaning of the word, versions, not translations. Anyone trying to translate Russian poetry is faced with an impossible dilemma, since English and Russian are not compatible languages. They have so little common vocabulary and grammar that if one tries to retain the rhyme and rhythm of the Russian, the meaning is distorted, and if the meaning is translated literally, the poetic form is lost. In earlier translations of the poetry of not only Mayakovsky but also Pasternak, Mandelstam, Esenin, and other Soviet poets, there was an effort to keep the rhyme scheme. The fashion at the moment is to translate with a sometimes tiresome literalness, ignoring the poetic form. In these versions I've given in, with some misgivings, to the new fashion, although at some points I've tried to suggest a little of the Russian form.

It is discouraging to realize that the earlier versions of the poetry didn't excite many Western readers. It is only in the new versions, which suggest that poets like Mayakovsky and Mandelstam wrote in open verse forms like the current styles in American and English poetry, that these poets have found a large audience. Their work has been used by a number of translators for whatever effect they wanted.

This dilemma has always been the bane of translators, and there has never been a satisfactory way around it. It is unfortunate that many modern translators have pretended that the problem didn't exist. One earlier solution I liked was a nineteenth-century edition of the poems of the Latin poet Martial. A poem was first given in Latin, then in a literal prose translation, and finally in a number of rhymed versions, leaving it to the reader to decide which he liked best. This method doesn't work with long poems, however. The whole situation was voluminously discussed when Vladimir Nabokov published his completely literal and flatly unpoetic version of Pushkin's *Eugene Onegin*, but it still lurks there in the shadows to haunt us.

With Mayakovsky the difficulties are further complicated by his habit of making up new words and punning on ordinary street language. This often gives his poetry, particularly his propaganda work, a broad and generally humorous tone, closer in feeling to someone like Ogden Nash than to more serious American and English writers. Mayakovsky, after all, even made up a pun for his suicide note. This humorous quality in his work is completely lost in literal versions, though it is versions of this kind that have made him readable to Westerners. He is often a very funny poet, and even the exaggerations of his early Futurist work were lightened with broad strokes of parody and conscious buffoonery that helped make him popular with his audiences.

The only true translations of Mayakovsky's work I've found that I like are the completely delightful versions the poet Edwin Morgan did. They are, however, in Scots rather than English—Scots seems to have a gustiness that English lacks. I get a very strong feeling of Mayakovsky in something like the opening of the poem "I'm Off"— or "I'm Aff," as Morgan has translated it.

> Ticket—
>   sneck.
>   Cheek—
>   peck.
> The whussle blaws,
>   we've breenged awa
> whaur
>   thae warld-troddlin wemen
>   traik
> like a herring-drave in their hose-net.
>   Caa
> the-day
>   wur weirdie-heidit guest,
> but gie fair focus
>   to the morn's-morn's pow . . .

I can't imagine a better way to end Mayakovsky's poem to the Brooklyn Bridge—or "Brig," as it is in Scots—than Morgan's

> And I'm gawpin still
>   like an Eskimo at an injin,
> like a cleg at the neck-band
>   drinkin it aa in.
> Brooklyn Brig—
> man . . .
>   that's BIG!

In English Morgan has to fend with the difficulties of bringing the rhyme across, and the meaning, as well as the tone, begins to veer toward a more conventional usage, as in his version of this early Mayakovsky poem:

> Along the pavement of my soul
>   worn out by feet
>   the steps of madmen beat
> their hard-heeled sentences . . .

Despite the seeming freedom of his forms, Mayakovsky generally worked with a four-beat line and an A-B-A-B rhyme scheme. He often achieved some of his effect by the simple device of splitting the lines so that the four-beat unit was visually broken up, even though in a reading the overall pattern is clear, especially as it was reinforced by regular rhyme. It would sometimes seem, from reading modern literal versions, that Mayakovsky must have written his poems easily, since they look like free verse. What everyone close to him remembers, however, is the grueling effort that went into his poetry. He worked on lines literally for days, trying new rhymes and new word structures, while still keeping to a clearly defined poetic scheme. It was only his enormous energy and stubborn persistence that made it possible for him to write as much as he did. Anecdotes about times of his life like the period in the summer of 1915 when he lived in a village in Finland and labored over the composition of the poem "The Cloud in Trousers" become much more understandable when one remembers that to write poetry with these given stylistic conditions is demanding, exasperating, and exhausting.

An example of the problems involved in working with Mayakovsky's poetry illustrates some of the difficulties. The opening lines of "The Cloud in Trousers" was one of his most successful audacities, causing as much reaction in audiences as Allen Ginsberg did later with his poem "Howl": "I saw the best minds of my generation destroyed by madness, starving hysterical naked." Mayakovsky's opening lines in Russian (in a latinized transcription by Bengt Jangfeldt) read:

> Vashu mýsl,
> mechtáýushuyu na razmyagchónnom mozgú,
> kak výzhirevshiy lakéy na zasálennoy kushétke,
> búdu draznít ob okrovávlennyi sérdtsa loskút,
> dósyta ízizdeváyus, nakhálnyi i yédkiy.

As often in Mayakovsky's poetry, the four-beat rhythm is spread over the first two lines; at the same time the dramatic effect is increased by putting the first words by themselves. The rhyme scheme, as it is for the whole poem, is A-B-A-B, although the poet has allowed himself the freedom of rhymes that are close but not precise in *mozgú—loskút* and *kushétke—yédkiy*.

A literal version of the lines in English immediately makes the problem clear. The lines read:

> Your thought,
> dreaming on the softened brain,
> like a fattened lackey on a greasy couch,
> I will tease against the bloody rag of the heart,
> (I will) mock till I am full (impertinent or obnoxious), and caustic.

There is no way that this can be twisted into his rhyme scheme; to achieve the rhymes means changing the meaning. A literal rendering, like the following translation by Max Hayward and George Reavey, is perhaps the best-known version of the poem in English:

> Your thought
> musing on a sodden brain
> like a bloated lackey on a greasy couch,
> I'll taunt with a bloody morsel of heart;
> and satiate my insolent, caustic contempt.

The Soviet translator Dorian Rottenberg's "Cloud in Pants" has this as a solution for these lines, keeping the rhymes:

> Your thoughts
> day-dreaming in a puddin'-soft head
> like an overfed lackey on a greasy sofa,
> I'll tease with my heart's blood-streaming shred,
> deride you, audacious, till you smart all over.

Another effort to deal with the problem is by Herbert Marshall:

> Your thoughts
> dreaming on a softened brain,
> like an over-fed lackey on a greasy settee,
> with my heart's bloody tatters I'll mock again;
> impudent and caustic, I'll jeer to superfluity.

They are heroic efforts which make it clear how difficult it is to find any satisfactory rendering.

My own sorrowful conclusion to all of this, after several years of struggle, is that in an essential way Mayakovsky's poetry can't be translated into English. Lili Brik felt that French, with its greater linguistic resources, could come closer to the style, but then all the rough force of the poetry would be lost. The best we can hope for is versions that come close to what Mayakovsky said, and if at any point there is a suggestion of the humor, the brilliant and original rhyme, and the roaring rhythm of the poetry, then perhaps a flavor of the original will come across.

SAMUEL CHARTERS

SOURCES

MAYAKOVSKY'S LIFE AND HIS RELATIONSHIP WITH LILI BRIK HAVE been the subject of scores of articles, memoirs, and critical studies by both Soviet and Western writers. Additional material about Mayakovsky's life with Lili Brik came from Lili herself in a series of interviews with her in Moscow in April 1972, December 1973, and April 1974, and in Peredelkino in June 1973. Quotations from Lili Brik and other references to Mayakovsky's life from these interviews appear throughout this book. Also interviewed were the two other women close to Mayakovsky at the end of his life, Tatiana Yakovleva and Nora Polonskaya, in New York City and Moscow.

In addition to the interviews, Lili Brik furnished chapters from her memoirs prepared in 1956 for *Literaturnoe nasledstvo*, including "The Last Months—My Recollections about Mayakovsky." Mayakovsky's letters to Lili Brik were published in Volume LXV of *Literaturnoe nasledstvo* (Moscow, 1958) with notes by V. A. Katanyan. Elsa Triolet's unpublished Russian memoir has also been incorporated into this book with Lili Brik's permission. Originally Elsa Triolet wrote it for the second volume on Mayakovsky for *Literaturnoe nasledstvo*. Lili Brik's tapes and memoirs, Elsa Triolet's memoirs, and Mayakovsky's letters to Lili Brik were translated from Russian to English by Alexandra Eiche, Rimma Vinnehova, and Ann Charters.

Rita Rait kindly translated her article "Mayakovsky and Pasternak: Fragments of Reminiscence," published in the *Oxford Slavonic Papers*, Volume XIII (1967). She also shared the letters and cards sent to her from Lili Brik and Mayakovsky, and talked in Moscow and Stockholm about her long friendship with them. In Moscow Vasya Katanyan contributed a chapter about Osip Brik from his unpublished memoirs, *Not Only Reminiscences*. Katanyan also gave copies of material in his Osip Brik archives to Bengt Jangfeldt, who shared his information with Ann Charters in Stockholm.

The most complete record of Mayakovsky's life is in V. A. Katanyan's *Majakovskij: Literaturnaja cronika*, fourth edition (Moscow, 1961), where Mayakovsky's activities from day to day are listed in chronological sequence. The factual details of Mayakovsky's life from the interviews and articles were checked against Katanyan's chronicle by Rimma Vinnehova and Ann Charters.

Another important source was Mayakovsky's autobiography, *I Myself*, translated from Russian to English by Rimma Vinnehova and Ann Charters. Viktor Shklovsky's *Mayakovsky and His Circle* (New York, 1972, translated by Lily Feiler) contains many insights and a sensitive evocation of Mayakovsky's life and times by one of his contemporaries. Wiktor Woroszylski's *The Life of Mayakovsky* (New York, 1971, translated from Polish by Boleslaw

Taborski) is a valuable collection of documentary sources arranged as a collage. It must be used carefully as source material since it was translated into English from the Polish edition, not the original Russian sources; whenever possible, the original Russian was consulted.

Edward J. Brown's *Mayakovsky—A Poet in the Revolution* (Princeton, 1973) is an academic study of Mayakovsky's poetry and a good survey of previous literary criticism. Patricia Blake's notes and brief introductory essay, "The Two Deaths of Vladimir Mayakovsky," in *The Bedbug and Selected Poetry* (New York, 1960) are a useful critical introduction to Mayakovsky's life.

The most complete available Russian edition of Mayakovsky's collected works is the thirteen-volume *Polnoe sobranie sochinenii* (Moscow, 1955–61, edited by V. A. Katanyan). The English versions of Mayakovsky's poems were done from this text by Samuel Charters, working with Bengt Jangfeldt, Rimma Vinnehova, and Rita Rait.

NOTES

CHAPTER 1

The lines beginning "If I am destined to be a tsar" are from Mayakovsky's "The Backbone Flute" in *Polnoe sobranie sochinenii* I (Moscow, 1955–59). This edition will hereafter be referred to as P.S.S.

The quotations from Lili Brik in this and subsequent chapters are from the series of interviews with her in Moscow and Peredelkino, 1972–74. She often paraphrased and repeated anecdotes she had published in earlier articles.

From the beginning of 1918 there was a new Russian calendar, which differed from the old by thirteen days. Dates in this book before 1918 are given according to the new calendar, unless specified otherwise.

CHAPTER 2

"First house remembered distinctly" and other quotations from Mayakovsky's autobiography *I Myself* have been translated from P.S.S. I. The autobiography was first written in 1922, but it was extended and revised in 1928.

"Youths have a lot of cramming to do . . ." is from Mayakovsky's poem "I Love," P.S.S. IV, p. 86.

Burliuk's description of Mayakovsky as a "brilliant poet" is quoted by Mayakovsky in *I Myself*.

The production of *Vladimir Mayakovsky: A Tragedy* is discussed in Susan P. Compton's *The World Backwards*.

The description of the activities and tours of the Moscow Futurists is from Markov's *Russian Futurism*.

Burliuk's description of Volodya's "achievements in debauchery" is from Woroszylski, *The Life of Mayakovsky*, p. 115, hereafter referred to as Woroszylski.

In *The Creative Experiment*, C. M. Bowra developed the idea that Mayakovsky mistrusted his emotions.

> Mayakovsky's poetry arises out of his conviction that he possesses special powers to create and transform, and for this reason he writes about himself. But this self-absorption is not matched by an equal self-confidence. At times he suggests he is not his own master, but the plaything of uncontrollable powers which will break him if he is not careful. He seems to have felt this especially about love. He knew all too well

what it meant, and he was uneasy about a passion which so undermined his self-confidence and made him the prey of incalculable forces . . . [The hyperbolic images of his poetry] move at a level of delightful absurdity, but [they are] built on a real fear, and this playfulness is Mayakovsky's escape from it (pp. 110–11).

Pasternak also commented that Mayakovsky fought "against the black velvet of the talent in himself, whose luscious dark-browned forms began to trouble him earlier than happens with less gifted people" (*Safe Conduct*, p. 113).

CHAPTER 3

Mayakovsky's poem about Elsa as "that meany witch" is from Shklovsky's *Mayakovsky and His Circle*, pp. 42–43, hereafter referred to as *Circle*.

Elsa Triolet's reminiscences about meeting Mayakovsky and about their early friendship are from her memoirs. Lili denied the possibility that Elsa and Volodya were lovers—"nothing like that could have happened"—in a letter to Ann Charters on December 17, 1977.

The incident of Mayakovsky and Chukovsky's attempt to find a publisher in Moscow is related in Katanyan's *Majakovskij: Literaturnaja cronika*, p. 78, hereafter referred to as Katanyan.

The quotations from Gorky's wife and Gorky's description of Mayakovsky in Finland are from Woroszylski, pp. 145 and 152.

CHAPTER 4

Mayakovsky's letter to his mother on November 9, 1915, is in Woroszylski, p. 161.

Shklovsky's notes on his first impressions of Lili are in *Circle*, pp. 75–79.

Mayakovsky's comment " 'The Cloud' proved feathery . . ." is from *I Myself*, P.S.S. I.

Pasternak's analysis of Mayakovsky's "wild shyness" and his description of their meeting in Petrograd before Volodya took him "to see the Briks for the first time" are in *Safe Conduct*, pp. 113 and 126–27.

CHAPTER 5

Pasternak's comment on Mayakovsky's sense of himself as "the subject of a lyric" is in *Safe Conduct*, p. 116.

Rita Rait translated Osip Brik's remark that "Mayakovsky understood love this way" during her talks with Ann Charters in Moscow in April 1974. A more complete text is:

Let me strum a little about love. Love can be very different. You can philosophize about it without ending. You give your life away for love. It's love when you comfort somebody. You pour out your soul to somebody—that's love. A person wants to seem better than he is—that's love. Another says, love me as I am—that's love too.

Let me strum a bit about this, about love. Mayakovsky understood love this way: if you love me, you are with me, for me, always, everywhere, in all circumstances. You can't be against me at any time, no matter how unjust or cruel I am. You always vote for me, even if it's a false witnessing. The least vacillation or change is treason. Love must be constant, like a law of nature which knows no exclusions. It can't be that I wait for the sunrise and the sun doesn't appear. It can't be that I bend down to a flower and she runs away. It can't be that I clasp a birch tree and she says don't. According to Mayakovsky, love was not an act of will, but the condition of life, like gravity. Were there women who loved him like that? Yes. Did he love them? No, he took them for granted.

Did he love anyone that way? Yes—but he was a genius. His power was stronger than the force of gravity. When he read his poems the ground rose toward him to hear better. Of course if one could find a planet impervious to poetry . . . But there wasn't a planet like that.

Shklovsky stated that "we were not expected to know what millennium it was outside" in *Circle*, p. 87.

There are many different accounts of the gala Futurist evening of poetry and art at the painter Lubavina's studio in Petrograd; see Woroszylski, pp. 151–54.

CHAPTER 6

Aseyev's description of Lili and Osya—"if the relationship between art and life was theoretical for them, Mayakovsky personified the real value in this relationship"—is included in *Den Vrålande Parnassen*, p. 166, and Woroszylski, p. 163.

Brik's article "Bread" is also in *Den Vrålande Parnassen*, pp. 141–42.

Herbert Marshall points out the poetic influence of Walt Whitman on Mayakovsky in his book *Mayakovsky*, pp. 47–48, hereafter referred to as Marshall.

CHAPTER 7

Mayakovsky's speech at the Mikhail Theater in March 1917 is quoted in Woroszylski, pp. 176–77.

Shklovsky described Mayakovsky's entering the Revolution "as he would his own home" and told the anecdote about Lili's handbag at the Stray Dog Café in *Circle*, pp. 97–98.

Woroszylski includes the story about Volodya's rushing out into the streets bareheaded and quotes Gorky's speech "Citizens, protect that inheritance" on pp. 174–75.

In *Safe Conduct*, pp. 127–29, Pasternak analyzes Mayakovsky's role as a romantic hero. See also Frank O'Hara's article "About Zhivago and His Poems," reprinted in *Standing Still and Walking in New York* (Bolinas, California, Grey Fox Press, 1975), pp. 99–109. O'Hara discusses Pasternak's relationship with Mayakovsky and their different involvements in the Revolution, concluding, "The chair of poetry must remain empty, for poetry does not collaborate with society, but with life. Soviet society is not alone in seducing the poet to deliver temporary half-truths which will shortly be cast aside for the excitement of a new celebration of nonlife. The danger is that life does not allow any substitute for love."

In Woroszylski, p. 182, Brik is mentioned as editor of Gorky's *Wheelbarrow* in Lunacharsky's letter to his wife on July 1, 1917.

Mayakovsky's letter to Lili and Osya on September 25, 1917, is translated from Volume LXV of *Literaturnoe nasledstvo* (Moscow, 1958), as are all of Mayakovsky's letters to the Briks quoted in this and subsequent chapters.

Mayakovsky's letter to his mother in October–November 1917 about having his teeth fixed is included in Woroszylski, p. 186. The same source has Lunacharsky's opinion of Mayakovsky as a "very talented near-giant" on p. 182.

Osip Brik's view of "a crime before culture" in Gorky's journal *New Life* is mentioned in Katanyan's note number 15 for Mayakovsky's letter number 2 in Volume LXV of *Literaturnoe nasledstvo*.

CHAPTER 8

Ilya Ehrenburg's description of the Moscow crowd reading the *Futurist Gazette* in March 1918 is quoted in Woroszylski, p. 195.

Mayakovsky's comment that the Neptune Studio made a mess of *Fettered by Film* is in *Russian Literature Triquarterly*, Volume 7.

The scenario for *Fettered by Film* was translated into English for this book by Rita Rait and Lili Brik in Moscow, April 1974.

On pp. 227–28 of Woroszylski are Alexandra Rebikova's reminiscence and Eugene Slavinsky's anecdote about Mayakovsky as a poet during his work on films.

CHAPTER 9

Woroszylski includes the appeal to "Comrade Actors" (p. 237) and Nikolai Punin's review of *Mystery-Bouffe* (p. 240).

In Woroszylski, p. 244, is Brik's account that "any reason was good enough to spark off a flare-up" and his belief that Mayakovsky realized "the struggle for new art could only be waged from within the Soviet institutional framework."

An extensive discussion of Mayakovsky and Brik's work for *Art of the Commune* is in Bengt Jangfeldt's *Mayakovsky and Futurism 1917–1921*

(Stockholm Studies in Russian Literature, 1976, reprinted by Ardis in the United States). Jangfeldt states:

> 1918 and 1919 were for the Futurists years of hard cultural ideological struggle. It was a time when they were forced to take a stand on the most urgent questions of art and culture and to fight for their views and positions . . . In the struggle between those who favored a Revolution of the Spirit and those who were enemies of such a Revolution, the latter triumphed. Mayakovsky had many opportunities to convince himself that the cultural revolution propagandized by the Futurists was not popular with the Party and many other groups in the young Soviet society: the never-ceasing campaigns against him and the other Futurists, the unwillingness (to put it mildly) on the part of the authorities to publish and stage his works, the closing of *Art of the Commune* and *Art*, and so on. 1919 was no doubt a difficult year for Mayakovsky . . . he understood not only that the Revolution of the Spirit was not close, but also that it was not wanted in the form in which the Futurists presented it.
>
> What, then, was he to do? It is my opinion that one of the reasons why Mayakovsky started to work at Rosta in the fall of 1919 was that he had realized the fruitlessness of posing the questions of art in such a general and provocative way as had been done in *Art of the Commune* and elsewhere. He understood that the new art had no possibilities of achieving victory at this moment; for this reason Mayakovsky chose more practical work and temporarily abandoned the theoretical debate.
>
> This, however, did not mean that Mayakovsky gave up his views. Futurism was not a poetic "school" but an attitude—a revolutionary attitude—to life and art. The Futurists had always fought against conservatism and stagnation. This struggle may, in fact, be seen as the very essence of "real" Futurism and the "real" Futurists. The struggle for the new against the old, therefore, was an integral part of Mayakovsky's life and work, both before and after the Revolution. This was a fight against *byt* and for the Revolution.

Jangfeldt's careful documentation of Mayakovsky's involvement in Futurism can be contrasted with Solzhenitsyn's sweeping condemnation of Mayakovsky and the Futurists in *The Gulag Archipelago* and elsewhere.

CHAPTER 10

Mayakovsky's argument "Why should literature occupy its own special corner?" is from *The Reminiscences of D. Lebedev*, quoted in Roman Yakobson's "On a Generation That Squandered Its Poets" in *Major Soviet Writers*, p. 14.

Lunacharsky's analysis of Mayakovsky's "double" personality is in Anatoly Lunacharsky's *On Literature and Art*, p. 196.

Shklovsky commented on Mayakovsky's feeling "well disposed toward the entire world" after the October Revolution in *Circle*, p. 151.

Lenin's note to Lunacharsky is quoted in Edward J. Brown's *Mayakovsky —A Poet in the Revolution*, p. 205, hereafter referred to as Brown.

Trotsky's *Literature and Revolution* has several long and highly critical passages on Mayakovsky's poetry and the Futurists.

CHAPTER 11

Rita Rait's reminiscences of her friendship with Mayakovsky and Lili in this and subsequent chapters are primarily from talks with her in 1973, 1974, and 1978, and from her article on Mayakovsky and Pasternak.

Lenin's speech to the Metal Workers' Conference is quoted in Marshall, p. 145.

Information about Osip Brik's loss of his Party card came from Bengt Jangfeldt.

Before the Russian literary critic Gennady Smakov left the Soviet Union, he read Kuzmin's account of his conversation with Pasternak in 1922 in Kuzmin's unpublished notebooks.

Mayakovsky's obituary for Alexander Blok is quoted in Woroszylski, p. 293.

Esenin's poem "I see everything" is translated from Russian to English by Geoffrey Thurley in *Confessions of a Hooligan*, pp. 66–67.

Mandelstam's statement that Mayakovsky "has absolutely no business impoverishing himself" appears in Clarence F. Brown's *Mandelstam*, p. 106. Rita Rait gave the reference to the term "marble fly."

Shklovsky commented that Brik's justification was "as precise as it was incorrect" in *Circle*, p. 150.

Rita Rait heard Mayakovsky envy "happy Pasternak" after they heard Pasternak read his poetry.

CHAPTER 12

"Vinokour," the person mentioned in Mayakovsky's letter to Lili on October 26, 1921, was a linguist and friend of the Briks.

CHAPTER 13

Lili wrote a letter to Rita on September 28, 1922, telling her to "be careful" about what she wrote "when we are all together."

Shklovsky's descriptions of Mayakovsky in Berlin and Norderney are in *Circle*, pp. 155, 161, and 162.

CHAPTER 15

Shklovsky described Brik at a workers' meeting when he said, "Poetry is not needed, anyway," on p. 172 of *Circle*.

Mayakovsky's letter to Chuzhak explaining that "Communist art . . . is still a vague concept" is included in Woroszylski, p. 315.

Mayakovsky's assertion that "meetings, speeches . . . are all equal and sometimes valuable examples of poetry" is quoted on p. 256 of Janko Lavrin's *A Panorama of Russian Literature*.

On July 25, 1923, Mayakovsky wrote his Berlin publisher: "For us, the masters of words for the Russian Soviets, the petty little problems of making lyric verses yield their place to the broad aims of the way the word helps to build the Commune." See Katanyan, p. 190.

Mayakovsky's shout to Mandelstam, "Like an Attic soldier," is in Clarence Brown's *Mandelstam*, p. 100. Forty years later the poet Boris Slutsky listened to Lili criticize Mandelstam's poetry, and he interrupted her to say, "When I attended Brik's workshop on Structuralism at the Literary Institute, he spoke highly of Mandelstam." There was a silence at the table, and then Lili replied softly, "Well, if Osya loved him, then I love him too." This anecdote was told by Rita Rait in Stockholm in June 1978.

Ilya Ehrenburg's comments on the Soviet Union during NEP, "We were naïve in those days" and "the belly had not only been rehabilitated but exalted," are in his *Memoirs 1921–1941*, pp. 66–70.

Aseyev on "the waves of NEP" and Mayakovsky on the brutal tone of his poems being "the answer to a similar brutality" in his subject are quoted in Woroszylski, pp. 299 and 411.

Mayakovsky joked to the Briks that if he became a Party member he'd be sent "to some God-forsaken place to edit the local newspaper."

CHAPTER 17

Burliuk's description of his meeting with Mayakovsky in New York City in 1925 is in Woroszylski, p. 367.

Mayakovsky's story about drinking tea at a New York party is quoted in Brown, pp. 296–97.

Mayakovsky's account "I love New York" is from P.S.S. VII, pp. 300–6. "The futurism of naked technology" is from P.S.S. VII, pp. 343–44.

While Mayakovsky was alive, he became a celebrity in the Soviet Union through his reading tours and his journalistic work. The bureaucracy hindered the publication of his books, which were usually printed in small editions of only three or four thousand copies.

CHAPTER 18

Theodore Dreiser described Lili Brik in *Dreiser Looks at Russia*, p. 201.

Shklovsky told the story about Mayakovsky "shaving an elephant" in *Circle*, p. 152.

Katanyan's remark about Brik's being "useful to many creative people" is from his unpublished memoirs, translated by Rimma Vinnehova and Ann Charters.

Chernyshevsky's characterization of the "new man" as exemplifying "common sense in action" is on p. 174 of *What Is to Be Done?*; his view of jealousy as "a distorted feeling" is on p. 254 of the novel; his definition of love is on p. 213.

Osip Brik told Rita Rait that he was upset after Lili's trip to Moscow with Volodya in 1916 but that he understood his jealousy was unimportant since "our long friendship and intimacy didn't depend on anything and couldn't end because of anything." When Rita received her medical degree, Osip drew a cartoon picture of himself with a round face, mustache, and glasses, and under it he wrote for Rita, "To the unruly pupil from her professor." He was joking about his attempt to teach her what he said was life's most important lesson and the basis of his self-control: his acceptance that "some things are temporary, and others are permanent."

Mayakovsky's comment on the limitations of *What Is to Be Done?* is quoted in Woroszylski, p. 352, as is his remark "Take care of poets," on p. 397.

CHAPTER 19

Brik's assertion that "art is nothing but vanity" is quoted by Shklovsky in *Circle*, p. 193.

The malicious review of "Good!" in the Rostov newspaper is in Woroszylski, p. 434, as is Pasternak's letter to Polonsky, on pp. 423–24.

Mayakovsky's angry remark "I don't give a damn whether I'm a poet" is in *Russian Literature Triquarterly*, Volume VII, p. 314.

Tatiana Yakovleva reminisced about Mayakovsky with Ann Charters in New York City in 1976.

CHAPTER 20

Quotations from *The Bedbug* are from Guy Daniels's translation in *The Complete Plays of Vladimir Mayakovsky*.

Preparations for the production of *The Bedbug* are described in Woroszylski, p. 440–41, and Patricia Blake's notes to *The Bedbug and Selected Poetry*, p. 314, hereafter referred to as Blake.

Mayakovsky's letter to Tatiana, "I work until my eyes go hazy," is in Woroszylski, p. 463.

Tatiana Yakovleva said that Mayakovsky "was completely disappointed in Communism" during the New York City interview in 1976.

Yury Annenkov related the story about his meeting in Nice with Mayakovsky in Nina Berberova's *The Italics Are Mine*.

Woroszylski includes Mayakovsky's letters to Tatiana about writing *The Bathhouse* on p. 465; his reason for not joining the Party because he had "acquired a lot of habits that cannot be reconciled with organized activity," p. 512; and his exchange with Bedny about the Renault.

Mayakovsky's statement that such talk was "useful for the purpose of revolutionizing art" is from Yakobson's "On a Generation That Squandered Its Poets," p. 14.

A discussion of how Brik modified his aesthetic theories is in Brown, p. 362, including Shklovsky's joke about Brik's legs. The quotation from Mayakovsky, "people reached for their handkerchiefs," is also in Brown, p. 302, as is Tatiana's letter to her mother about the "awful lot of dramas" in her life (p. 338) and Volodya's telegram AM VERY DEPRESSED (p. 339).

Mayakovsky answering the hecklers "I kept quiet!" is quoted in Woroszylski, pp. 470–71; the same source includes his speech at the Dynamo Stadium, pp. 471–72.

CHAPTER 21

Lili's diary notes are from her article "The Last Months—My Recollections about Mayakovsky," translated by Rimma Vinnehova and Ann Charters.

The description of the party for Volodya on December 30, 1929, is from Woroszylski, pp. 473–76, and Marshall, p. 25.

Lev Nikulin's reminiscence about Mayakovsky is in Woroszylski, p. 466; the same source includes Mayakovsky's discovery that he had strained his vocal cords (p. 455) and Zoshchenko's description of the failure of *The Bathhouse* (pp. 478 and 483).

Osip Brik's explanation of Volodya's depression was quoted in Lili's article "The Last Months."

RAPP's division into two groups, the "October Caucus" and Mayakovsky, is described in Woroszylski, p. 505. See also Brown's discussion, pp. 359–68.

CHAPTER 22

"Why does death occur so frequently in the spring" is on p. 240 of Andrei Sinyavsky's *A Voice from the Chorus* (New York, 1976).

Nora Polonskaya's remark that Mayakovsky "seemed a little old" and her account of their last days together are from her interview with Ann Charters in Moscow, April 1974.

Mayakovsky's poem "Every cow has a nest" is quoted in *Circle*, p. 185, and retranslated here by Rita Rait.

Woroszylski includes Lavut's description of how Mayakovsky wrote his suicide letter in bed (pp. 521–22); Aseyev's memory of their conversation, "We must put it off to some other day" (p. 523); and the incident of Mayakovsky at the State Circus (p. 527).

Valentin Katayev's account, "My memory has retained nothing of the most important details," is quoted in Konstantin Bazarov's article "Mayakovsky: Poet of the Revolution" in *Books and Bookmen*, March 1972, p. 6.

Mayakovsky's suicide letter is included in Brown, pp. 352–53.

Pasternak described Mayakovsky's suicide in *Safe Conduct*, pp. 140–44. His comment on Volodya's face, "the expression with which one begins life," is quoted in Bazarov's article, p. 6.

Osip Brik's reminiscence of being in Berlin with Lili when they learned of Volodya's suicide is from Lili's article "The Last Months."

Rita Rait translated her account of April 14, 15, and 16, 1930, into English with Ann Charters in Moscow, April 1974.

CHAPTER 23

Roman Yakobson wrote that Mayakovsky's suicide "was spontaneously felt by his contemporaries as the finale of a whole literary epoch" in *Harvard Library Bulletin*, Volume IX, p. 2, Spring 1955. See also Pasternak's *Safe Conduct*, in which he visualized Mayakovsky as personally representing the Revolution.

Mayakovsky's purpose in writing "To Sergei Esenin" is quoted in Blake, pp. 28–29.

Lunacharsky's analysis of Mayakovsky's double personality is on pp. 199–200 of *On Literature and Art*. The official Soviet explanation of his suicide was "extreme nervous stress," as presented in K. Zelinsky's *Soviet Literature/ Problems and People* (Moscow: Progress Press, 1970), p. 63. The latest unofficial explanation is that the "great Soviet poet" was destroyed by his "false friends" the Briks. See Brown, pp. 346–47.

Marina Tsvetayeva's statement that "Mayakovsky did away with himself the way he would with an enemy" is from *Russian Literature Triquarterly*, number 13, pp. 536–37.

Details of Mayakovsky's funeral are in Katanyan, pp. 402–4. Soviet scientists also removed Mayakovsky's brain for study before he was cremated; they found it was unusually large.

Lili Brik gave a copy of her letter to Stalin to Rita Rait, who translated it with Ann Charters.

Pasternak wrote about Mayakovsky's "second death" in *I Remember*, pp. 99–101.

After Mayakovsky's death in 1930, Brik "blossomed out" a little, according to Rita Rait. Among his projects was a play that justified the cruelty of Ivan the Terrible's infamous executioner, and a cynical essay praising Stalin, arguing that repression and suffering were temporary conditions necessary for the ultimate triumph of world Communism. To his closest friends he confided that he believed only in literature, "the highest product of the human brain."

The lines "Everything will perish" are from "Man," P.S.S. I, p. 272.

BIBLIOGRAPHY

Barooshian, Vahan D. *Russian Cubo-Futurism 1910–1930*. The Hague, 1976.

Berberova, Nina. *The Italics Are Mine*. New York, 1969.

Bojko, Syzmon. *New Graphic Design in Revolutionary Russia*. London, 1972.

Bowlt, John E. (editor). *The Documents of 20th-Century Art—Russian Art of the Avant-Garde*. New York, 1976.

Bowra, C. M. *The Creative Experiment*. London, 1948.

Brik, Lili. "Majakovskij i chuzhie stikhi." *Znamya*, 3 (1940).

—— "Predlozhenie issledovatelyam." *Voprosy literatury*, 4 (1966).

Brik, Osip M. "Majakovskij redaktor i organizator." *Literaturny kritik*, 4 (1936).

—— "On Khlebnikov." *Russian Literature Triquarterly* 12 (Winter 1975). Translated by V. D. Barooshian.

—— "The Picture, the Photograph and the Movie Still." *Russian Literature Triquarterly* 7 (Winter 1974). Translated by V. D. Barooshian and C. MacCormack.

—— "She's Not a Fellow-Traveler." *Russian Literature Triquarterly* 13 (Spring 1975). Translated by Anya Kroth.

Brown, Clarence F. *Mandelstam*. Cambridge, 1973.

Brown, Edward J. *Major Soviet Writers—Essays in Criticism*. New York, 1973.

—— *Mayakovsky—A Poet in the Revolution*. Princeton, 1973.

—— *Russian Literature Since the Revolution*. New York, 1969.

Burliuk, David. *Color and Rhyme*. Numbers 31, 41, 49. New York, 1956–66.

Camus, Albert. *The Rebel—An Essay on Man in Revolt*. New York, 1956. Translated by Anthony Bower.

Carlisle, Olga (editor). *Poets on Street Corners*. New York, 1970.

Cary, Joseph. "Futurism and the French Theatre D'Avant-Garde." *Modern Philology* LVII, 2 (November 1959).

Chernyshevsky, Nikolai. *What Is to Be Done?* New York, 1961.

Compton, Susan P. *The World Backwards—Russian Futurist Books 1912–1916*. London, 1978.

Constantine, Mildred, and Fern, Alan (editors). *Revolutionary Soviet Film Posters*. Baltimore, 1974.

Cork, Richard. *Vorticism and Abstract Art in the First Machine Age*. Berkeley, 1976.

Darring, Gerald. "Mayakovsky: A Bibliography of Criticism (1912–1930)." *Russian Literature Triquarterly* 2 (Winter 1972).

Dreier, Katherine. *Burliuk*. New York, 1944.

Dreiser, Theodore. *Dreiser Looks at Russia*. New York, 1928.

Ehrenburg, Ilya. *Memoirs 1921–1941*. New York, 1964. Translated by T. Shabunia and Y. Kapp.

—— *People and Life 1891–1921*. New York, 1962.

Ehrlich, Victor. "The Dead Hand of the Future" in *The Double Image*. Baltimore, 1964.

—— *Russian Formalism*. The Hague, 1969.

—— (editor). *Twentieth-Century Russian Literary Criticism*. New Haven, 1975.

Esenin, Sergei. *Confessions of a Hooligan*. Cheshire, 1973. Translated by Geoffrey Thurley.

Fitzpatrick, Sheila. *The Commissariat of Enlightenment*. Cambridge, 1970.

Gorky, Maxim. *Fragments from My Diary*. New York, 1972. Translated by Moura Budberg.

Gray, Camilla. *The Great Experiment: Russian Art 1863–1922*. New York, 1962.

Hackel, Sergei. *The Poet and the Revolution—Aleksandr Blok's "The Twelve."* Oxford, 1975.

Harding, Gunnar, and Jangfeldt, Bengt (editors). *Den Vrålande Parnassen*. Stockholm, 1976.

Henderson, Elizabeth. "Shackled by Film: The Cinema in the Career of Mayakovsky." *Russian Literature Triquarterly* 7 (Winter 1974).

Humesky, Assya. *Mayakovsky and His Neologisms*. New York, 1964.

Hyde, H. Montgomery. *Stalin—The History of a Dictator*. New York, 1972.

Jangfeldt, Bengt. *Lili Brik—Ur Minnen av Majakovskij*. Stockholm, 1974.

—— *Mayakovsky and Russian Futurism*. Ann Arbor, 1976.

Katanyan, V. A. *Mayakovsky as an Artist*. Moscow, 1963.

Lavrin, Janko. *A Panorama of Russian Literature*. London, 1973.

Lettres de Maiakovski à Lili Brik. Paris, 1969. Translated into French by Andrée Robel.

Levin, Dan. *Stormy Petrel—The Life and Work of Maxim Gorky*. New York, 1965.

Lissitzky-Kuppers, Sophie. *El Lissitzky: Life-Letters-Texts*. Greenwich, 1968.

Lunacharsky, Anatoly. *On Literature and Art*. Moscow, 1965.

Maguire, Robert A. *Red Virgin Soil*. Princeton, 1968.

Marinetti, Filippo. *Selected Writings*. New York, 1972. Translated by R. W. Flint and A. A. Coppotelli.

Markov, Vladimir. *Russian Futurism: A History*. Berkeley, 1968.

Marshall, Herbert (editor and translator). *Mayakovsky*. London, 1965.

Mayakovsky, Vladimir. *The Bedbug and Selected Poetry*. New York, 1960. Translated by Max Hayward and George Reavey and edited by Patricia Blake.

—— *The Complete Plays*. New York, 1968. Translated by Guy Daniels.

—— *Essays on Paris*. Austin, 1975. Translated by Paul Schmidt.

—— *How Are Verses Made?* London, 1970. Translated by G. M. Hyde.

—— "A Man." *Russian Literature Triquarterly* 12 (Spring 1975). Translated by Paul Schmidt.

—— *Poems*. Moscow, 1972. Translated by Dorian Rottenberg.

——*Wi the Haill Voice*. Oxford, 1972. Translated into Scots by Edwin Morgan.

—— *Die Wirbelsäulenflöte*. Frankfurt, 1971. German translation and notes by Karl Dedecius.

McVay, Gordon. *Esenin—A Life*. Ann Arbor, 1976.

Mirsky, D. S. *A History of Russian Literature*. New York, 1958.

Moorehead, Alan. *The Russian Revolution*. New York, 1958.

Muchnic, Helen. *From Gorky to Pasternak*. New York, 1962.

Nag, Martin. "Fantastical Realism: The Problem of Realism in Mayakovsky's *Pro Eto*." *Scando-Slavica* IV (1959).

Obolensky, Dimitri (editor). *The Penguin Book of Russian Verse*. London, 1962.

Pasternak, Boris. "The Art of Fiction" (Interview with Olga Carlisle). *Paris Review* 24 (Summer/Fall 1960).

—— *Doctor Zhivago*. London, 1958. Translated by Max Hayward and Manya Harari.

—— *I Remember—Sketch for an Autobiography*. New York, 1959. Translated by David Magarshack.

—— *Safe Conduct: An Autobiography*. New York, 1958. Translated by Beatrice Scott.

Reed, John. *Ten Days That Shook the World*. New York, 1960.

Rickey, George. *Constructivism—Origins and Evolution*. New York, 1967.

Salisbury, Harrison (editor). *The Soviet Union—The First Fifty Years*. New York, 1967.

Sinyavsky, Andrei. *For Freedom of Imagination*. New York, 1971. Translated by Laszlo Tikos and Murray Peppard.

—— *A Voice from the Chorus*. New York, 1976. Translated by Kyril FitzLyon and Max Hayward.

Slonim, Mark. *Modern Russian Literature*. New York, 1953.

—— *Soviet Russian Literature*. New York, 1964.

Solomon, Maynard (editor). *Marxism and Art*. New York, 1974.

Solzhenitsyn, Alexander. *The Gulag Archipelago I–II*. New York, 1973. Translated by Thomas P. Whitney.

Stahlberger, Lawrence. *The Symbolic System of Majakovskij.* The Hague, 1964.

Stillman, Beatrice. "Sofya Kovalevskaya: Growing Up in the Sixties." *Russian Literature Triquarterly* 9 (Spring 1974).

Thomson, Boris. *The Premature Revolution: Russian Literature and Society 1917–1946.* London, 1972.

Thomson, R. D. B. "Mayakovsky and His Time Imagery." *Slavic and East European Review* XLVIII (1970).

Triolet, Elsa. *Maiakovski, Poète Russe.* Paris, 1945.

Trotsky, Leon. *Literature and Revolution.* Michigan, 1960. Translated by Rose Strunsky.

Tsvetayeva, Marina. "Epic and Lyric in Contemporary Russia: Mayakovsky and Pasternak." *Russian Literature Triquarterly* 13 (Fall 1975).

Vladimir Mayakovsky 1894–1930. The American Quarterly on the Soviet Union. Volume III, 1 (July 1940).

Vladimir Tatlin. Modern Museet, Stockholm, 1968.

Volkov-Lannyt, L. *Alexander Rodchenko.* Moscow, 1968.

Weiss, Evelyn. *Alexander Rodtschenko, Fotografien 1920–1938.* Cologne, 1978.

Yakobson, Roman. Commentary on poem "Letter to Tatiana Yakovleva." *Russki Literaturnyi Arkhiv. Harvard College Library Bulletin,* No. I, 1956.

―――― "On a Generation That Squandered Its Poets." In Brown, *Major Soviet Writers.*

―――― "Unpublished Mayakovsky." *Harvard College Library Bulletin,* No. IX, 1955.

INDEX